The Consciousness Quotient

The Consciousness Quotient

Leadership and Social Justice for the 21st Century

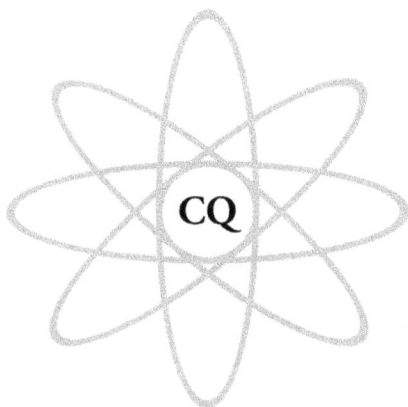

CQ

C. J. Cloutier

HEARTSTONE

Published by HeartStone,
an imprint of CJC Consulting Ltd.
Maple Ridge, British Columbia, Canada
www.transmutational-leadership.com

Library and Archives Canada Cataloguing in Publication
Cloutier, C. J., 1958-, author
    The consciousness quotient : leadership and social justice
        for the 21st century / C.J. Cloutier.
Includes bibliographical references and index.
ISBN 978-0-9920634-0-5 (pbk.)
    1. Leadership. 2. Leadership—Moral and ethical aspects.
    3. Leadership—Social aspects. I. Title.
HD57.7.C56 2013   658.4'092   C2013-906005-7

Edit and text/cover design by Simone Gabbay Associates
www.simonegabbay.com

HeartStone will donate 10 percent of profits from this book to
charities that work to raise consciousness in the world.

For Our Children and Humanity
And for Susan and Danielle

Contents

List of Figures

✵

TRANSMUTATION

The water becomes oil.

In the moment between, it forgets.

It is silk.

I calm myself—my alchemist choice.

Smooth and black, polished obsidian;

My water imperceptible, ready to erupt,

At the slightest touch.

On the edge, I dip my finger,

The ripples reveal: oil and water are one.

✵

Why I Wrote This Book

THERE IS A DEEPENING anxiety in the world today. This book has been a work in progress for many years as I have watched this anxiety grow and have reflected upon it. As I write the final drafts in 2013, I reference many books and events. Documenting everything and keeping it up to date is an impossible task, of course, since so much is happening, and research must be stopped at some point.

I am very concerned about the future of our children and humanity and how leadership has contributed to the precarious situation we've created. The list of problems we face at the local and global levels is overwhelming. How did we get from the bliss of the Garden of Eden to the global problems of today? Perhaps our nostalgic view of the past is not so accurate. Past eras had their dirt and brutality too, maybe more so. Today's problems are no different, except perhaps for their scale, simply because of the size of the population and modern technology. It is well known that the global population is consuming resources faster than they can be replenished. Sustainability has become a serious concern, but the population and consumption continue to increase.

In many places, we have an excellent quality of life as compared to past societies. We can thank leadership for that because it is leadership that has created this progress and success, but we can also blame leadership for the problems. Furthermore, we continue to behave quite badly toward each other in manifest ways. Artists around the world have documented these anxieties in many forms. This is reflected, for example, in the Black Eyed Peas' song, *Where Is the Love?*

Along with this musical group, many people have asked why we have great beauty in the world and great ugliness, too. This is a form of binary (i.e., polarized) thinking. Humans have a natural tendency to polarize every issue and thereby judge all things and all people as good or bad, including leadership. This creates an *us* versus *them* approach to problem solving.

What applies to us individually applies to our organizations. It is well understood that we have a need to belong to social groups by choice (i.e., our organizations) or by birth (e.g., family, nation), and these social groups are often in conflict with others.

History has shown that there is an uneasy balance between competition and cooperation. In many ways, cooperation is just another flavor of competition as groups of people cooperate in order to compete more effectively with other groups. This is true of all types of organizations, including some of the largest systems of cooperation, such as military alliances. The cold war's alliances are an example of this type of competition.

At the global level, it's a game with high stakes. When it's between nations, these high-stakes games often lead to conflict and war. We want our leaders to be ethical and fair, but we don't have a problem when they behave unscrupulously if it benefits our social group. An example of this type of behavior during the cold war was Russia's and the United States' intelligence agencies interfering in the politics of less powerful nations. These types of actions, taken for self-interested purposes in what would otherwise be unacceptable behavior, are what I call complicit hypocrisy, and they are a significant contributor to social injustice.

We all do this sort of thing because we are self-interested as individuals and as groups. Complicit hypocrisy is independent of race, creed, color, gender, sexual orientation, and so on because it is in our nature to satisfy our self-interested desires. The root cause of this behavior, in my opinion, is the need for our physical survival. Thus, our brains are designed and have evolved to do this magnificently, which is how we've become extremely successful as a species.

Traditional leadership, what I call *brain-mind* leadership, usually acts to promote the self-interest of the group at the expense of other groups simply because we always compete for scarce resources. Therefore, leadership as traditionally practiced is the very thing we must overcome to address our global problems. Overcoming an aspect of our very nature is the paradox of our times. Fortunately, I believe that our mind is capable of doing so. I've done what I can to figure this out, and this book and the transmutational leadership model presented herein are the result of that journey.

This book is not for everyone. It is for those who care about ethics, morality, social justice, and personal integrity, and have the courage to look inside themselves. What I have to say may be very controversial to some, perhaps even disturbing, and will make a lot of people uncomfortable. It would be unethical of me not to warn the reader about this. Once an idea is transferred across to the reader, it cannot be put back in the book.

Be Warned, I'm Biased

I must admit my biases. I am a male, ex-military officer, entrepreneur, CEO of a small engineering company, very analytical, and introverted. I have a somewhat romantic view of the world. For example, the legend of King Arthur and the Knights of the Round Table is an archetype that lives in my subconscious. But I'm also a bit cynical and skeptical. I believe that might does not make right, but it is often the way of the world. Leaders constantly exploit power differentials. So, I am generally critical of leadership as practiced today. I believe that these practices are embedded in our many existing systems and serve to prop them up. I belong to a minority group in my country and was bullied a lot growing up. I have some understanding of prejudice and bigotry. I suffer from self-interest, just like everyone else. I am Canadian, and the Canadian culture influences my perspective and interpretation of the world and the times we live in. I believe that brain and mind gender differences run deep and are primary contributors to the glass ceiling that females struggle against. I believe that gender equality is a significant social justice issue. I believe that all organizations compete at some level. Whenever organizations compete, there is always a winner and a loser, and this is another impediment to social justice. All these things, and more, shape and inform who I am and how I write about leadership. These ideas represent my reality and the truth as I see it, and my biases.

Limitations

There are limitations to this work. I can't possibly know everything there is to know about the subject of leadership. Perhaps someone somewhere or sometime has already thought of and expressed my ideas exactly how I see them. I am sure the knowledge contained in this book already existed before it emerged from my awareness. There are, in my opinion, numerous people who are converging on these ideas today, so I'm only lending my voice and perspective to the ongoing conversation. Furthermore, I'm only fluent in English and functional in French. I'm quite sure that there is a plethora of works in other languages (past and present) that are inaccessible to me. I'm thankful for those scholars who have translated some of the texts I've read. I only have a lifetime and, regrettably, I read slowly!

The ideas expressed in this book are the synthesis of many ideas from multiple disciplines, including spirituality, philosophy, and science. The concept of the Consciousness Quotient (CQ) and the transmutational leadership model are the result of this synthesis and represent a new notion of leadership, what I call *soul-mind* leadership.

The transmutational leadership model illustrates the CQ process and provides a framework to advance the conversation. The other aspect of the model illustrates that leadership operates within a continuum whereby leaders can exercise free will regarding at what place in the continuum they choose to be and make their decisions. The evolutionary nature of the concept and the depth of the model are the reason they are part of a conversation and not a final answer.

I am particularly grateful to all the authors whose works I've read and all the people who have taught me, many of whom are referenced in this book. Perhaps more than anything else, how ideas build upon one another and how these ideas are debated vigorously is an indication of the advancement of civilization and how ideas progress. I hope you will join the conversation. If nothing else, by reading with an open mind, you will have done so.

Finally, I struggled with how to write this book. I'm afraid that those who are looking for a scholarly treatise on this subject may be disappointed, but perhaps those who aren't will be relieved. Furthermore, my sources are not generally academic, but mostly consist of published books and Internet sources and my own observations and thoughts. These are not always the most reliable from an academic sense, and much of the information and knowledge contained in these sources is often highly controversial and has been heavily criticized. This will happen to this book, too, I'm sure. Nevertheless, I wrote it in such a way as to satisfy my desire to appeal to the widest possible audience, since an idea has little value unless it is shared widely. Consequently, I have chosen a more personal style that I hope will engage the reader and make these ideas more accessible. To that end, I've included some poetry in between chapters and a short story in the final chapter to bring balance to all the technical mumbo jumbo.

Basically, I've tried to keep it simple and provide something for all readers and leaders. As in every endeavor, there is something lost and something gained by any choice one makes. As a reader, how you choose to engage with the content of this book is an example of this. Either way, I hope that I've achieved my intent.

Mutual understanding and the use of language to achieve it are so very important. In Appendix A, you will find a list of key terms and definitions. I've included them there and where they most logically fit in the text in an effort to accomplish shared meaning and mutual understanding.

A Humble Request

I challenge you to leave any skepticism you may have in the parking lot and to keep an open mind on how I define things and what I believe. I would still ask you to read and think critically. However, not only am I asking you to consider openly what *I* believe; I am also asking you to deeply question what *you* believe.

I hope you enjoy the journey of reading this book, and the conversation. I always welcome feedback at www.transmutational-leadership.com.

✻

NEXUS

Look to your passions; you will find their opposites.

In between, nothing and everything coexists.

It is the nexus of infinite possibility,

Where we live our truth and discover our greatest potentials:

Compassion, Fearlessness, Love.

Journey to infinite possibility.

Journey there and find peace.

✻

Overview of Leadership

I STRONGLY BELIEVE that leadership is greatly misunderstood. In fact, I think most people would agree that the term *leadership* has been so overused and abused that there no longer is general agreement on its meaning. Nevertheless, we know great leadership when we see it, but there is always some context or situation that defines what great leadership is.*

You'd think that after the last few hundred years, at least since the Age of Reason, we would have come to grips with the leadership selection process and found a way to promote only good leaders. So, how is it that we continue to have both good and bad leaders? Is it a problem with the selection process, as well as with how leaders make decisions, or is our definition of what is good and what is bad faulty? Why is it that we constantly witness leaders being unscrupulous and abusing power? Why can't we consistently select only good leaders? This is nothing new. Throughout recorded history, many leaders have behaved poorly. What is the source of this recurring theme about

---

* For a more detailed discussion of leadership, please refer to Appendix B.

human beings, and leaders in particular, that contributes to such things as unscrupulousness, abuse of power, and social injustice?

It is questions such as these that have led me to conclude that leadership and the process of selecting leaders contain an inconvenient truth. This inconvenient truth is directly related to how we are as human beings.

Throughout history, the selection of leaders and leadership has been based on inequality of ability, which results in unequal distribution of power, wealth, and glory. This inequality of ability and distribution of resources* is independent of political or economic systems or any other form of organization.

Leaders get these extra resources because both leaders and followers believe that they deserve the extra resources as a reward for the group's ongoing success and ultimately its survival. Thus, *the purpose of leadership, the leadership selection process, and the act of leadership are, in effect, the exploitation of inequality for the benefit of the people belonging to the group.* A group of people always form, and belong to, various organizations. It is no wonder that organizations are often considered to be exploitative.

Throughout history, competition for resources and efforts to repel threats to survival has driven the need to exploit inequality. This type of exploitation ultimately creates social justice issues because some people and some groups end up with more resources than others. Thus, down deep, the *ultimate purpose of leadership* is to satisfy the need for survival of the organization for the benefit of the group, and there is nothing as effective as dominating competing groups to ensure that this happens.

As mentioned, this fundamental inequality and its exploitation are inherently in conflict with social justice. This is so because *social justice is founded on equality of persons and a just distribution of resources.*

---

* Note: I view power, wealth, and glory as resources.

This inherent conflict between leadership and social justice is the inconvenient truth of leadership. Our very nature is the cause of social justice issues, and leadership is our instrument. Yet, somehow we want leadership to solve social justice issues. I believe that the traditional leadership practices we've had so far are incapable of doing so because leadership is the instrument and not the root source of the problem. I believe there is too much complicit hypocrisy when trying to implement social justice throughout the world.

There is also a social justice issue internal to organizations. If there is a significant and unfair imbalance or a rampant abuse of resources on the part of a leader, the group will do what they can to remove the leader. What is deemed fair and unfair is culturally driven and defined by the values and norms of society and of the organization. Therefore, social justice within organizations is not understood in the same way as it is externally. For example, when it comes to social justice, how we behave toward the citizens of our country is very different when it comes to foreigners.

As to the selection process, leaders are often chosen because their traits correlate with the organization's goals and how the group or organization defines success. By defining the meaning of success, an organization creates a polarity of good and bad by which to measure progress toward achieving the goal that is defined by success.

A leader's task within this framework is to maximize internal cooperation in the pursuit of the organization's purpose and goals, which are outwardly competitive. For example, a country is a type of organization that manifests these attributes. When war happens, the country's leadership will work hard to maximize internal cooperation in order to defeat the external threat. The enemy country is doing the same thing. Thus, each type of organization competes with other organizations of the same type that are pursuing a similar purpose and goals. The fundamental purpose of this competitive framework is to dominate, which ultimately is for the organization's survival. This is true to varying degrees for all types of organizations. As we know from experience, competition can be healthy and is a significant contributor to increases in quality of products and quality of life. However, it can be very unhealthy too, as we've seen far too often.

A consequence of the selection process is that some leaders see themselves and their traits as superior and worthy of the extra power, wealth, and glory that success brings. Folks such as these will claim that they deserve the extra resources and that it was their hard work that got them there. This is in part true, but they were also lucky to be born with certain traits, in a certain country, in a certain age, to certain parents, and so on. Having a lot of wealth, power, and glory feels good and is self-reinforcing. Many leaders develop a sense of entitlement that leads to hubris. As the saying goes, power corrupts, and absolute power corrupts absolutely.

When a corrupt leader is threatened in any way that may cause the perks of leadership to be lost, that leader works hard to resist these threats. These types of leaders want to maintain the status quo or even strengthen their dominant position. This determination to remain dominant contributes to both positive and negative behaviors. We call these people the dominant few, a somewhat derisive term. If negative behaviors in the dominant few, such as unscrupulousness and abuse of power, become too much for followers, it often produces a painful reaction for everyone. Examples of such situations at the nation level are revolutions and civil wars (e.g., the French revolution of 1789). An example at the corporate level is termination of employment, which is sometimes followed by incarceration (e.g., the Enron scandal).

It's important to understand that what applies to the individual scales up to humanity. I believe that *all organizations have been created by us in our self-image to serve our self-interests*. Corporations, for instance, have the same rights and obligations as individuals. From a people perspective, organizations are simply a collective of people, and so they have a collective personality and character. For example, some are greedy and exploitative, and some are charitable. This applies to all forms of organizations. Our nation-states have a collective personality and character, too.

The *ultimate purpose of our many organizations* is to serve our self-interest, and how they operate reflects our need, and their need, for survival. Consequently, organizations behave as we do. They want to survive just as we do, and will resist when their survival is threatened. Since a primary task for traditional leaders is to satisfy the primary rule of survival, those who excel at this are held in high esteem and rewarded accordingly. Leaders' success reinforces the organization they belong to, just as our ascendency to the top of the food chain has reinforced our "successful" behaviors. Thus, even organizations can develop hubris and behave unscrupulously and abuse their power.

Leadership quality is always contextual. Whom we consider to be a good leader for today's conditions may not be good for tomorrow's conditions. Thus, leadership and the selection and removal of leaders contain a lot of paradoxes, dilemmas, and conundrums in a competitive world of diminishing resources. Indeed, rapid change requires us to be more thoughtful about how to remove leaders with dignity and respect, so that we don't inadvertently create a serious conflict.

I strongly believe that leadership is a function of our brains and our minds. If we don't understand the underlying processes of how these work, we have a serious problem overcoming our tendencies. So, understanding what leadership is, how it emerges, how we select leaders, how we remove them, what constitutes a legitimate* leadership decision, how our brains and minds work as it relates to leadership, and so on, matters a lot. All of these can only get more difficult in the presence of rapid change and diminishing resources. What hangs in the balance is social justice for all people, all species, and the environment we call planet Earth.

This book is an examination of how our brain and mind operate as a system and how that creates leadership dilemmas. Consequently, I put forward a hypothesis, a model, and techniques to overcome our many leadership and social justice issues. As previously mentioned, I call these the Consciousness Quotient and the transmutational leadership model.

---

* Note: By *legitimate,* I mean ethical, moral, and just.

✵

BUSY BEE
(Homage to Dr. Seuss' Style)

Oh the choices we make
As leaders we fake

Learn to live well
As you stare down your well

So pack your bags and go on that journey
And be your own mind as you witness the tourney

You'll come back alive
As you reenter the hive

✵

1

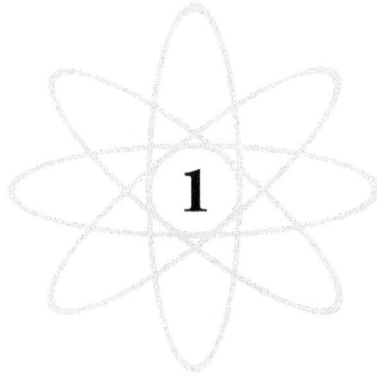

Hypothesis of Mind and Consciousness

NOBODY CAN CLAIM to know the truth! We have ideas. We have beliefs. But we really don't know. That's why a hypothesis is needed. It's needed because we need to put a stake in the ground so that we can argue logically from the main assumption that forms the hypothesis. If the assumption proves true, then what follows logically must be true. This is a form of truth by coherence.*

> TRUTH:
> 1. *A collected set of opinions and sometimes not even that*
> 2. See also *"Mind"* and *"Belief"*

My hypothesis of body, brain, mind, soul, and consciousness and how they work together is the basis for CQ and the transmutational leadership model.

---

* For more about truth and errors, see Appendix C.

The primary focus of the hypothesis is the nature of mind. My assumption is that mind is a form of energy that is separate from, yet fully intertwined with, every cell of our body. This assumption cannot currently, and may never, be proven true or false. Nevertheless, if the assumption and resulting hypothesis turn out to be true, they have interesting consequences for the practice of leadership and the alleviation of social justice issues.

> **MIND:**
> 1. *An ethereal and eternal energy that defies full definition and understanding*
> 2. *An eternal and infinite intelligence or energy that is everywhere and infused into everything simultaneously; see "Consciousness"*
> 3. *A form of energy accessed by the human brain and the human soul that contains a person's beliefs, memories, experiences, and personality*
> 4. *The source of all knowledge and possibility*

Philosophers and scientists have struggled with the nature of mind for a long time, and there is much uncertainty regarding the interrelationships between body, brain, mind, soul, and consciousness. The debate about these issues continues today. The basic question being investigated is whether the mind emerges from the electrochemical processes of our brain or from the energy world of our souls.

As can be imagined, there are deep philosophical, religious, and scientific debates about this. Typical Western thinking is that mind is a *thing* that is unique to us.

> **BRAIN:**
> 1. *The entire nervous system distributed throughout the human body (could also include the immune and endocrine systems, according to some people)*
> 2. *Part of the central nervous system enclosed in the cranium of humans serving to control and coordinate mental and physical actions*

This idea makes the assumption that the mind has a physical source (is located in and forms part of our body) and emerges from the electrochemical processes in our brain. As such, it is considered separate from other minds, just as our body is considered separate from other bodies. This approach and assumption are largely driven by our Greek heritage and our education in the rational-reductionist approach of Western science and way of thinking during the last few hundred years.

Typical Eastern thinking is that mind is a *process* that emerges from the dynamic ongoing changes of the universe. This idea makes the assumption that the mind exists both inside and outside of the body and is a subset of the *Infinite Mind*, which is part of the fabric of the universe and its creative source of energy. So, contrary to Western thought, Eastern thinking sees the mind as simultaneously interconnected with, and inseparable from, everything in the universe. This intuitive-holistic thinking has been largely driven by the Eastern philosophies of Hinduism, Buddhism, and Taoism. Interestingly, parallels have been drawn between the Eastern view of mind and physics, particularly quantum mechanics.

These two dominant forms of thinking, one rational and the other intuitive, may simply be a matter of perspective and are, in my opinion, both true. Indeed, there is a debate, as a result of work in modern physics, that these two views may be two sides of the same coin. Some physicists have even argued that consciousness (what I define as mind) should be included in particle physics models of the four fundamental forces of nature: electromagnetism, gravity, weak nuclear, and strong nuclear. So, perhaps there is a fifth fundamental force that we perceive right under our noses, or should I say behind it: Mind.

I side with Eastern philosophy when it comes to how I view the mind, and this is reflected in the hypothesis and the model.

The transmutational leadership model, presented in Chapter 4, is in part a synthesis of certain aspects of Western and Eastern philosophies. The main assumption in the model is that mind is a form of energy that is constantly undergoing dynamic change, and it is mind energy from which consciousness emerges. Thus, we become aware of mind energy through consciousness. The more consciousness we have, the more mind energy we perceive. Since our mind and our body are fully entangled, we also have more awareness of what our brain and body are doing as we increase our consciousness.

CONSCIOUSNESS:
1. *An emergent process and ability by which we become aware of mind*
2. *Self-awareness*
3. *A universal property of awareness that is infused in all things that emerges as self-awareness at a certain level of complexity*

The model assumes, then, that mind energy is capable of creating and changing matter, and we use consciousness to do so. For example, it is proven that meditative practices create new neurons and synapses. We can also change a negative emotion into a positive one through free will. This is the source of the term *transmutational*. It is transmutational because our mind can intentionally change (i.e., transmute) our physical attributes and how we view reality.

> **TRANSMUTATIONAL:**
> *The ability of a substance or thing that permits a change of its fundamental characteristic, for example, as in changing one form of energy into another form of energy or using energy to effect a change in matter*[*]

The model is analogous to certain theories found in particle physics, as it is known that particles are first and foremost a form of energy that coalesces or congeals into matter. It is also analogous with ideas of entanglement and symmetry that are being investigated by scientists. As tantalizing as it is to see the parallels with quantum physics, it's important to note that we are simply looking at an analogy. A lot more research is needed before anyone can claim that all five forces are aspects of the fundamental nature and fabric of the universe.

The consequence of the synthesis of philosophies and the assumptions made in the transmutational leadership model is that the mind is not physically separate in the way that we believe our body to be physically separate.

The concept of our brain and mind operating together— what I call the brain-mind, the source of traditional leadership—causes us to see our body as separate, unique,

---

[*] Note: It is proven that thought and intention change the physical brain by creating new neurons and connections.

and distinct in the physical world. What I call our soul-mind sees us as fully interconnected with all things. There is no real separation of brain-mind or soul-mind, but it is convenient to describe them this way because it is natural for us to separate things and ideas into this or that. Indeed, brain-mind and soul-mind are simply levels within a continuum.

Thus, our brain-mind and soul-mind are connected simultaneously and continuously to the Infinite Mind of the universe. This Infinite Mind has infinite possibilities. Figure 1 illustrates how I see it. It is a Venn diagram of mind and possibilities that emerge from the fabric of the universe.* The brain-mind and soul-mind, as I label them in the diagram, represent our unique identity. As our mind expands, our identity expands and we become more capable because we have more possibilities at our disposal.

Our minds (i.e., both brain-mind and soul-mind) are an extremely small subset of the Infinite Mind—the intelligence of the universe or, if you prefer, God by whatever name you feel comfortable with. The level of access an individual has to the Infinite Mind is completely determined by how much consciousness exists in that individual, and this determines the number of possibilities available for problem solving and decision making. For those who see themselves as separate from the world and act in a very self-centered way, the bubble of brain-mind possibilities is small. In terms of possibilities, it is my opinion that the size of the soul-mind bubble far exceeds the size of the brain-mind bubble but, alas, that is difficult to illustrate on a small two-dimensional page. The Infinite Mind, of course, is everything. It is the Tao as described below. How inadequate my illustration!

---

* A Venn diagram shows all possible logical relations between a finite collection of sets (aggregation of things).

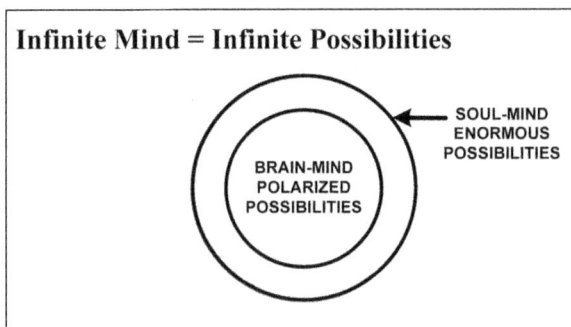

Figure 1: Venn Diagram of Mind and Possibilities

I think of the mind (the Infinite Mind as shown in Figure 1) as Lao Tzu describes it in the Tao Te Ching:[1] Tao is the supreme reality, and Te is its manifestation on earth. Te is a subset of Tao, just as our brain-mind and soul-mind together are a subset of the Infinite Mind. Ching is the book about Tao and Te. Tao is not knowable in its entirety, but can be glimpsed by virtue of the fact that Te is a subset of Tao. We must be satisfied that we can never fully know Tao, accept that fact, yet strive for greater understanding of Tao, as that will lead us to greater possibility and enlightenment. CQ consists of a number of techniques, and transmutational leadership is the underlying model for that journey.

The scientific theory that I like to use as an analogy to illustrate the brain-mind and soul-mind is physicists' theory about wave-particle duality[2] from quantum physics. Think of the brain-mind as a particle and the soul-mind as a wave. They are not separate, but one and the same together. They are correlated, but can only be measured or observed one at a time. As a matter of fact, it is the act of observation that causes one or the other to manifest in our perception.

> **TRANSMUTATIONAL LEADERSHIP:**
> **1.** *A process and a number of methods, tools, and techniques designed to increase awareness of mind and to open numerous additional possibilities to support problem solving and decision making*
> **2.** *A theory or hypothesis that posits that a paradigm shift of consciousness will fundamentally change existing systems*
> **3.** *A state of being*
> **4.** *Alchemy of the mind and brain*

Extending the analogy as it relates to us, we could say that the brain-mind can only perceive the physical world as a particle, whereas the soul-mind perceives the world as a wave, and doing both simultaneously is not possible. As humans, we are very adept at seeing the world as particles, since our brain-mind dominates us.

Another metaphor I like to use is that our minds are like the ocean. A single wave is a unique phenomenon that can be seen and measured for its characteristics at a specific point in time. Yet, it is inseparable from the ocean and connected to every other water molecule in the ocean (and to all other things in the universe) by virtue of its fundamental properties. The brain-mind sees the wave, the soul-mind sees the ocean, and the Infinite Mind sees all.

Our body eventually dies, but I believe that our mind lives on. As a fragment (i.e., a unique pattern of energy), our mind energy is separate, unique, and distinct in the ethereal world, as it has a unique energy signature, just as our body has a unique signature. It is a harmonic of energy, if you will, just as a chorus is made up of individual voices. As energy, it is eternal. When the body dies, the mind lives on as the soul's intelligence and self-knowledge. This has very interesting consequences.

> **SOUL:***
> 1. *A unique and eternal entity in the form of intelligent undefinable energy separate from our physical body; our spiritual self*
> 2. *The quantum level (i.e., intelligent energy) aspect of a human*
> 3. *Consciousness*

We do not yet understand how our mind energy and our physical body's matter are entangled, but together they form our unique identity. The mind is associated, in part, with our beliefs, memories, experiences, and personality. We draw on all of these when leading. They are all aspects of our mind and are subject to feedback and continuous change. We can intentionally enable feedback and change via consciousness. Consciousness is a way for us to deliberately observe and participate in our mind's development and is the method by which we exercise free will. Consequently, *the more consciousness one has, the more free will one has.* So, there is continuous unconscious feedback and change, and there is intentional conscious feedback and change. The metaphor I think of is the difference between flying on autopilot and flying manually.

As I see it, there are three components of consciousness, namely conscious thought, unconscious thought, and no thought. *Conscious thought* is associated with the *logical brain* and is rational intelligence (i.e., IQ). *Unconscious*

---

* Note: I do not intend "soul" to be interpreted as a religious idea or associated with any religion. In most contexts in this book, I intend "soul" to mean our spiritual self.

> **CONSCIOUSNESS QUOTIENT:**
> *CQ is the intentional oscillation between the mind and brain for the purpose of increasing self-awareness. The higher the oscillation, the higher the CQ.*

thought is associated with the *reptilian and mammalian brain* and is emotional intelligence (i.e., EQ). *No thought* is associated with awareness of *mind energy only*, (i.e., a heightened state of awareness and a complete absence of thought, as experienced when meditating), and is spiritual intelligence (i.e., SQ). The concept of all three operating as a system is associated with systems intelligence (i.e., SysQ). Various techniques that permit us to rapidly oscillate between the brain and mind constitute the exercise of consciousness (i.e., CQ). The transmutational leadership model incorporates all of these intelligences.

> **THOUGHT (CONSCIOUS):***
> **1.** *The process of accessing and focusing aspects of mind to satisfy a purpose or intention, for example, accessing beliefs, memories, experiences, and personality as they relate to problem solving and decision making*
> **2.** *Reasoning*

As you may have determined, the model contains the basic elements of a system model, namely the input,

---

* Note: Conscious thought and consciousness are often used interchangeably in many texts, but, as discussed in this book, I define consciousness as being much more than conscious thought.

process, product, output, and feedback loop. I visualize the mind as a system in which feedback is used for learning and growth. Indeed, many believe that our physical self is nothing more than a physical vessel to accomplish this learning for our spiritual self to incrementally grow toward, and finally achieve, enlightenment.

Consequently, if this hypothesis is true, our entire experience is integrated, however subtly, into the fabric of the universe (via the Infinite Mind), automatically and immediately.

Even neuroscientists who seek an exclusively physical explanation for the source of the mind will admit there is no unequivocal scientific proof yet and that a complete understanding of the brain's function still eludes them.

Whenever there are theories or models about something, there are limits to their application. This means that exception cases will exist beyond the limits of applicability. Exception cases reveal deficiencies in the theory or model being applied and illustrate in what manner it is incorrect. For example, quantum mechanics has shown that Newtonian physics is incorrect. That does not invalidate Newtonian physics, but simply reveals the limits of its applicability.

Existing theories regarding brain and mind are no different. For example, we have models of the structure of the brain, but the nature of memory is very uncertain. We know that experiments can stimulate an area of the brain to elicit a memory, and scientists have identified where things get processed, but how does one explain the person who has only a thin layer of brain cells about a millimeter thick in his cranium and yet leads a perfectly normal life?[3] More exception cases, such as energy healing, the placebo effect, and psychic phenomena come to our attention every day.

Exception cases such as these always point out to us that we don't understand it all and may be quite wrong regarding our models, theories, and hypotheses.

My hypothesis is no different. It is subject to debate, although I believe it accommodates certain exception cases, though it has limits too. There are no known ways of experimentally proving it true or false—short of dying, that is. Even here, however, I would point to near-death experiences, psychic and paranormal phenomena, and in-between life regressions as non-rigorous probabilistic evidence supporting my hypothesis.

And yet, science is progressively shedding light on how these exceptional cases and unexplainable phenomena may be possible. For example, some believe the mind to be holographic (i.e., nonlocal and distributed) and the brain fractal in its design (i.e., specialized, local, and very deep), although this is controversial, to say the least. These holographic and fractal concepts of mind and brain respectively support the transmutational leadership model and my hypothesis.

Given the fact that the hypothesis cannot be proven true or false, it must be taken on faith. If you set aside your beliefs for a time and allow that all this is possible, however unlikely you may consider it to be, and perhaps even true if you are generous with me, then this belief will alter how you lead and how you define leadership.

> **BELIEF:**
> **1.** *An opinion (as in the validity or truth of a statement or fact) or conviction (as in a value judgment about a person's action being good or evil)*
> **2.** *Confidence in a truth (as in a scientific theory backed by empirical evidence) or existence of something not immediately susceptible to rigorous proof (as in religious faith)*

I want to be clear that it is not my intent to tell anyone how to lead. My intent is to simply ask you to reflect on and consider these ideas seriously. This is possibly the most important thing you could do to derive the maximum value from this book.

CQ is the ability to transcend an aspect of our very nature. CQ is the rapid oscillation between the mind and the brain using various consciousness techniques. The faster the mind and brain oscillate, the higher the CQ and, I claim, the better we are as leaders. Surely, this is of value even if the underlying hypothesis of mind turns out to be wrong. If the ongoing debate and research prove that it is wrong, then the tree of knowledge will be suitably pruned and these ideas and the model quickly forgotten. So be it.

KNOWLEDGE:
1. *Facts about a thing believed to be true*
2. *An opinion shared by a majority of observers*
3. *Information held in the fabric of the universe*

Is It Controversial? You Bet!

As mentioned, none of the above can be stated as categorically true. Many years ago, I came up with the following notion: The truth is a collected set of opinions and sometimes not even that. It's what keeps my mind open to possibility. Therefore, this book is simply my opinion and is intended to generate thought and conversation and not to promote some silver-bullet solution. Someone else down the line might find it useful to generate other ideas and generate even more conversation. Who knows, I might be completely wrong. But even so, I hope that learning and advancement will result.

Purpose of Brain and Mind

I believe the brain-mind exists in, and for, the physical world. It sees itself as a separate entity among other separate entities, and its primary purpose is its own survival, which manifests as competition and fear.

The brain-mind is exquisitely designed to judge everything very quickly. The brain-mind has a sense of time and space because of how it processes input from the external environment. It perceives a past, a present, and a future and wants ultimate control over everything to satisfy its self-interest. The brain-mind's design very quickly polarizes all input into a binary choice that results in a decision. I believe the brain-mind is the root cause of our suffering by virtue of its design and how it operates.

I believe the soul-mind exists in, and for, the spiritual world. It sees itself as connected to everything at all times, and its primary purpose is self-development, which manifests as unconditional forgiveness, compassion, and love. The soul-mind is nonjudgmental and does not polarize input. The soul-mind does not have a sense of time and desires ultimate creativity for its own development on its path to enlightenment. The soul-mind does not suffer.

I cannot know the Infinite Mind or its purpose, but I believe that increasing consciousness in the universe is an aspect of its creativity.

The brain-mind and the soul-mind together strive for balance. The brain-mind converts input into this *or* that, whereas the soul-mind converts input into this *and* that. Thus, we do see shades of gray in many situations. That ability is the manifestation of the dynamic nature of brain-mind and soul-mind working together.

Regrettably, at this stage of our evolution, the brain-mind still dominates us because we have created systems to satisfy it, reinforce it, and have entrenched our beliefs accordingly. Furthermore, in terms of energy, the brain-mind is very noisy compared to the soul-mind, which is very quiet. As we know, loud sounds usually overcome soft sounds.

For a very good description of how the brain and mind relate to each other, I highly recommend Chopra and Tanzi's book *Super Brain: Unleashing the Explosive Power of Your Mind to Maximize Health, Happiness, and Spiritual Well-Being.*[4] Their description of the brain, mind, and consciousness is consistent with my hypothesis and model.

Consciousness Quotient and the Transmutational Leadership Model

Leadership today and into the future will require people who are adept at using both the brain-mind and soul-mind in a more balanced way. There already are a number of great soul-mind leaders in the world today, and it is clear that the direction of leadership development is toward the soul-mind. However, I have no illusions that exclusive soul-mind leadership is a panacea for all our ills. Soul-mind leaders will be seriously challenged by the competition and fear that will occur as humanity experiences diminishing resources and the global Tragedy of the Commons, which is explained in Chapter 3.

As you will see in Figure 14 and Figure 15 in Chapter 4, the transmutational leadership model consists of a process (Figure 14) whereby our brain and mind get input and produce output, and it also consists of various outcomes of leadership practices and capabilities (Figure 15) that are found somewhere on a continuum of one possibility to infinite possibilities.

Once you have read the book, there are two questions that I would ask you to reflect on:

1. At what level in the continuum are most of your decisions made?
2. How high is your CQ?

Answering these two basic questions will help you situate your degree of self-awareness as a leader.

Remember that there are no right answers, only appropriate or inappropriate responses to the situation and to the prevailing ideas and philosophies that guide our ethics, morality, and social justice.

As you make decisions, consider them as either legitimate or not. I believe that a legitimate leadership decision must satisfy the mandatory elements of consent, reciprocity, and community. Followers give you, the leader, their consent that you have the right and power to make decisions on their behalf, and followers must be fully informed to prevent abuse of power. Reciprocity is needed to ensure that both leader and followers receive some benefit from the decision. The degree of benefits (typically wealth, power, and glory) accruing to the various people affected by the decision within the group must be guided by the culture of society and the norms of the organization. Finally, the decision must benefit community. This not only means the community within the organization, but also society as a whole and, ultimately, all of humanity, other species, and the environment.

Thus, leadership and making legitimate leadership decisions are very hard work that is filled with dilemmas, paradoxes, and conundrums as leaders face multiple competing criteria in all of their decisions. Therefore, finding balance is crucial, and having a model that situates these decisions is valuable. That's where I see the true value of CQ and the transmutational leadership model, because there are no completely right answers, just as there are no completely right models.

I hope that this uncertainty will stimulate your critical thinking and assessment of the model, and how you relate to it.

MAKTUB

The here and now is but momentary choice

Connecting past and future.

Choose the path that calls you

Every waking moment.

Sharpen your mind's eye.

Meditate on its teachings.

Feel the hum of convergence along the path.

Your path is unique and your most trusted companion;
its counsel is wise.

Your journey awaits; follow your path.

It is written!

2

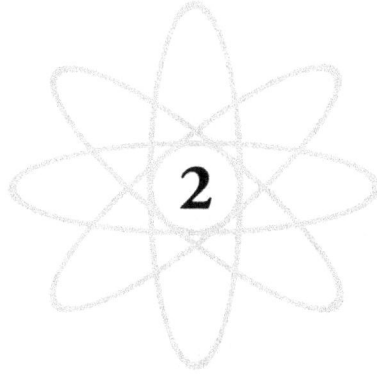

Getting to Know Your Brain and Mind

The Root of the Problem

AS MARSHALL McLUHAN famously said, *"The last thing a fish notices is the water it's swimming in."*

Applying McLuhan's saying to us, our issue is that we are generally unaware of what our brain and mind are doing. In my opinion, the root problem of our suffering and often poor decisions is the very nature of our brain's design and how our brain and mind operate.

When the brain receives input, it puts these through a nonlinear (i.e., chaotic) process, then filters them in a number of ways to create polarities that appear as orderly conscious thought, and these thoughts are the basis for some form of output; that is, a decision and some type of action. For example, for a given input, we don't know if we will feel the emotion "happy" or "sad" until the solution presents itself to our consciousness.

There are three primary areas that I will discuss, namely polarity thinking, chaos-order oscillation, and beliefs.

Polarity Thinking

Consider the following opposites created by our three primary brain structures: Chopra[*] informs us that our reptilian brain, some 300 million years old, directs us to flee or fight. Our limbic (mammalian) brain, some 100 million years old, tells us whether we should be happy or sad. Our cognitive (logical) brain, some 4 million years old, advises us whether something is good or bad. So, the binary solution space is resolved through a decision made consciously and/or subconsciously. That means that consciousness, which appears to be a more recent phenomenon, evolutionarily speaking, cannot change a brain design that is hundreds of millions of years old. The brain will do what it is designed to do. Our consciousness can only allow us to be self-aware of what our brain is doing in order to overcome its polarizing tendency—a tendency that leads to seeing everything as separate rather than interconnected and to judge all things as good or bad in less than a second, both consciously and unconsciously. It is no wonder that it is hard work to be fully conscious of one's self.

Thus, whether we are conscious of it or not, we judge things as good or bad, and we determine very quickly if we're happy or sad about something and whether or not we'll run away or fight when threatened. There are many beliefs that we convert into implicit and explicit rules in all of our organizations and systems, such as how we define progress and success, good behavior and bad behavior. Our beliefs guide whom we choose as leaders, how we choose them, and how we make leadership decisions; for

---

[*] Chopra, D. (2008). My personal notes from a talk given by Deepak Chopra in Vancouver, Canada

example, how we determine rules of democracy regarding voting and related procedures.

> **PROGRESS:**
> 1. *A change in an entity or thing whereby the difference is judged to be positive by the observer of the change*
> 2. *A values-based assessment of change*

We use our rules (i.e., beliefs) to create a value system to justify ourselves and to make sense of our decisions. This is true individually and organizationally. For example, you will notice that a country's foreign policies are based on self-interest, a root cause of conflict between nations and a reflection of our individual and collective self-interest. It is very challenging for leaders to balance this self-interest against internal and external social justice.

These binary or polarized judgments fuel our hatreds and make us feel good. They give us the pleasant feeling of moral superiority over others when we think we are right, especially when they've been reinforced by success. Even if we can perceive a potential solution as both this and that, only one or the other will prevail at the end of a forced choice. It's important to know that we make these choices both consciously and unconsciously.

Jung showed us that much can be learned about our subconscious through dreams. Here's a personal example of a dream I had while writing this book. In my dream, I was a company executive in a boardroom with my finance manager, and across the table were two insurance representatives—one very senior and one junior. The senior guy was training the junior guy. We were going over the policy, and I was picking it apart and being very difficult. I was focusing on a minor detail and was going on and on about it relentlessly. Although it was negligible in the grand scheme of things, it represented to me what I disliked about banks and insurance companies. I saw it as nickel-and-diming clients and finding ways to greatly increase premiums (i.e., ensure their profitability) at my expense. What bothered me is that I could not get almost-guaranteed profits from my clients. As I saw it, loyalty to them meant abusing their clients, whereas loyalty to me meant discounts. Cynically, I thought loyalty represented a stickiness factor: "Great; they're loyal, we'll stick it to them!" Anyway, I was going on and on about it, haranguing him relentlessly, like a dog with bone that won't let go. The senior guy was getting visibly upset. I could tell that he didn't like my obstinacy. He was there to train the junior guy, so he was not looking good, and his ego was getting bruised in the process. He was also thinking that this ridiculously small amount of commission was not worth this much pain. I decided to take a time-out and went to the bathroom.

I realized during my time-out that my behavior had not been ideal. I realized I had acted despicably. My buttons had been pushed, and neither he nor I liked what was going on. I knew that he hated clients like me who wasted his time for things that had virtually no commission. I realized that I hated what he represented to me: a greedy corporation that had an effective monopoly and an almost guaranteed way of making profit, whereas my company did not. I saw the situation as being one in which his corporation was abusing my corporation. That's what really annoyed me. Neither one of us was really in control of anything that was going on in the room. I also saw myself finally giving in and signing the contract.

Sometimes dreams are reflective of real-life situations and sometimes not. In this case, it was the former. In fact, just two weeks earlier, I had received my home insurance notice. The premium was going up ten percent with no changes to the policy. With inflation running at about two-and-a-half percent, I saw this as typical of insurance companies gouging clients, and so my dream was not exactly out of the blue.

From this true story, you can see the three brain levels at work. The reptilian brain with its fight-or-flight response was certainly there, and I was primarily in fight mode. The mammalian brain of emotions was there. Anger, frustration, and other negative feelings were manifesting themselves. It made me feel good to take out my anger on the insurance reps and standing on my soapbox to make me feel better. My logical brain was there arguing about the logic of big increases and the need to have them justified to my satisfaction.

The scenario I paint by relating my dream shows the importance of how our brain-minds can capture us in the moment and what can happen if one is not self-aware and mindful at all times. Competitive situations are antagonistic by nature, and we can easily get caught up in the moment.

As it applies to the subconscious, leadership exists as an archetype, or as archetypes, in our psyche. I believe that this is why we recognize leadership when we see it in the context of a situation, but otherwise can't define it logically because it is dependent on the situation.

> **LEADERSHIP:**
> 1. *An abstract construct of a person's mind*
> 2. *A unique combination of attributes within a person or organization recognized by the majority of observers as superior within a specific context or system*

It follows then that we need to be very aware of our subconscious, because a lot of our decisions are influenced by archetypes that we are not even aware of. That is difficult at best and requires a certain amount of courage and fortitude to investigate honestly. I believe that Carl Jung and his colleagues would agree with me, and I highly recommend Jung's book *Man and his Symbols.*[1]

For a more in-depth discussion of what I believe are some key leadership issues, please refer to Appendix B.

What I describe above is a system of perceiving reality that is designed, or has evolved, to benefit us individually and collectively to ensure survival. This system scales up from the individual to whatever form of organization we create to benefit us. Whether it is individual against individual, tribe against tribe, nation against nation, or religion against religion, the fundamental way the brain's system works is via polarized thinking (both conscious and unconscious). By and large, leaders are influenced by, and exploit, the fundamental properties of this system.

This form of systemic response to our perceived external environment has served us well. Our intelligence and opposable thumbs have allowed us to create technologies that have exploited our superior capabilities. We are very much the dominant species at the top of the food chain. Our success has greatly contributed to a deteriorating environment and our fast depleting resources.

Those leaders who have been the best at the leadership game have risen to the top, like cream does in milk, and have been showered with wealth, power, and glory. History books are littered with these folks, which proves the point. Some of them weren't so nice, though many of them were very "successful."

For more on polarized brain-mind thinking and a possible way out, I highly recommend you read Tolle (2004)[2, 3] and encourage you to read Rychkun (2012).[4]

Chaos-Order Oscillation

As I mentioned at the beginning of this chapter, the brain is actually chaotic in its design.

In between an input to the brain and its output is the time period when the brain is in a chaotic state concerning that given input. During that brief moment, many possibilities are "fighting" it out to determine which one will prevail.

As is known about chaotic systems, the system's initial condition or, as we would put it in reference to our brain, our "state of mind" prior to input, has a lot of influence on the outcome—this being which polarity will dominate as perceived by our conscious thought. This is what then drives our decisions and our actions.

The analogy I like to use is that the brain is like the atmosphere and a cloud at the same time. Consider a nice fluffy white cumulus cloud of the type that is often seen in the summertime. The cloud is constantly receiving energy as a result of the sun's heating, and it moves along with the wind. At any given moment, it is impossible to predict exactly what it will look like next; the process is far too complex. That nice fluffy cumulus cloud, however, given the right input, can turn into a nasty tornado. But a tornado, like the atmosphere in general, naturally returns to a stable state when its energy has dissipated. For the brain, we call this state homeostasis. As we all know, no one can sustain an angry rage for very long, but we can hold the anger in our minds for a long time. This is part of our beliefs and how our brains and minds can bias future input.

It's important to realize that this chaotic state—the time between the input and our perception of outcome—is the space and time where ultimate creativity resides and more possibilities exist. This is so because no polarity is equal to no thought. This is why meditative practices are so powerful. Meditative practices are able to stop the brain and allow us to become self-aware. I believe that quieting the brain in this manner is how "higher" levels of mind are accessed.

All human beings are able to access this space on their own. This is good news for everyone, not just leaders. The reason it is good news is that, when we intentionally use techniques such as meditation, we stop seeing the world in polarities, as in *us* versus *them*, and begin to sense the interconnectedness of all things and our place in it. We begin to see and understand how we affect everything by our mere presence, let alone our actions, and how everything else does the same thing, too. We begin to understand how diverse and beautiful the possibilities are and how wondrous the world really is. We begin to understand our complicity in events, and learn how to forgive ourselves and others and learn to love. If you can pause your brain-mind to observe without fear or judgment, then you will see every situation quite differently.

The consequence of this design is that we cannot predict exactly how we or others will react to any given situation. It is also a great design if adaptability is the goal. We do adapt very well, which is one reason we are so successful as a species. However, the situation in the world is such that we need to get off autopilot and fly manually now by using our CQ.

I discuss chaos and order as it applies to systems in more detail in the chapter on systems (Chapter 3). For an enlightening discussion of nonlinear systems and the science of chaos in general, I highly recommend the book *Chaos: Making a New Science* by James Gleick.[5]

How We Are Biased by Our Beliefs

Belief and knowledge are related. There are things we know, things we don't know, and things we think we know. Knowing the difference is a form of intellectual competence. Knowledge has deep philosophical roots.

The allegory of the cave in Plato's *The Republic* illustrates how beliefs, knowledge, and systems interrelate. In the allegory, the cave is the system and our beliefs and knowledge result from our experience in the cave. Here's how it goes:

People are chained to a wall and facing it. A fire is blazing behind them, casting light. People and other objects are walking or moving back and forth between the fire and the people chained to the wall. The chained people cannot see the people and objects moving back and forth or sense them in any other way. Their reality is that the world consists of shadows on the wall. They have no concept of other people or the objects that are creating the shadows. One day, an individual is miraculously freed from his chains and turns around to see what is really happening. As a result of his new awareness, four fundamental scenarios become possible:

> ➤ First, the individual is so traumatized by the truth that he turns back and chains up again so that he can remain comfortably numb. The whole experience is interpreted as a nightmare.

> ➤ Second, the individual, now knowing a different reality, attempts to tell his friends about it. They discuss it and determine that their friend is deranged and don't accept the new vision of reality. So, they dismiss it and go back to looking at the shadows. They attempt to make the individual conform and stop spreading seditious ideas. They tell him to rejoin the group. Failing that, and as difficult as it may be to do while chained to a wall, they may even attempt kill him in an attempt to kill the idea.

> ➤   Third, having failed at convincing his
>   colleagues of the new truth, the individual
>   either reintegrates into the previous system
>   or heads out on his own. Being alone is scary
>   and threatens survival, so the chances of
>   the maverick heading out are less than for
>   a reintegration. Consequently, the maverick
>   chains himself up, buries the idea in the
>   subconscious, and forever doubts the decision
>   to return to the fold.

> ➤   Fourth, the maverick convinces some or all
>   of the others of the new truth, so that they
>   allow him to unchain them. With courage and
>   trepidation, they step away from the wall and
>   turn around, so that they can experience this
>   new reality. This new reality now becomes the
>   new dominant opinion because they haven't
>   ventured out of the cave yet to see that there's
>   a whole other reality outside.

Anyone who does not share the opinion of the majority is a maverick in the allegory. You will notice that all of our religious prophets fit this maverick image.

What happens to the maverick in the allegory tends to happen to all those who would question the status quo and the belief system that supports it. Indeed, anyone who does not agree with a generally accepted truth is sometimes treated in a very hostile way.

Organizations are ambivalent toward mavericks; they make use of them in the short term, but then they get rid of them when the change is accomplished. Rule breakers are despised because they destabilize. They're a lot of trouble! They are just like ideas or experiences that don't fit a scientific model. They are often speaking and writing inconvenient truths. And yet, these people are invaluable. Change often happens because of the tension created between believers and nonbelievers.

At any given moment, for any input, the brain's state is biased by the mind's beliefs, memories, experiences, and personality. So, while the input to the system goes through a non-deterministic and nonlinear or chaotic process, it is biased toward a particular solution. Thus, we cannot predict with certainty how we will react to any given situation, but we have a bias driven by such things as our dominant beliefs and personality. This gives us consistency of behavior most of the time. Knowing our personality type helps us understand how we prefer to respond to the external environment. For instance, introverts and extroverts respond differently to the same stimuli originating from the external environment.* However, when we learn about others' personality types, we start to see them in a particular way, and our beliefs bias how we interact with them. Sometimes, leaders use this information to persuade and influence in a good way and sometimes they use it to manipulate in a bad way, depending on what they want to accomplish. This is how all beliefs end up biasing our behavior.

Some beliefs are extremely difficult to change. A lot of the time, we are not even aware that some of our behaviors are due to unconscious beliefs that we hold.

Operation of the Brain and Mind and Its Consequences

It is perhaps not surprising that the brain has evolved in this manner. Making quick decisions about an unknown noise in the night or about a competitive situation is good for survival of the individual and the species. It's a rather fast process. The time between input and output is measured

---

* For information on personality typing, please see "Example 1 – Myers-Briggs Type Indicator" in Chapter 5.

in less than a second; you might characterize the process as thoughtless! Certainly, it's thoughtless when most of the processing is subconscious.

During an experiment reported by Talbot,[6] a stimulus (start) was detected in the brain 0.0001 seconds after it occurred, the response occurred 0.1 seconds after start, and the person only became aware of the stimulus or the response 0.5 seconds afterward. So, unless we are paying conscious attention, we sometimes do things or make a decision without really knowing why. For example, if you are an experienced driver, you will often have driven without conscious awareness. Routine driving is treated like noise by the brain until something forces you to pay attention. The ability to treat background information as noise in order to focus on what's perceived to be important can be a very positive attribute for us. Unfortunately, it also means that we are vulnerable to missing important information too.

The ultimate consequence of this aspect of our nature is that we judge people rather quickly, and we judge ourselves, too. In no time at all, we judge whether we like someone or not, and we often beat ourselves up unnecessarily. For the most part, we don't even notice we're doing it. All of a sudden, we'll wake up in the middle of the night with that voice in our head going over the same negative events over and over. That voice in your head is not you. You are the person who is aware of the voice in your head.

A perceived successful system self-reinforces leadership behaviors, but once critical conditions in the system change, leadership must also change. Unfortunately, there is always a lot of resistance to change, especially by the dominant few who don't want to easily give up their wealth, power, and glory. But trouble starts when the majority of people recognize increasingly that their interests, guided by their fundamental beliefs, are no longer served by the dominant few. Consequently, some type of crisis usually ensues.

Leaders are constrained as well as empowered by rules that are based on beliefs and ingrained into the culture of society. Thus, leaders have a difficult problem on their hands. The external system is constantly changing, and the internal rules may not be right for the circumstances. The leader's traits may no longer be viable for the new conditions. The leader has tough decisions to make and also will look after their self-interest. Leaders must not only decide difficult matters, they must also ask tough questions. Shall we compete or authentically cooperate? What legacy shall we leave our children? Shall we sacrifice the well-being of our group in favor of others? Shall we leave our children materially worse off than our generation? How do we resolve the conflict of the "American" dream, shared by many, to ensure that our children are better off than we were if we are to sacrifice our material well-being in favor of others? Can we really cooperate when there are insufficient resources for all? (I also believe we need to redefine what we mean by "better off than we were.") In our current situation, how do we enable social justice for all? How do these questions get resolved within the current framework of our rules?

None of these questions is easy to answer. Do we really have the courage to abolish all our armies? I think not, and as long as we are or feel threatened in some way, we won't. We easily forget that we sometimes use our various forms of power to compete at the highest levels to secure our economic future (i.e., our modern symbol of survival). Even if we have good intentions, we maintain standing armies, if only to warn others of our ability to defend and avenge as needed.

I mentioned that leaders have a considerable problem balancing the needs of the group with the needs of other groups. They also have a problem with their own brain and mind. In the Introduction, I raised the issue of leadership abuse of power, which not only applies to the individual, but also to all forms of organization up to humanity as a whole. Clearly, humanity is abusing other species and the environment.

Thus, our very nature is at the core of the problem, and the exploitation of inequality is why abuse is rampant. An example of such abuse is the tobacco industry. Quite some time ago, the so-called leaders of this industry perjured themselves in front of Congress and in multiple court-rooms swearing up and down and on any bible you would care to choose that cigarette smoking was not harmful to health. They did this even though their own records clearly contradicted their statements. It took many lawsuits and litigation for the truth to emerge: smoking cigarettes is harmful to health. Cigarettes are still being manufactured and marketed today.

I believe that when a for-profit organization considers its reason for existence to be profit only and its "leaders" are rewarded accordingly, then that's what we get. Thus, what an organization believes to be its ultimate purpose makes a significant difference in its conduct.

The distinction between traditional capitalism lead-ership practices (as I see it, brain-mind driven) versus conscious capitalism practices (as I see it, soul-mind driven) and their respective belief systems is outlined by Mackey and Sisodia in their book *Conscious Capitalism: Liberating the Heroic Spirit of Business*.[7]

Leaders are generally rewarded for achieving their orga-nization's charter, rather than for how it affects humanity. Thus, leaders are not always rewarded for doing the "right" thing for humanity and the planet; quite to the contrary, in fact, and that's a serious issue. Therefore, mindful fol-lowers should examine the purpose of their organization and how it serves humanity and how they want their leaders to lead. Mackey and Sisodia clearly show that align-ment of purpose with consistency of leadership practices intended to achieve a higher purpose is a powerful method for reinforcing positive energy and generating outstanding results that are not just financial. However, there are many who believe that profits will always suffer if the for-profit motive is compromised in any way. In particular, if for-profit corporations saw their reason for existence as providing a net positive value to society, as Hawken suggests in his book *The Ecology of Commerce: A Declaration of Sustainability*,[8] or if we required them to do so, then this would change their behavior. But many also believe that this would necessarily increase cost, and therefore price, to the end customer. This concern is not unfounded, and so many organizations resist sustainability intiatives.

Hawken points out that a lot of the cost of a product does not take into account the costs of remediating the environment, which ends up being paid for by taxpayers. Open-pit mining and the health care costs resulting from cigarette smoking are two examples. Note that the price to the consumer is not the total cost. And even if the result of a cost-benefit analysis is positive, as Phillip Morris once argued in the case of cigarettes, there are other non-economic issues at stake.

So, if we shift our beliefs about the purpose of for-profit corporations as being profit only to being for-profit in the service of humanity and the planet, it would certainly change behavior. This is especially true if we really required our organizations to demonstrate to us how they serve beyond their immediate mandate and then reward them for it. The positive feedback loop in the reward system would reinforce such behavior. Of course, this is not a simple problem.

Nevertheless, it seems obvious in this day and age that all organizations should be mindful of the planet and humanity. So, why do for-profit organizations and leaders behave badly? Because it's usually significantly cheaper or more profitable! Besides, their immediate mandate is to serve their paying customers, not the general public.

So, even though some of them might feel badly about negative outcomes, they aren't rewarded for doing something about it. Part of the problem is that the global economic system, and capitalism in particular, is based primarily on the seventeenth-century philosophy of utilitarianism. Utilitarianism is otherwise known as the cost-benefit model, and it is a big part of our belief system. Given a number of choices, an individual or organization selects the option that provides the highest benefit for the least cost, thus yielding the highest value or profit.

But there are things that go beyond financial considerations on which we cannot put a financial value, though we certainly try to do so. There is no question that cost-benefit is very important, but ethics, morality, and social justice need to be equally considered as part of every leadership decision. One would think that the Pinto car scandal many years ago would have served notice to all companies that this type of behavior is a slippery slope and won't be tolerated, especially in this age of social media and rapid communication, but this does not appear to be the case. When you observe an organization, ask the following questions: Who are its clients? Whom does it serve? Why does it exist? What is its purpose? What do leaders consider when making decisions?

Here's an example of shameful abuse. On 10 March 2013, an episode of the *60 Minutes* TV show featured a story involving NECC, a pharmaceutical company behind a tainted steroid that caused a deadly outbreak of fungal meningitis. Many people died, and many others will remain ill for the rest of their lives. It all started when the United States federal government deregulated this type of pharmaceutical production company. The FDA was vehemently opposed to the deregulation, but was forced to comply. As a result of the deregulation, the rapid increase in demand caused quality issues at NECC's manufacturing plant. Employees raised concerns regarding excessively high production requirements and quality. These concerns were met with shrugs by managers, who told the employees to get on with it. What could the workers at NECC do when they felt they could lose their jobs if they pushed too far? These are serious dilemmas when you have a mortgage to pay and a family to feed. NECC made a lot of money. The sad story doesn't end there. NECC executives took several million dollars, 16 million as I recall, out of the company shortly before filing for bankruptcy. If you're not familiar with how this works—it's a great way to avoid paying for lawsuits. It wasn't clear from the episode where exactly these executives and the money ended up. How do we stop this type of unscrupulous behavior?

Please do not get me wrong. I am totally in favor of for-profit corporations. I firmly believe that wealth creation is a very necessary aspect of transforming our society for the better and to advance civilization. I also believe that it is crucial for capital to be available in the amounts necessary for great projects to be accomplished. Someone has to put up the money if the government won't, and those folks deserve some kind of return for the risks they take. That's what I believe as a capitalist with a social conscience.

Whatever the case, we're dealing with very complex systems and contexts. Since we can't understand these complex problems, we turn to our experts and leaders to help us solve them. It is, after all, what we pay them for and why they deserve extra wealth, power, and glory. In some ways, this also allows us to point fingers and assign blame when something goes wrong, rather than hold ourselves accountable.

It's also easy to play the victim; none of us had a choice about the systems we were born into. It's easier to go with the flow and not question anything. Our brain-mind goes out of its way to protect its self-esteem, self-worth, and survival. Isn't it just easier to delegate our power and responsibility to our leaders? It gives us a way out and someone to blame. That's how the brain-mind operates.

And so the wheel turns and symptoms get moved around with no real progress, and leaders indulge in "blamesmanship" to protect their personal interests and egos. Everyone is intrinsically motivated to protect their self-interest, self-esteem, and self-worth. The ego of the brain-mind assures it. So, a great way to distract us and prevent us from seeing the true nature of a problem is when a leader blames something or someone for some failure or crisis; of course, the humorous part is that they take full credit when things go well. What is the absolute truth and what is propaganda are immensely blurred. Regardless, they are usually blaming or taking credit for a symptom! So, nothing substantial gets done to solve the fundamental problem. No learning takes place, or the wrong learning takes place. As some Eastern philosophers would say, "all is illusion."

One politician I know has said this about a contentious issue, and I paraphrase, "The people don't care, and I will do what I want to do." This leader is dismantling environmental laws for economic reasons. When a leader behaves in such a way that a dominant system gets entrenched and reinforced at the expense of other systems, the dominant system over time gets closer and closer to a cataclysmic event. For example, if an economic system puts jobs over the environment to such an extent that both renewable and nonrenewable resources are no longer available, the economic system ultimately collapses. You are probably asking where these systems come from. You guessed it— they are of human origin.

As a CEO entrepreneur, I can assure you that part of an organization's culture is its unwritten rules. These are a reflection of the founding leader's values, character, and personality. Thus, organizations contain both the good and the bad in all of us. Regardless of all that, they manifest the most competitive and fearful aspects of our brain-minds into a variety of behaviors, individually and collectively. Collectively, the organization cares a lot about its survival and will resist "going out of business," even when the value to society is shown to be negative by any standard. Drug cartels are an example. An organization that is failing reflects the process of grief much like we all do when we suffer loss. Elizabeth Kübler-Ross was a pioneer in identifying the grieving process: denial, anger, bargaining, depression, and acceptance.[9] This applies to our beliefs at a personal level, too. Indeed, when faced with a truth that is completely contrary to our most closely held beliefs, we meet it with denial first. Thus, facing ourselves takes work.

The older the system, the more entrenched it is in our subconscious psyche as a belief system. Note that none of us is truly free in the sense that we are born into many preexisting systems. Whether it is a nationality, an ethnic group, a family, an economic system, or otherwise, we are encouraged to adapt very quickly into our many systems in order to "succeed." In the West, this is mainly understood as economic success.

> **SUCCESS:**
> *A set of criteria whereby change or progress is judged as positive. Its antithesis is failure and is judged as negative.*

Many of our systems were created hundreds and even thousands of years ago. Consequently, true free will and informed choice can only be exercised if an understanding of the system(s) and self exists. This requires a certain amount of courage.

Many of us know that organizations that go unchecked will often do as they please and end up negatively impacting the world in multiple ways. That type of unfettered organization always seeks to dominate if it can. Perhaps that explains, in part, the adventures of Genghis Khan and Alexander the Great.

Fortunately, if we recognize the system and how it affects us and fundamentally change how we lead, we will automatically change how our organizations function. Why? Because fundamentally changing how we lead changes the rules of the system by definition. *We* are the system. Increasing our consciousness is our tool to change the rules of the system.

A word of caution is warranted. I don't believe that this is a magical silver bullet. Change always carries with it a variety of tough issues for everyone. There's a gap between here and there. Change is threatening to a lot of people, and we fear it, just as did the chained-up people in Plato's cave. We need to feel safe in order to participate in the change.[10, 11] Transmutational leadership is the bridge that spans the chasm.

Summary

As mentioned, our brain-mind state is constantly changing from moment to moment. It is a dynamic process and as such is consistent with the dominant Eastern view of mind. This process results in a specific state and as such is consistent with the dominant Western view of mind as a thing. They are both true.

We cannot change our fundamental design or how our brain processes input, but we can change our biases through consciousness and various feedback techniques. This is why education is so critical. Not just education in general, but leadership education in particular. Leadership education can create biases whose influence on our decisions may make the result quite harmful.

Thus, knowing one's beliefs is vital to leadership, and self-awareness of both brain and mind is crucial in making sound and legitimate leadership decisions.

A critical issue for leaders is that a lot of the foregoing is not accessible to our conscious thought unless we pay close attention. It is well known that conscious thought is only 10 percent of the system's processing capacity. The other 90 percent is unconscious. Beliefs are held in both locations. Beliefs, combined with chaos-order oscillation, make it difficult for leaders and followers alike to know themselves and to behave authentically. Only higher levels of consciousness are capable of facilitating the difficult task of knowing one's self. This is how transmutational leadership is capable of empowering us to overcome the problems created by traditional leadership. As Albert Einstein said, "No problem can be solved from the same level of consciousness that created it."

You've Been Busy

I see you've been busy.
I hear of the things you've been doing.
Marvelous work, you tend your gardens well.
With all the change you've experienced you must have
Filled your life with joy and sorrow.
It's your many cares, but you know that, don't you?
Yes, you cannot hide the truth from me.
I see you as you are: strong and vulnerable.
I hear your cries: Who looks after me?
So, I've often wondered where you get your energy.
Where's that source of renewal?
What is your secret?
I see the passion that speaks of a life well lived.
So, you're tired.
It's not surprising; each creative act dissipates energy
And you've had many creative moments.
Creative acts cause change,
And change causes joy but grief, too.
So, it's okay to pause for renewal.
Happiness lies in growth—the next step.
Exciting, isn't it?
Just like a caterpillar that needs to pupate
to become a butterfly.
Remember, a butterfly flapping its ephemeral wings
can change the weather.
You make a difference, too!
The seeds you've sown will echo through eternity—
the concert of your soul.

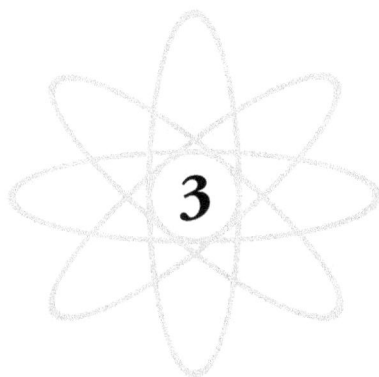

3

Systems

MY BOOK CAN ONLY represent a small subset of the leadership body of knowledge. Thousands of books have been written on leadership and the subjects associated with it (e.g., philosophy). I am simply shining a spotlight on what I think the key issues and ideas of today are, based on my beliefs that the brain left to itself acts like a zombie. In addition, leadership education and training are difficult to accomplish, simply because the scope is so vast and everyone so unique. What to focus on is a constant debate, and only so much depth is possible in any given area. It's true of this book, too!

Systems are, regrettably, one of those often overlooked leadership training topics. There are many books on systems, so this is just a summary of what I think are the most relevant points as they relate to transmutational leadership. This discussion is important, in my opinion, because our brain and our mind are systems. So, understanding systems is essential to understanding our brains and minds, as well as our organizations.

> **SYSTEM:**
> **1.** *An assembly or combination of things or parts forming a complex or unitary whole (as in an economic system or an aircraft or a human)*
> **2.** *An ordered and comprehensive assemblage of facts, principles, doctrines, or the like in a particular field of knowledge or thought (as in a system of philosophy or a religious system)*
> **3.** *A coordinated body of methods or a scheme or plan of procedure; an organizational scheme (as in a system of government or a company)*
> **4.** *Any formulated, regular, or special method or plan of procedure to achieve success (as in a gambling system or a performance-enhancing drug system or a learning system)*

In a practical sense, just how effective leadership traits and practices are is irrelevant unless the system context is examined simultaneously. This is because a system's rules drive our behavior. Leaders are not separate from the systems they lead and are affected by them just like everyone else, but they also have some ability to affect how the system functions, and the truly powerful leader is able to make new rules and change the behavior of the system. Therefore, it's important to have an understanding of what a system is and for me to explain how I see the mind and brain as a system.

I believe that there is general agreement that good leadership is, in part, about achieving change in a positive way. I believe that leading change is one of the foremost tasks for a leader because change is constant. Whether it's internal or external, change involves one or more systems, and change affects one or more people, including the leader. Change always affects people, and the system is always the context that drives decisions. Whether it's internal, as in a belief system, or external, as in competition that threatens survival of the individual or organization, change is inevitable. Even if we don't want to change, entropy assures that change is happening. Entropy, which I describe later, is the Second Law of Thermodynamics initially formulated by Sadi Carnot, and it applies to all things in the physical world. Essentially, it says that all physical things increase in entropy over time. That means that all physical things eventually disintegrate. This is consistent with Eastern philosophy's belief that everything is impermanent. Even the great pyramids at Giza, if left alone, will return to the desert someday.

All systems have a point of leverage that is usually obscure to those embedded in the system. A point of leverage is defined as a factor or aspect of a system whereby a big change occurs for a very small amount of energy applied to the point of leverage. Archimedes was the first to mathematically define the lever. He boasted that if he had a big-enough lever, he could move the Earth. For our typical mundane system, such as an organization, a lever could be a small change imposed by a leader that results in a change in behavior of people or the structure of the system. These small changes, applied correctly, produce extraordinary results.

For example, a small change could be legislation removing or adding the need to do environmental studies before proceeding with industrial projects. It may only be a paragraph or a sentence that are added or removed, but the change can have dramatic effects. It's important to perceive how everything is connected in a system and how decisions about a part can affect the whole.

A big aspect of leadership is the leader's ability to spot

points of leverage and cause fundamental and lasting change to occur. It's typically very hard to see this point, or points, of leverage when you are embedded in the system. If you can't spot them, you just push symptoms around and don't make any significant progress. Often, leaders try various methods because they don't understand what they are fundamentally doing. They will often use a valid method incorrectly and be surprised and confused by the result. The length of time required for results to occur can contribute to the uncertainty regarding the reasons for the results. A certain amount of patience is required— something that is in short supply in this day and age of instant messaging.

For example, reorganizing is a possible leverage point method that is sometimes good and sometimes not. Gaius Petronius Arbiter was a consul of Rome during the reign of Nero. He had this to say about reorganization, as used incorrectly: "We trained hard, but it seemed that every time we were beginning to form up into teams, we would be reorganized. I was to learn later in life that we tend to meet any new situation by reorganizing, and a wonderful method it can be for creating the illusion of progress while producing confusion, inefficiency, and demoralization."[1] Tragically enough, this is common practice today with project teams. It seems that high-performance teams are always broken up following the conclusion of a project and reorganized with new members for the next project. Maybe that's okay and maybe it's not.

So, it's important that leaders understand systems and how to perceive them, what the key leverage point is, and the best way to put it to work. So, what's a system?

Types of Systems

A system is a concept created by us to put a boundary around a thing for some purpose. I won't be discussing products as systems in this book. Transportation systems, such as aircraft and boats and so on, are not relevant to this discussion. Things such as information systems, computers, and real-time systems only support the larger systems we've created, such as our economic systems. I won't talk about computers and the like, either.

All systems share common traits, namely structure, behavior, interconnectivity of subsystems or parts, and rules governing the structure and/or behavior. For instance, a commercial corporation is a structure; it behaves a certain way toward its external environment; it has parts, such as the finance department, and its rules, both written (e.g., procedures) and unwritten (e.g., culture), drive the behavior of the people within it and how it operates. An example would be a public company's procedures that need to follow the Securities and Exchange Commission's rules. Subsystems or parts are often systems unto themselves.

What constitutes the system or subsystem depends on perspective. In my example of the corporation, the said corporation may have a significant subsystem, such as a complex manufacturing system, and it may interface externally to other systems, which create meta-systems at the global level. For example, the global economic system consists of many parts that are also called systems, including, but not limited to, institutions such as the banking and insurance systems, for every nation. We are another example. A human being is a system, but we can also recognize major subsystems, such as the central nervous system, as a system unto itself. Many humans together are also a system. We call a collection of humans a society with social rules (e.g., laws) and a culture. Our systems are everywhere, and we interact with them on multiple levels and in multiple ways. Our constant interaction with our systems via feedback loops causes us to learn continuously, both good and bad.

Conceptually, there are three types of systems, namely

Isolated, *Closed*, and *Open* systems. There are many subtypes or classifications of these systems, for example, natural or human-made systems. Given the purpose of this book, I'll focus on the brain and the mind.

By definition, a system always has a boundary, as shown in Figure 2 below. This basic diagram can be applied to an individual cell or to the largest structure imaginable (e.g., our galaxy and beyond). The boundary is especially important because that is where learning primarily takes place, as Bruce Lipton explains in his book *The Biology of Belief.*[2]

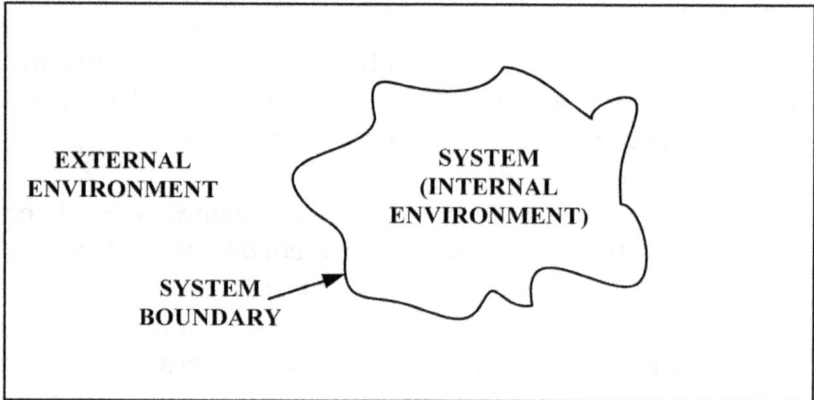

Figure 2: Basic System

An Isolated System is a theoretical system that does not exchange matter or energy. The only isolated system we can conceive of is all of everything and nothing together. If the universe describes all of everything and nothing together, then it is an isolated system. It follows that the Infinite Mind may be an isolated system and we are embedded in it. An isolated system would not have a boundary, since a boundary implies there is something else. Perhaps the only isolated system conceivable has been expressed by Lao Tzu. As he would say, it is the Tao.

A Closed System, as shown in Figure 3, is a system that

only exchanges energy across its boundary. The Earth is thought of as a closed system for practical purposes, but it's well known that this is not true. The Earth receives large amounts of matter (i.e., micrometeorites) every day. We know for a fact that asteroids have hit the Earth periodically. Planets are not closed systems. We've seen a comet impact Jupiter. Closed systems have feedback loops, just like open systems. By my definition, the human mind, being energy only, is a closed system. This should not be confused with the notion of having an open or closed mind, which means something altogether different.

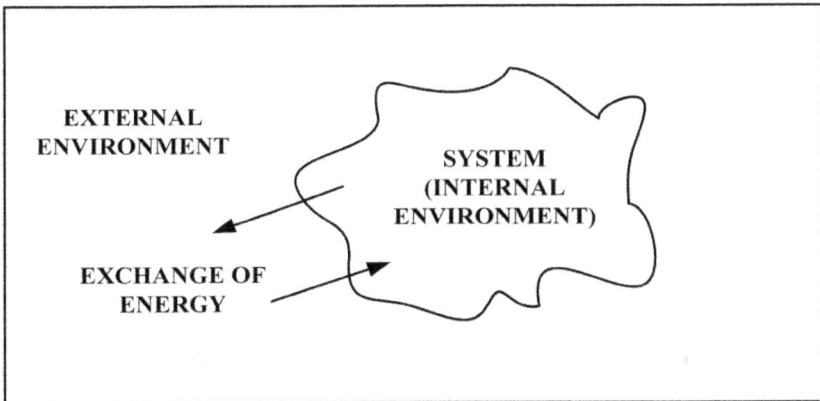

Figure 3: Closed System

An Open System, as shown in Figure 4, exchanges both matter and energy across its boundary. Whether natural or human-made, open systems are affected by both positive and negative feedback. Further, all physical systems decay over time and ultimately perish because of entropy, time being measured from seconds to eons. Mountains become plains, forests come and go, our physical bodies die, species vanish, corporations extinguish, and someday, all that is the Earth and its inhabitants will plummet into the Sun.

In the meantime, we are caretakers of our systems. Our

energy and our resources keep entropy at bay. The human brain is an open system, as is our entire body.

As you can probably now understand, one of the major reasons for me to distinguish the mind as being separate from the body is that they are not the same type of system. The brain is an open system.

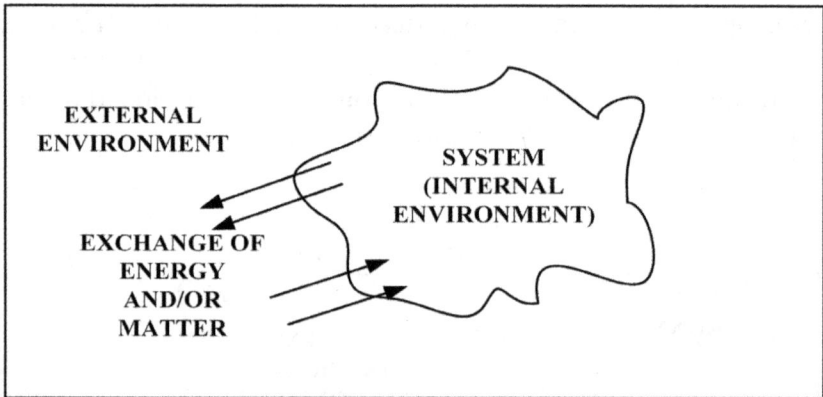

Figure 4: Open System

Natural and Human-Made Systems

Natural systems are all around us. They are what we often call our environment and our ecosystems. Without these, we could not exist. Some of them do quite well without our help, and others are hindered by us.

The beaver pond is often used by ecologists as a way to describe an ecosystem undergoing the process of entropy. The beaver builds his dams, and the world of his pond is created. The pond is an ecosystem and gives habitat and life to other species, such as birds, fish, and insects. But the water is always trickling through and eroding the dam (this is entropy in action), and unless an equal amount of water is coming in from feeder streams and/or unless the beaver continuously expends energy and resources (i.e., mud, reeds, grasses, and tree branches) to repair the dam, it will eventually fail and the water returned to its original level.

The beaver moves on to a new location once it has eaten all the available edible trees within reach. Once the beaver moves on, eventually, all of the beaver's creations will return to their quantum creative soup. Assuming another location can readily be found, the beaver has avoided the Tragedy of the Commons.[3] I will explain the idea of the Tragedy of the Commons later on.

Unlike the beaver that can move on to greener pastures, humans have only one planet. Once resources are expended or cannot reproduce in a timely and sustainable way, tragedy will occur and all of our creations will succumb to entropy. We think that's what may have happened on Easter Island.

Our human-made systems are also all around us. Civilization has been built brick by brick with these systems. We cannot escape them. We are born into a set of systems and have a set of beliefs conditioned into us by these systems and our experiences within them since birth. We remember the rules of these systems.

It's instructive to know that memories carry with them the rules of the system that existed when the memory was created. When you remember someone, for instance a family member, you remember the person in relationship to you. A relationship is a system, too. That relationship is a system that has rules attached to it by definition. These memories are constantly being added to every moment of our existence, whether we are aware of this or not.

Assuming that we are maintaining our systems by expending energy and resources to keep entropy at bay, and assuming that the entropy is growing, a system that is changing is responding to feedback. Feedback is how a system learns from its experience. The boundary is where this happens primarily in the same way as we learn by interacting with our external environment. This learning causes adaptation to occur. Feedback has to be timely for optimal learning—neither too fast nor too slow. Generally, assuming the learning is timely, the faster the feedback, the faster the system learns.

Feedback Loops—Positive and Negative Reinforcement

We've all experienced feedback, both directly and indirectly. There are lots of examples, and I'll mention a few. You've probably studied or heard of Pavlov's dog experiment, the classic example of positive reinforcement. Other examples abound. When you were young and did something your mother asked you to do, she might have given you some ice cream as a reward. Perhaps you worked hard at school and turned that mid-term C grade into a final B grade and got great comments from your teacher and another reward from your parents. Maybe when you were a kid, you threw a baseball through a neighbor's window and got grounded for a week. Now that you're a parent, perhaps you're adding monthly texting minutes to your kid's cell phone or threatening to take them away! When you went to your cousin's wedding, the entertainer got his microphone too close to the speaker and the amplifier howled painfully. When you lost your money in the stock market, you swore you would never buy individual stocks again!

Positive and negative feedback should not be thought of as pleasant or unpleasant, respectively. Positive feedback creates a system that is self-reinforcing. Negative feedback creates a system that is self-correcting. Our mind and our brain have both negative and positive feedback loops.

A howling amplifier is a system exhibiting positive feedback. The microphone picks up the loudspeaker's signals and causes the amplifier gain to go to its maximum output very quickly. An uncontrolled positive feedback loop can cause a system to transition to chaos mode and self-destruct.

The Tragedy of the Commons is a metaphor for a positive feedback loop that ends badly. In terms of our situation today, it is the depletion of a shared resource by individuals, acting independently and rationally according to each one's self-interest, despite their understanding that depleting the common resource is contrary to the group's long-term best interests.

The example often cited is one of a group of farmers who own cows. There is a common area fenced in that is the only place for the cows to graze. The farmer's cows that can graze the most are the most productive with milk and off-spring. In this society, more milk and more offspring mean more wealth and power. A larger herd for a given farmer means more pasture is devoted to that specific farmer at the expense of other farmers. A larger herd grows faster than a smaller herd in absolute numbers. For example, a herd of 10 cows experiencing 10 percent growth in a year means that the herd will be 11 cows in one year's time. A herd of 100 cows experiencing the same 10 percent growth in the same year means the herd will have grown to 110 cows in one year's time. As you can see, the more success-ful the farmer, the faster he/she gets rich at the expense of other farmers, because his/her herd eats up more pasture in absolute numbers.

So, power and wealth accumulate more and more rap-idly in fewer people under certain conditions. Thus, it is in the farmer's self-interest to find a way to get more pasture from the commons than other farmers. Since this is a positive feedback loop, everyone acts similarly, the resource is soon depleted, cannot reproduce itself fast enough, and everyone loses. As you might imagine, this causes a lot of conflict within the society. This very thing happened to the cod fishery off the east coast of Canada many years ago. The cod are not likely to ever recover to the levels seen by the Portuguese fishermen who discovered the Grand Banks and the Flemish Cap. That is, as long as humans are around!

The arguments around shared resources in the Tragedy of the Commons mirror the capitalism-versus-socialism argument within a finite resource we call planet Earth. Hence, there is a lot of talk about sustainable organizations and sustainability in general and how wealth is to be shared. There's a big debate about what sustainability really means.

The Tragedy of the Commons metaphor operates continuously in our systems, since it is a reflection of our nature. For example, it applies to money. Money represents cows because it's the number of cows that define the farmer's wealth. Money begets money in the same way as the Tragedy of the Commons metaphor, as follows: All things being equal, people who have $100,000 and earn 10 percent interest have $110,000 at the end of a year. People who have $1,000,000,000 and earn 10 percent have $1,100,000,000 at the end of the same year. The person who earned the $10,000 might need to spend it to pay the ordinary bills of living or might use it to go on a nice holiday with the family. The person who earned $100,000,000 doesn't need all that money to live in extreme luxury by any standards. Ergo, that's how the rich get richer. Once you have enough to live to the standard you desire, the excess accumulates really fast. In addition, money-smart people know that money needs to be put to work, so it needs a debtor. As the poor get further and further into debt, the rich accumulate money that much faster. At some point a crisis occurs.

That's why a democratic process and taxes work reasonably well because they are effectively a negative feedback loop that attempts to maintain some sort of balance. It is a peaceful transfer of wealth that recognizes that the wealthy are the beneficiaries of a relatively stable system that recognizes talent. The "have-nots" outnumber the "haves" in almost all societies. In a true democracy, the transfer of wealth cannot be stopped because of the principle of one person equaling one vote. It's deemed fair by "have-nots" and confiscatory by the "haves." Regardless, if the "haves" should take control of the democratic process, the positive feedback loop will overcome the negative feedback loop and accelerate the accumulation of wealth in fewer and fewer individuals, thus creating a dangerous imbalance. This is how the system moves closer to a chaotic event. The argument over taxes in the United States and how to deal with the national debt is a case in point.

This is no revelation for our times, and I believe the economic crisis of 2008/2009 was just a repeat of past patterns. For example, in ancient democratic Athens, the disparity between rich and poor was so great that the city was on the verge of a civil war. Using dictatorial power, Solon reset the economic situation and saved Athens from self-destruction. Of course, there was immense conflict while these changes were being imposed, but within a generation, almost all Athenians agreed that the act had prevented a revolution. For a more detailed account of the history of Athens during the period, I highly recommend Will Durant's book *The Story of Civilization, Volume II: The Life of Greece.*[4]

It is very disturbing to read articles such as the one titled "Are 'extractive elites' sucking the life out of Canada's economy?" by Diane Francis,[5] which essentially states that we've already been hijacked by the "haves." I recommend that you look up this article. While I don't believe that we are anywhere near a situation like that faced by Solon in ancient Athens, we need a global Solon for our times, though his methods may not be as appropriate today. I also recommend *The Lessons of History* by Will and Ariel Durant and their entire brilliant series *The Story of Civilization*.

It is through the magic of compounding that the rich get really richer over long periods of time. Capitalism and a high degree of freedom from rules and regulations accelerate the process of wealth transfer from the many to the few. This is exactly what capitalists with a libertarian philosophy want.

It would be really funny if it were not so sad that banking deregulation (demanded by the rich) was blamed for the fiscal disaster of 2008/2009. The few use this wealth to buy up the pasture, which impoverishes the many. That's what Karl Marx railed against and what all people who prefer socialism and communism will point to. Fortunately or unfortunately, depending on your perspective and judgment, many communist countries have been hijacked by what looks like monarchies today. That's one of the reasons we have democracy and taxation; they regulate the economic pendulum of life in the interests of long-term social stability. I believe it was Winston Churchill who said that democracy was the worst form of government, but the best we've come up with so far. This doesn't say much for the other forms. Again, fortunately or unfortunately, depending on your perspective and judgment, democracy is starting to look like monarchies, too. The brain-mind will have its way, no matter what type of economic or political system you care to choose. I hope we won't be faced with having to globally relive the story of Europe of the last few centuries!

Negative Feedback Loop

A negative feedback loop causes a system to self-correct. It reverses trends. Your home heating and cooling thermostat is a negative feedback loop. A thermostat has a set temperature, its goal, which it seeks to maintain. If you set the house temperature at 72 degrees Fahrenheit, the thermostat measures if it's too hot or too cold within a range of 72 degrees, say +/- 1 degree. If the temperature gets to 73 degrees, the furnace turns off. If the temperature gets to 71 degrees, the furnace turns on. If you're cooling to that temperature, the air conditioner will work the temperature in the opposite way to the furnace.

The culture of the organization is reinforced by promoting those people whose values and ability to make money were consistent with the organization's goals. We do tend to surround ourselves with like-minded people. Sometimes it works and sometimes it doesn't. The rules of the organization and how they are applied constitute both negative and positive feedback loops. Be careful how you go about creating this type of organizational and individual learning. There's a famous Nordstrom case study that I discuss below under "Types of Leverage Points to Intervene in a System" that examines reward systems and how they can turn out badly.

The person who can change the rules, apply some leverage, or change feedback loops is the one with the true power to change the organization. The effectiveness of all these things depends on what time frame you care to consider, since there are both short- and long-term consequences. If that is not complicated enough, conditions change and things like feedback loops that were appropriate when they were created may not be appropriate now, but people will resist changing them nonetheless. Compensation plans are one thing that people will resist changing, unless it's about getting more! Leadership is in large part about overcoming the friction of disagreement.

As I stated earlier, memories carry with them the rules of the system that existed when the memory was created. For example, each of our families have rules regarding various combinations of parent(s)-and-child(ren) and child-to-sibling(s) relationships. These are embedded in our memories. They surface whenever we think about our families or when we get together with them. Those rules may no longer be appropriate now that we're all adults, but they are there nevertheless, just waiting to surface at the most appropriate or inappropriate moment.

For a good overview of feedback and reinforcement, have a look at this Wikipedia entry: http://en.wikipedia.org/wiki/Feedback_loops.

Learning System Model

I've extracted and modified the following discussion about learning from my Master of Arts thesis. My thesis was specific to learning from projects, but how organizations learn is the same, whether or not it's project-based experience.

Figure 5 illustrates single-loop and double-loop learning. The traditional "lessons learned" exercise can be seen as single-loop learning, as shown in Figure 5. This is so primarily because individuals are risk-averse to the potential consequences of discussing sensitive topics or of wanting to admit to the truth. Double-loop learning is the ability to go beyond immediate cause and effect and thereby be able to examine system-level causes, including the organization's culture. There is also triple-loop learning, which I describe later. Generally, I consider single-loop learning to be symptom-effect (i.e., brain-mind) learning, whereas I consider triple-loop learning to be deepest root-cause (i.e., soul-mind) learning. I will explain the reason later.

Most learning is the result of interactions at the boundary of a system. What I mean by that is that an organism, or an organization, learns from its experience by interacting with the external environment. What it learns is based on its beliefs and the meaning it ascribes to its experiences. To learn correctly and quickly requires a safe environment for core beliefs to be questioned, so that the organism, or the organization, can adapt quickly to external realities.

Leadership is crucial for this process to be successful. Leaders must provide a safe environment. They must have the courage to admit how their contributions contributed to failure and success. They must ensure that the recognition and reward system is in alignment with the desired learning culture. Finally, they must implement the necessary changes resulting from the lessons learned. As you will see later, both leaders and followers have choices to make to ensure all these things are done well. CQ and the transmutational leadership model support these requirements.

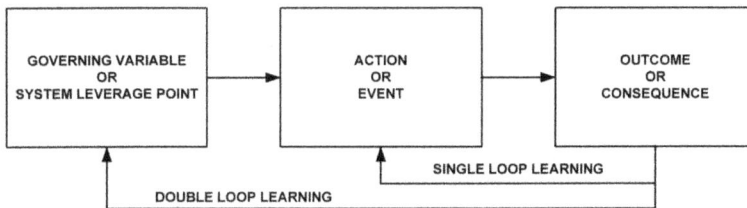

Figure 5: Single-Loop and Double-Loop Learning

The rules of the system influence directly whether learning takes place and how it takes place. Individuals, teams, and organizations need to move beyond single-loop learning and incorporate double-loop learning by fostering a safe and healthy environment conducive to risk taking. Each level must take this approach if the organization is to ultimately learn from its successes and failures, but it must start with senior leadership/management. It is my opinion that lack of understanding of the brain-mind in action results in "organizations...unintentionally reinforcing single-loop learning" (Morgan, 1998).[6] Whenever we indulge in blaming others, we are doing single-loop learning. We may, quite likely, be reinforcing the wrong lessons!

To achieve sustainable learning and change, an organization must understand the governing variable or the system leverage point for any given situation, especially how its own organizational culture impedes its learning. If senior management is not committed to change, employees will consider any new approach to lessons learned with some cynicism.

The following statement is a fine example of the need for double-loop learning. It is a direct quote from a transcript examining project closure issues and originates from my MA thesis. The participant, when speaking about the need for formal closure, stated, "Yes, especially in the sense that if any of the causes of failure were with the employer [leader], then an employee [follower] needs to have some recognition that the employer is aware of it and is taking steps to remedy it and is able to, because otherwise ultimately you may have attrition due to that or you may—if there's a problem with management, if there's a problem with the culture in the organization, you will lose."

Single-loop learning can readily address explicit rules, while double-loop learning is needed to address the implicit rules of an organization, especially those regarding its culture. Indeed, double-loop learning is critical to identify the leverage point in the system at each level of inquiry to turn tacit (i.e., implicit) knowledge into explicit knowledge.

Structural and psychological barriers prevent individuals and organizations from learning from their experiences. Structural barriers include issues such as organization structure, rules regarding communication, and an organization's reward and recognition system. Psychological barriers include various emotions such as fear, anger, cynicism, and bitterness. These structural and psychological barriers prevent an organization from experiencing double-loop learning. It is categorically clear that double-loop learning is critical for individuals and organizations to adapt and survive over the long term.

If you think that single-loop, double-loop, and triple-loop learning apply only to organizations and how they learn, think again. They are completely applicable to a single individual. For example, blaming others is single-loop learning done, sometimes, to protect self-esteem. Avoidance of the truth leads to improper learning, although it might make us feel better. The ego is powerful. We must be very wary of it.

As I mentioned earlier, systems and people learn via their feedback loops. I derived Figure 6 from Figure 5. I separated out the leaders and the followers, since the leaders are generally responsible for the rules of the system and how it learns. Indeed, from a learning perspective, the rules of the system determine how effectively feedback works, if at all. For the rules may not allow feedback to occur. An example of preventing negative feedback is not doing lessons learned at the conclusion of a project, and another example is terminating employees who have been labeled "troublemakers." But make no mistake, the absence of feedback, deliberate or otherwise, is feedback in and of itself and is equivalent to inaction by a leader; the system and the people learn from this, too! Leaders who won't listen to followers can end up creating a cynical, unmotivated, low-energy, and low-productivity followership. Leaders who do care must create a safe environment for followers. If they don't, well, as the saying goes, you can lead a horse to water, but you cannot make it drink.

Figure 6 shows that there are brain-mind barriers to learning that both leaders and followers must overcome for the organization to learn effectively and efficiently. Brain-mind thinking is usually symptom-effect thinking (i.e., single-loop learning in the illustration). It doesn't get at the root cause or the leverage point in the system because no one wants to question the rules of the system or put their ego at risk, or their job, for that matter. Usually, the barriers can only be overcome with soul-mind thinking, and both leaders and followers need to choose that. There is some overlap in double- and triple-loop learning, as all things are interconnected. However, I define double-loop as getting at the external environment of the system (e.g., the culture of the organization and its rules) and triple-loop as getting at the deeper personal environment and beliefs and how these contributed to the outcome. The dotted lines get "leakier" because accomplishing learning gets progressively harder to do the deeper you go.

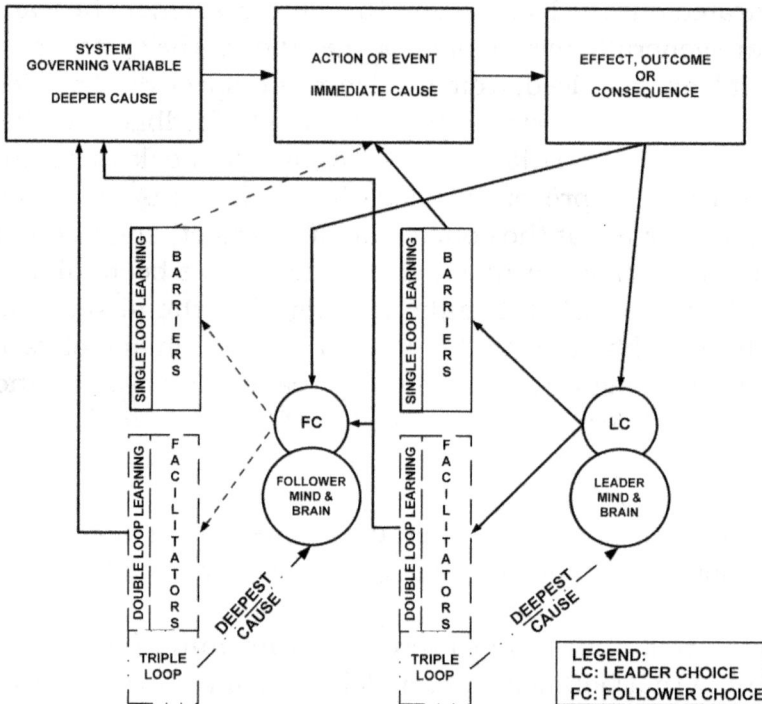

Figure 6: Single, Double and Triple-Loop Learning—Leadership and Follower Choice

As I have stated previously, soul-mind thinking contributes to courage, forgiveness, compassion, and love and gets people to see the system as it is and their complicit contribution to outcomes under review. But first of all, it takes courage.

Consider the following that I derived from Drucker's[7] examination of organizational politics and culture. It is a composite picture of some of the situations I have personally experienced as well.

A project is late and going over budget. The individuals on the team are asked to work overtime to stem the losses and, through heroic effort, finally achieve their technical objective. On closeout, the project team gets together for a lessons-learned session and determines there were not enough resources to achieve the originally intended objectives. Nobody suggests that poor team morale and too much schedule pressure were the real causes of the low productivity achieved. Nobody suggests that management might have deliberately underestimated the cost to get approval for their pet project, or that higher priority projects and organizational barriers bled the team of resources and expertise. The team is not rewarded for their commitment, and some members leave the organization. The rest are so fatigued and upset that poor morale and motivation is the entry norm on the next project, thus making it difficult to create a high-performance team and achieve high productivity. Nobody works overtime on the new project. Later in time, the product does not achieve its market expectations or return on investment. In a review of the situation, the specification was seen to be incomplete. Nobody suggests that poor idea and project selection methods doomed the project in the first place. Nobody suggests that poor leadership and political machinations are at the heart of the failure. Nobody suggests that fear and competition exist at all levels of the organization and are a fundamental barrier to the learning. Nobody suggests that corporate culture is the culprit.

In my experience, these types of suggestions are considered by many to be career-limiting moves. However, as Quinn[8] and Oshry[9] point out, having the courage (i.e., letting go of fear and competition) to create an environment of deep learning can be liberating and can unleash creativity. That kind of courage is asking a lot of leaders and followers, in my opinion. Yet, it must be done. Suffice it to say that organizational learning and the way learning is conducted are inextricably linked to extrinsic and intrinsic motivation and behavior in individuals, teams, and organizations, and ultimately leadership. Creating an environment of deep learning is a choice; it is free will!

There is also another way to interpret Figure 6, which is similar to Figure 7 later. Figure 6 can also be seen as feedback loops in a quality management system to illustrate preventive and corrective action. Preventive action means applying changes to the process. This is making decisions before the outcome is produced. It has been shown repeatedly that the cost of preventive action is usually much lower than corrective action. Corrective action is applied to the result of a process, which is the product or outcome, whichever you prefer. In people terms, the product is a behavior. Corrective action means it is too late, since the product has already been produced. The Space Shuttle Columbia disaster is often used to illustrate this principle and how organizational culture and leadership contribute to failures. Corrective action is related to single-loop learning, and preventive action is related to double-loop and triple-loop learning.

The type of deep learning required to truly move an organization forward is not necessarily easy to do, depending on the situation. It often requires an external and independent observer that will guarantee anonymity for those who have the courage to admit their personal complicity in failures.

Stability and Instability—Order and Chaos

All systems oscillate, like a pendulum, between stability and instability or between order and chaos, if you prefer.

Each system has a "region" of stability and a "region" of instability and a transition point or tipping point in between in either direction. The tipping point is called a bifurcation, and it's a lot like the brain making a decision between two alternatives. A system can go from chaos to order or from order to chaos, depending on its natural characteristics. The nature of the feedback loop, whether positive or negative, and other characteristics drive the system toward stability or toward instability. There is virtually no equilibrium possible, especially in complex systems, except for defined periods of time wherein a range of values is perceived as equilibrium. In most cases, that is sufficient for the system to accomplish its goals, but eventually nature will have its way and the system will transition to its opposite state.

This aspect of systems is a key idea in the transmutational leadership model that is outlined in Chapter 4. Think back to the beaver pond example. The dam is constantly eroding because the water flows through it. The beaver responds to the sound of water and expends its energy and resources plugging the leak. Assuming there is no inflow or outflow of water, the system is stable. If something happens, an earthquake for example, the dam can fail catastrophically. If it fails, the system becomes instantly unstable and fails entirely. Another way the dam can fail is if the flow of water into the pond rapidly increases to a point where it flows over the dam, eroding it quickly and causing it to fail catastrophically. Systems can enter a chaotic state in multiple ways, and they can fail in multiple ways. The levees that failed around New Orleans as a result of Hurricane Katrina are a case in point. Human systems are designed by humans to operate within a defined zone of stability. When pushed beyond their design limits, they too will go into chaos mode and self-destruct. This applies to our organizations and to individuals equally. A common expression that we all know is "the straw that broke the camel's back." It is the event that is the tipping point that causes the system to transition from stability to instability, from predictable behavior to unpredictable behavior. The event is usually a symptom of the system and not the root cause. The symptom is often mistaken for the cause. It's easy to blame the straw! Politicians do it all the time, as do we.

Consequently, leaders must be able to perceive the forces driving the system and act or not act to achieve their purpose. Sometimes, a leader's purpose is to inject a little chaos into the system to cause change to occur. Either way, a leader's actions or inaction will always move the system toward stability or instability. There is no neutral position possible, since change is constant; it's only a degree of balance. Sometimes, inaction can have as much effect as action. In my opinion, the important thing is for the leader to act or not act with purpose and with ethical intent in the best interest of the organization and humanity (i.e., social justice). This is difficult at best in this modern world of ours, as there are a lot of competing issues in complex systems, including the leader's own self-interested philosophy of convenience and perception of duty. Let us not forget Machiavelli's contribution in *The Prince*!

The Drive for Efficiency May Be the Road to Success but also to Chaos

Commercial organizations that are operating at maximum efficiency to compete (e.g., in a commodity such as PCs) become vulnerable to any disruption, for instance in their supply and manufacturing system. Dell, the PC manufacturer, is an example of that. In their drive for maximum efficiency to satisfy the profit motive of their owners (shareholders), they carried a minimum amount of inventory and relied on their suppliers to keep a ready, just-in-time supply of parts available. I don't know if this has changed, but a few years ago, if you ordered a Dell computer online, the parts weren't necessarily in the Dell system, but were more likely with the suppliers. That meant that Dell did not have to use its money to stock a lot of parts in its inventory, but had your money up front through the credit card company, and probably had 30 to 120 days credit with the suppliers as well. This arrangement was quite profitable in its day.

Money is to business as rain water is to the ocean; it will always seek the easiest and most efficient way to achieve its destination (i.e., goals). Money is neither good nor evil and has no conscience. Yet, it is necessary to achieve "progress" and advance civilization. It is important to believe that abundance for all is possible. Money is simply a surrogate for wealth. It represents the ability to do things. How a system accumulates and distributes both wealth and poverty is a key leadership issue.

A highly optimized, 100-percent efficient, and highly controlled system is always vulnerable to unanticipated external events. Furthermore, you create chaos when you drive the system beyond its design parameters, as we see in the Lorenz Water Wheel model described below. To get more performance then requires a fundamental paradigm shift to the system. Dell experienced these types of events from time to time.

I think that Dell executives were well aware of all this, but had to create their system's characteristics in order to compete effectively and keep the shareholders happy. A lot of people got rich while things were good. Now that the PC market is slumping, Dell is trying to exit the public market and go private by selling itself for some 24 billion dollars, as seen in the news on 5 February 2013. Apparently, it can no longer meet shareholders' expectations within the rules set for a public company and a deteriorating market. It needs to reinvent itself, and being tied to a fickle public capital market won't do. I discuss reorganization under leverage points below. As the well-known Leonard Cohen song says, everybody knows—that's how it goes.

Linear and Nonlinear Systems—The Lorenz Water Wheel

I consider *Chaos* by Gleick, mentioned in Chapter 2, as a magnificent book and highly recommend it. Gleick describes linear and nonlinear systems quite nicely. He uses the Lorenz* water wheel model to describe how a system's characteristics and its feedback loops can cause it to go from stability to instability. A water wheel is a device used to take the energy from water and gravity, and convert it into some kind of mechanical energy. Energy comes into the system, and energy goes out by being used up to grind the grains.

The water wheel that was modeled reflected the real-life experience of what can happen to a similarly designed and operated system. For a range of driving energy it remains stable, but there is a point where it exceeds is stable linear range and enters into a chaotic nonlinear state. In other words, beyond a certain degree of driving energy, the outcome is no longer predictable.

Figure 7 illustrates linear and nonlinear systems. The difference between a linear and a nonlinear system is that a linear system is predictable over a wide range of parameters over relatively long periods of time. Its initial state does not have a great effect on the outcome. Our solar system is such a system. The orbits of the planets are predictably estimated by Newtonian physics. We can calculate what the sky looked like to the Mayans thousands of years ago, and we can calculate what it will look like thousands of years from now. This gives us the appearance that it is stable, but it is only an approximation and may not be true when time is measured in billions of years. Nevertheless, for our purposes, it's close enough. It's what allows NASA to send the Voyager spacecraft to visit the planets safely and send

---

* Note: Edward Lorenz was a meteorologist who was a pioneer of the science of chaos. Chaos science is a multidisciplinary approach for the study of the global nature of systems, in particular the nonlinear variety.

back those great pictures. It's what enables us to put GPS satellites in orbit, so that we can find our way through our urban jungles. A linear system is stable over long periods of time and input parameters. The key idea is that its current state, or initial condition, does not influence the outcome.

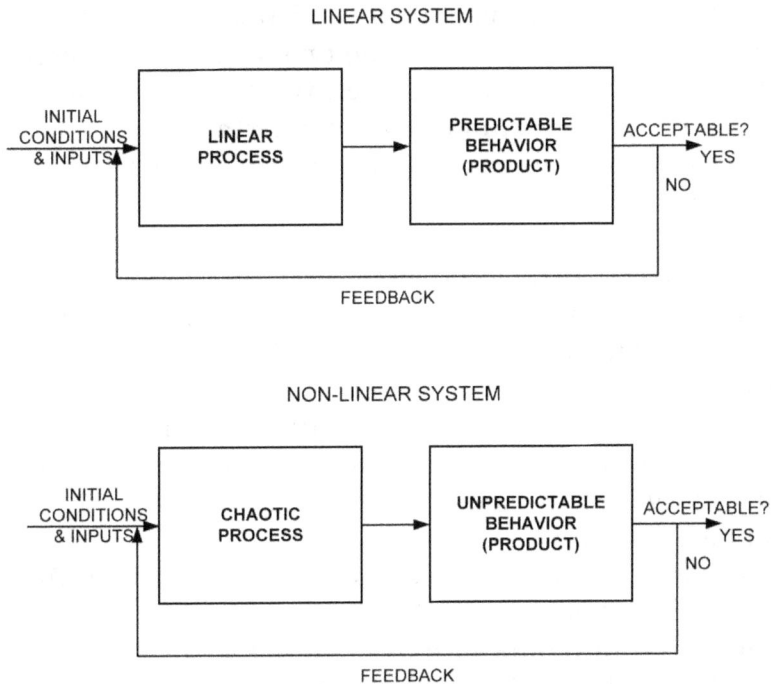

LINEAR SYSTEM

| INITIAL CONDITIONS & INPUTS | → | LINEAR PROCESS | → | PREDICTABLE BEHAVIOR (PRODUCT) | ACCEPTABLE? YES / NO |

FEEDBACK

NON-LINEAR SYSTEM

| INITIAL CONDITIONS & INPUTS | → | CHAOTIC PROCESS | → | UNPREDICTABLE BEHAVIOR (PRODUCT) | ACCEPTABLE? YES / NO |

FEEDBACK

Figure 7: Linear and Nonlinear Systems

Nonlinear systems, on the other hand, are highly sensitive to initial conditions. How they will behave is about probability, not certainty. They do have a range of parameters and/or time frame where they are stable, or appear to be, but they are chaotic by nature; it's never totally predictable what the outcome might be for any given input.

The human brain is a nonlinear system. It is highly sensitive to initial conditions. Because the mind and the brain work together as one system, together they are nonlinear by nature. While a person may appear to be predictable most of the time, we are never quite sure how people will behave in the moment. Normally, people behave more or less the same in a given situation because the system is biased by a number of attributes, including beliefs. For example, when someone is being considered for a job, it's believed that past performance is indicative of future performance. The major assumption is that the two work environments are somewhat the same, but often that's a big stretch. It can only be an approximation, not a certainty.

Our brain originates from the natural world; therefore, it oscillates between order and chaos, just as the atmosphere, sea, and wildlife populations do. For example, the chaotic nature of the atmosphere changes from moment to moment, which means that its initial condition at every location is continuously changing. This is why weather forecasting is so difficult. When was the last time that a long-term weather forecast was 100 percent accurate? Never, of course; it is not possible to make accurate long-term weather predictions because weather is nonlinear (chaotic) by nature.

Weather forecasts are based on mathematical algorithms of weather models. As in all models of nonlinear systems, the outcome is highly sensitive to the initial conditions. This has led to the metaphor of the butterfly effect. The butterfly effect is the idea that a butterfly can flap its wings in Tokyo in May and be the root cause of a Caribbean hurricane in August. This applies to us, too. We never know how the smallest of actions, such as holding a door open for someone, or giving up our seat on the bus, or yelling at someone out of frustration, will reverberate throughout history.

We believe that most of us are rational and orderly people, but that is simply our perception of the output of our brain-minds because of learning and the apparent stability of the systems we've created. We adapt quickly to the rules of the system that tell us what behavior is acceptable and what is not. Our systems reinforce this learning in multiple ways. So, we seem to be predictable, normal, rational, and orderly only most of the time, in the short term. For example, the way stock prices move is based on the assumption that rational human beings are making logical decisions out of financial self-interest. Given equal knowledge, all investors should make the same decision. The truth, however uncomfortable it may be, is that our behaviors are only the winning probability among multiple possibilities. Stock markets oscillate just as our brains do. Sometimes the herd stampedes, and nobody knows why, although it's easy to blame one thing or another.

Which behavioral possibility wins out is very sensitive to what we call our state of mind, that is, initial conditions. Our beliefs are an initial condition. Manipulators know this.

Free will is the (hopefully) thoughtful choice of which belief is chosen to be true. We can listen to our own self and change the outcome (i.e., our minds). Our beliefs limit our choices, but if we change our beliefs, our creativity flourishes. The mind is a beautiful thing, and beauty truly is in the eye of the beholder. Consciousness enables us to see this.

Listening to our own self is a feedback loop. It is being mindful. We can observe ourselves in action. When we know we are in an agitated state, we can calm ourselves at any moment, thus changing the initial conditions before the input happens.

We can choose what we believe, but only if we are aware of our biases (these are also beliefs) in the first place. Overriding our preprogrammed responses using CQ techniques is the practice of free will. However, the more entrenched a belief is, the harder it is to change it.

This is even truer when we hold a belief collectively. There's a famous saying that goes like this: "We hold these truths to be self-evident." All nations are built on an idea and a belief system. It usually takes a crisis of some kind to change these. It seems that letting go of a belief follows the Kübler-Ross process of grief: denial, anger, bargaining, depression, and acceptance.

For example, the current global economic system is deeply entrenched. Who in the western industrialized world questions our current capitalist system? Certainly, the majority do not. It's sobering to realize that various flavors of capitalism and socialism have existed throughout history. They are not new.

Capitalism and socialism oscillate like a pendulum, as does the brain-mind. It's not surprising because capitalism and socialism are economic ideas and systems created by our collective brain-minds. How fast they oscillate depends to a certain extent on how much economic freedom people have. Relatively speaking, there are probably as many super-wealthy individuals in China and Russia today as there are in America. Karl Marx would be appalled to know how many billionaires are in government office in China today. Is there truly a substantive difference between the outcomes of each ideology in practice today? I'll be vilified for even asking that question or suggesting our system is the same, but it seems to me that each have their dominant few and their relatively poor many. As Durant and Durant say, "In progressive societies the concentration [of wealth] may reach a point where the strength of number in the many poor rivals the strength of ability in the few rich; then the unstable equilibrium generates a critical situation, which history has diversely met by legislation redistributing wealth or by revolution distributing poverty." [10]

I believe that the 99-percent movement that emerged after the 2008 economic crisis is a precursor of more to come—a tremor prior to the volcano erupting. It is the many trying to send a message of peaceful reform to the few. If the few do not listen, we'll enter chaos mode at some point in the future. Trouble is, I'm not sure if anyone really understands what system we're talking about! The global economic system is a symptom and not a root cause. We need a paradigm mind-shift to solve this problem, as Einstein would tell us. Changing our paradigms and our beliefs are system leverage points, as I describe below.

Physically, a belief held in the brain-mind is a whole bunch of neurons ganging up to prevent a new input from rewiring the brain-mind into a new belief system. The ego does not like anything that threatens its self-interest! We tend to welcome information that agrees with us and discount information that doesn't. Many accidents (e.g., aircraft crashes, car accidents) have happened as a result of this phenomenon. Ergo, this tendency results in bad decisions.

The "stronger" the neurons are, the harder it is to overcome them. A belief is like friction. The more friction a system has, the more energy it takes to get the system moving. As Claude Bernard said, "It is what we think we know already that often prevents us from learning."[11]

Just like Lorenz' water wheel, a belief can be driven through a transition point into chaos and self-destruction. That's called a crisis. That is the wisdom and essence of T'ai-chi T'u or Diagram of the Supreme Ultimate, otherwise known as yin and yang. Yin and yang are complementary polar opposites. Yet, each one contains the seed of its own destruction. Take anger, for instance. Anger, when driven hard, can cause someone to self-destruct.

Figure 8: T'ai-chi T'u (aka Yin and Yang), System Context

Types of Leverage Points to Intervene in a System

As discussed earlier, every system has a key leverage point whereby a small change in one part of the system can result in extraordinary change in the direction intended, but only if applied correctly. Donella Meadows[12, 13] was a pioneer in understanding leverage points. I highly recommend her work. As she points out, the two most effective leverage points in a system are related to mindset and belief.

A mindset or paradigm creates our organizations and systems. For example, a society is founded and built upon an idea and a philosophy, which constitute, in part, its mindset and paradigm. Mindsets and paradigms are very hard to change, but there are also no limits to possible changes. Donella Meadows indicates that paradigms might be changed by repeatedly and consistently pointing out anomalies and failures in the current paradigm to those with open minds.

The ability to question our most deeply held beliefs is an ability we all share. We just need to choose to do so. For example, there has been a seemingly widespread belief in our society that the Earth is here for us to exploit. This belief is long held and its origin is not necessarily clear, though some would argue its modern foundation is derived from religion and economics. Even Aristotle concluded that lower forms of organisms existed to serve higher forms when he remarked about the hierarchy of animals. Unstated in this belief is that humankind is the most important creature on Earth because of our abilities, and everything else is there to exploit.

We often choose to believe what we want to in order to serve our brain-mind purpose. Somehow the arrogant belief of our importance at the top of the food chain seems to allow us to destroy our habitat to such an extent that it may cause our own demise. Fortunately, this underlying belief is being challenged today both explicitly and implicitly. Nevertheless, there are still many leaders who set up the choice we are to make as a polarity, for example, jobs *or* the environment! A lot of people agitate to reframe the problem to be solved as "jobs *and* the environment." For various reasons, politicians and big business try to isolate and marginalize these agitators. Thank goodness for a free press.

When the problem to be solved is framed with an *and*, the possibilities move from two to potentially many.

Donella Meadows pointed out that the most potent lever is the power to transcend paradigms. Transcending paradigms may go beyond challenging fundamental assumptions into the realm of changing the values and priorities that lead to the assumptions, and being able to choose among value sets at will. Related to my examples regarding mind-sets and paradigms above, many today see Nature as a stock of resources to be converted to human purpose. Others see Nature as a living god, to be loved, worshipped, and lived with. These views are incompatible, but perhaps another viewpoint could incorporate them both, along with other viewpoints. The power to transcend paradigms is held completely in the mind. Transmutational leadership is by definition changing the paradigm of how we lead.

There's No Free Lunch

The ability to consider a larger number of possibilities sounds really good, doesn't it? As for most things in life, the answer is yes and no. Yes, more possibilities on average lead to a better choice, but too many choices can have a lot of downsides and cause decision paralysis. Having too many choices really complicates decision making. It's especially difficult for indecisive people and can cause regret about not choosing other alternatives. It can cause severe disagreement among those making a decision. It can help self-interested people and organizations delay a decision by asking for more study when the leading choice is not consistent with their interests.

There is always a lot of disagreement around change and which lever the leader should use to achieve progress toward a new vision. Having many choices does lead to higher expectations. It can cause disappointment around unmet expectations. Change means letting go of the old and embracing the new way of being. This can be quite challenging. There is a gap, or chasm, between the old and the new that must be crossed. A change that is perceived as scary requires courage. The other side of the gap is uncertain; nobody can predict the future. It's scary territory for many people. That's why most people opt for the status quo and why leadership that is able to move followers across the gap is so important.

From a brain perspective, a lot of choice can mean the brain stays in chaos mode for a longer period before it settles itself down to the order implied by choice. That means that leaders need to be comfortable with discomfort. It's one of those difficult paradoxes for leaders.

Notice that some propaganda exploits the too-many-choices problems. By not agreeing to a single perspective or a truth, any number of issues remain unresolved and therefore not acted upon—global warming, for instance.

A word of caution is warranted. Followers don't like indecisive leaders, so it's important to not become paralyzed by indecision. Followers want the rules of the system clearly spelled out when an ambiguous situation occurs.

Consequently, leaders must be able to go in and out of order-chaos mode fairly quickly. They must be able to balance chaos and order not only in their minds, but also in the minds of their followers and in the systems of their organization. The faster they are able to do this, the faster the system learns and adapts to its emergent reality. Fast and small adaptations make a system less prone to crises and massive change. The one exception is unexpected external events. A comet or asteroid hitting the earth is such an event. If humans had been around with the dinosaurs when the last big one hit, I might not be here talking about it. At the same time, I might not be here if it hadn't!

Leadership Styles and Influencing Change

Leaders who rise to the top of their organizations are typically extremely smart people. Consider the President of the United States or the Prime Minister of Canada. They probably know that they are the product of their system, finely tuned to it, rewarded by it, asked to keep it stable in the presence of external challenges, and yet required to continually change it to compete effectively in the global economy. They might even admit that they are simply lucky—right place, right time, right traits, right relationships, and so on.

Regardless of what their followers might desire and what the polls reveal, they may have a vision of the future toward which they are driving. They may or may not want to reveal too much of it. It's not clear, for example, what the current Prime Minister of Canada, Stephen Harper, wants to do. My father read his book and he related to me that when he (Prime Minister Harper) would be finished with Canada, we wouldn't recognize it. Prime Minister Harper is the guy who has dismantled some of the environmental laws protecting fish habitat. While I don't agree with this change, I'm not criticizing. It's a difficult job to lead a nation, and our leaders are caught up in the system. Be kind to them. The beauty of democracy is that if you don't agree, you can always replace them peacefully, whereas this would not be possible in a place like Syria, for instance. Don't be fooled, however. No matter who leads your nation, they are caught up in the larger global system, and there is only so much they can do.

Most of our human-made systems were created long ago by some very smart people and are led today by equally smart people. For example, some smart dude came up with the concept of money a long time ago. This concept has evolved such that today, we have a globalized economic system.

The dominant few who run this system don't really want it to change in the same sense that rich people don't really want to pay more taxes, and they'll find ways of avoiding to do so if they can. Each generation of leader/ manager has inherited this system and tries to evolve it so that it's bigger, stronger, faster, and more profitable or, if you are a not-for-profit organization, more successful. But no matter how hard they try, the system becomes unstable from time to time. There is always some form of natural or human-made resistance. They lament it and work hard to overcome it. They strive to achieve a single currency, a single market, a single government, a single religion. It seems sometimes that there is a belief that if only we had one of each of these things, we could control everything and keep it all stable forever, but the question is, stable for whom and for what purpose? The dominant few want to remain dominant. Their attempt to control crushes creativity. Eventually, such a system will go into chaos mode. I believe the 99-percent movement is like a small tremor that precedes a volcanic eruption. As with a volcano, we cannot predict when it will erupt.

I'm not suggesting that one economic system is better than another, nor am I advocating the removal of the dominant few. If you read history, you'll notice that the two main forms of economic systems, centrally planned and controlled (i.e., socialism generally associated with communism) and free-market capitalism (i.e., capitalism as generally associated with democracy) are the two extremes of a swinging pendulum. Capitalism's excesses lead to socialism, and socialism's excesses lead to capitalism. These two forms are part of our fundamental belief system. The dominant few within each ideology fight each other for supremacy; that's the way it goes. It is based on brain-mind polarity processing after all. Just read Durant and Durant.[14]

The global economic system has been spectacularly successful regardless of ideology. Nevertheless, as in every system, there are some cracks. For example, some people interpret New Age consciousness as a move toward socialism. Others interpret the 99-percent movement, a reaction to the 2008 economic crisis, as also a move toward socialism. There is no question that these movements are reactions to irresponsible governance and unethical behavior and a global economic system that reaps benefits by keeping people and nations in debt.

I interpret all these things as a reaction to a global system (primarily economic) that was created long ago and exquisitely reinforced by the brain-mind. Capitalism's temporary triumph is the triumph of a democratic political system and the freedom permitted our exploitative brain-mind. Freedom is simply more creative. There is no chicken or egg question here. The brain-mind came first and the system(s) we have invented and inherited came second to serve it. I'm not trying to beat up capitalism. Quite to the contrary, I describe myself as a capitalist with a social conscience.

I'm simply interpreting our current economic pendulum position. As a matter of fact, all of us should be grateful for the economic system's ability to create the civilization we know today. Grateful? Yes. Wary of it? Yes.

Balancing Chaos and Order

So, how does a system progress? Changes to a system vary considerably and may be gradual and smooth or rapid, chaotic, and catastrophic. The progress of human civilization certainly hasn't been smooth; we've had "dark" ages. Since belief is so important, how do we define progress?

I am not sure whether an objective definition of progress is possible. I don't believe true objectivity is even attainable. The victors write the history, and they fill it with propaganda. It seems like the Goebbels school of big lies and half-truths is alive and well. We all know that most historians are truthful, but biased in what they select to record or what they are told to do by the leaders. Napoleon was a master of the public relations campaign following his victories and defeats alike. His opponents saw it differently. For an example that is closer to home, Benedict Arnold could either be seen as a patriot or a traitor, depending on perspective. Time allows us a different perspective of individuals and both their choices and achievements. Historical "facts" are vulnerable to derision, review, revision, and reinterpretation ad infinitum. Enough said. Let's get back to progress.

We can only measure progress by observing the difference between where we are now and what it was like previously. For example, when the Mongols destroyed the might of Islam around 1200 AD, and thereby kept catholic Europe safe and peaceful for generations, was it progress? Westerners would believe so. If one species wipes out another, is that progress? A new road built by humans could be hailed as a great achievement of progress, but how does the ant colony feel about it as it is being bulldozed away, or the tribe in the Amazon rainforest making way for oil tycoons? Sure, we've progressed technologically and to a great degree have conquered the environment and other species. However, at what cost to our own selves and our habitat?

If we destroy our environment because of some odd belief in what constitutes progress and thereby self-destruct, is that progress? There are no winners in this type of progress, though some will get fabulously rich.

Every increase in control and irresponsible behavior carries with it its short- and long-term consequences. Nuclear technology is a case in point. Setting aside the issue of waste, nuclear technology may heat our homes, but our nuclear weapons may destroy humanity if we allow our brain-minds to dominate us. Another example closer to everyone's home is the plastics disposal problem around the world.[15] Again, those who are profiting by it want to study (i.e., delay) the problem to continue profiting. Please let's take action to protect all species' habitats. Let's find creative solutions that result in win-win-win. Otherwise, we won't be balancing the order-chaos continuum anytime soon.

The veneer of civilization is very thin, and we can succumb to brutality at a moment's notice. The transmutational leadership model clearly shows that brutal brain-mind leadership is at everyone's disposal and is the typical default response when things get difficult.

Diversity is nature's way of creating a complex system. There is order in the chaos and chaos in the order. Which one manifests most of the time depends on many things. One thing is very clear: diversity allows for more creativity. Diversity means an elegant balance between order and chaos so that something beautiful emerges. We must coexist, rather than dominate. If our habitat is destroyed for the sake of "progress," and this leads to human self-destruction, how can that be called progress? And yet, that is exactly what we are doing in the name of "progress."

Too much control reduces diversity. If we are to get out of our current problems, we need to have less control. It is the paradox of our times that only a paradigm shift in our individual and collective minds can solve. It is one of the collective leadership's greatest challenges. It doesn't help when our governments demonstrate a preference for control.

Freedom of speech is one way for diversity and creativity of ideas to flourish. Then, freedom and control are opposites. Thus, as we apply more control, we get progressively less creativity until we reach the breaking point. That breaking point is the bifurcation in the system. It is when the system transitions very rapidly from order to chaos. This becomes uncontrolled creativity. A tragic example of this type of transition is what immediately happened in France during the French revolution.

Here's an excerpt regarding the importance of freedom of the press and information by MacLeod: "...still today, governments continue to try to control and manipulate the information the citizenry can get...all these acts have as their purpose the control of the message and the making of government look as good as possible, while limiting actual real scrutiny and public knowledge."[16] It matters not where you look, all forms of government want control. It's just that democracies have at least attempted to keep our press free, and the fact that we can even publicly publish an article like MacLeod's should be cause for celebration and hope.

The key is diversity. Sir Ken Robinson said this: "If all the insects were to disappear from the Earth, within 50 years, all life on Earth would end. If all human beings disappeared from the Earth, within 50 years, all forms of life would flourish."[17] There are many others who have said this, too.

I submit that the reason for this is that creativity requires diversity and freedom—not control. Since we humans seek to control everything out of fear and ego to satisfy our survival instinct, we have a tendency to destroy habitats and other species. We also do this in subtle ways in our societies and organizations. For example, bullying is a form of control that is rampant. I don't mean the adolescent kind exclusively. I believe that bullying comes from the desire to dominate and the fear of things that are different or beyond our current level of understanding. It can manifest itself at the individual level and also at the group level. At the group level, it is the majority trying to make the minority conform. Long ago, it was burning so-called witches, today it is "shunning." We have a lot of synonyms for bullying!

Pluralism of races and of ideas is difficult. It is messy and difficult to manage. Despite all our cognitive work, bullying continues to exist in all walks of life and in all organizations. In the end, we destroy our creativity and ourselves in the process. It is the brain-mind doing its thing! The soul-mind would never consider it; hence, our internal conflict. That doesn't mean abandoning the wisdom of the many for all the weird ideas of the few. Let us not throw out the baby with the bath water. We must advance carefully and not swing too quickly or too far to the chaos side of the order-chaos continuum.

I define progress as *a change in an entity or thing whereby the difference is judged to be positive by the observer of the change.* Since we construct our own reality, how we interpret progress will meet with a lot of disagreement. What is positive progress to one thoughtful person may be perceived as the exact opposite by an equally thoughtful person. It depends on time frames, too. It may very well be that what the best answer would be in the long term will simply not be agreed to by the majority in the present circumstances. What then? A leader's job is not easy.

I don't think a definition of progress can be anything but subjective because, as I said, all of us construct our own reality. Of course, since each observer constructs their unique reality, my definition will cause a significant amount of disagreement about any given change constituting progress. We see this today between environmental scientists and industrialists regarding plastics, for example. Such a situation will cause a lot of disagreement.

Disagreement is a messy yet beautiful thing. Beauty and creativity are in the space of the disagreement. Disagreement and dissatisfaction are what causes change to take place. Honest debate ensures that a new reality of mutual understanding will be born. It is a process rather than a destination.

This process requires freedom of information, free speech, honesty, safety of conversation for all, respect for everyone, including the current leaders, and zero bullying. What are you doing as a leader to create this process and culture in your organization? If you are a follower, it also requires compliance once a change is agreed to and the outcomes/effects become clear, until the next debate. Freedom doesn't mind its chains of responsibility. The process will have a rhythm of its own, depending on the nature of the organization and how it interacts with its external environment. A tall order, perhaps, but a dream I have for a new leadership. It reminds me of how important it is for the world's leaders to come to a mutual agreement about what the word "progress" means. Now there's a lever that will move the world! That applies to the word sustainability, too. We certainly can't leave that to industrialists exclusively!

My view provides for a relativistic definition. It's more tuned to the context or system under consideration and includes perspective. As sentient beings capable of thought and logic, we can take the point of view of anything or anyone we want. What was progress to the now extinct

Dodo bird as compared to the humans who slaughtered it? I suspect that many CEOs of public companies agree with me. The short-term thinking of public markets and fickle shareholders are driving more and more companies to go or stay private in order to be able to balance both short- and long-term objectives. Even the successful billionaire Mark Cuban said that Wall Street capital markets no longer serve their original purpose. The entire banking system is also being questioned by some pretty senior people. Here's what Mark Carney, the recent Bank of Canada Governor, said: "To restore trust in banks and in the broader financial system, global financial institutions need to rediscover their values... For companies, this responsibility begins with their boards and senior management. They need to define clearly the purpose of their organizations and promote a culture of ethical business throughout them."[18]

It's not all dismal, ugly, and cause for giving up. There are many leaders in the world today who are moving toward transmutational leadership in their own quiet and unassuming way. Oddly enough, we don't hear much about these people. They are working hard to balance their organization's interests with environmental and social responsibility. The leaders at Whole Foods are a great example. They are very active in the conscious capitalism movement. Also, there are many billionaires today who have pledged at least half their wealth to philanthropy. Notable names include Warren Buffet, Bill and Melinda Gates, Richard Branson, Vladimir Potanin, and Axim Premji. Perhaps they did some things from time to time they aren't necessarily proud of—that's the nature of running an organization and having a brain-mind—but they are taking action today and are making the effort to walk the talk.

I like to think that there are many more accomplished leaders than the number of those who aren't socially and environmentally responsible. These leaders go about their business quietly and without fanfare. That is why we don't know them. I hope they'll speak up more, and here's why I say this: It is known that peer pressure is strong. We are social animals. For example, it turns out that the number one reason people recycle is because their neighbors do it. Sure, it feels good to be environmentally responsible, but that is not reason enough for doing it consistently. People want to belong and do their share and be seen to do their share. That is culture (unwritten rules) in action. So, conscious leaders need to speak up more.

That's going to be difficult to do for some people in certain parts of the world. This is particularly true in nations and organizations run by dictators. By definition, they tend to crush disagreement.

Most people try to do what is right based on their beliefs and the rules of the system. However, there are some who do not subscribe to the beliefs of the majority. We label these dissenters with many names, including "criminals." Dissenters have many advantages because they don't follow the rules. So, we need to be constantly vigilant and take action when something outrageous occurs, but we need to be patient with others. How we respond is crucial. I'm not proposing that we be mean about it and thereby sink to the level of "an eye for an eye" or offer complete forgiveness. Reacting to abuses with compassion and love does not imply inaction or acceptance. But what do you do with repeated outrageous offenses? What do you do if someone sets off a nuclear device in New York City? What do you do with people who knowingly buy elephant ivory today? Regardless of all the laws we've passed, elephants are still being slaughtered. What do you do with people when malice is intended? How we respond matters a lot. I will discuss "game" responses later.

We must also be vigilant about ourselves. There are some rule breakers and people labeled as dissenters and fools who are leaders in their own right and are simply showing the majority that they are wrong. Honest debate is okay. We need to embrace those who disagree. We sometimes question their methods, and sometimes we applaud them. Either way, we and they usually get caught up in brain-mind responses of methods and value judgments. We must be forever mindful of ourselves.

I am actually optimistic. Transmutational leadership practiced by many has the potential to minimize fear and competition, increase authentic cooperation, increase diversity, and increase creativity. As a result, organizations are likely to be less ego-driven and more creative because more people will be involved in the leadership and thereby the solution space greatly enhanced.

Social Systems and Game Theory

How do we respond to those who are stuck at the brain-mind level and, because of their self-interest, hurt us? How do we respond to those organizations that are stuck at the brain-mind level and, because of their self-interest, destroy the planet?

We can look to game theory for some answers. The gaming strategy we use is dependent upon our beliefs, our predicament, and what we are trying to achieve. How our brain works is how our organizations behave, too. Ball provides an excellent discussion of these points in his book *Critical Mass: How One Thing Leads to Another*.[19] I highly recommend this book.

How we behave in the moment reflects what we've learned, what we believe, and our chaotic minds. Ergo, initial conditions have a significant effect on the result, those being how we respond.

What you've learned from philosophers is a case in point. If you believe in the utilitarianism philosophy of Jeremy Bentham and John Stuart Mill, you believe that all things have a cost-benefit ratio and that if benefit outweighs cost, then it's an easy decision and human rights don't matter too much. If you believe in the libertarianism of John Locke, then you'll believe in the innate good in humans and that decisions should take into account their inalienable rights to life, liberty, and pursuit of property. These two philosophies, among many others, are alive and well today.

There you have it—what you believe is the initial condition of your brain-mind system and determines to a great extent the tendencies you have regarding how you see the world and how you respond to it. These beliefs may not be conscious reasoning, but may emerge from archetypes existing in the subconscious, as Carl Jung would say.

Some see it all as a game with high stakes. Political scientists study this area of thought, as do mathematicians trying to determine how social systems can be modeled and why they operate as they do. Their models likely assume that everyone is rational and shares the same values. If they tried to use linear equations, they'd probably be as good as weather forecasters.

A leader must decide what game strategy to use when responding to events. The outcome of the leader's choice will result in feedback. How we receive the positive or negative feedback will depend a great deal on what and how we choose to believe, including how we feel, and what "facts" we pay attention to.

There are four essential strategies that people use in competitive situations. We should understand each one, namely Tit for Tat, Generous or Partial Tit for Tat, Pavlov, and Complete Forgiveness. Ball describes each of these brilliantly in his book *Critical Mass*, which I mentioned earlier.

We should also discuss a widely used situation called the Prisoner's Dilemma to frame how self-interest works relative to these strategies. These apply to us today as self-interested individuals and organizations compete for diminishing resources. It's important to understand these strategies, since a transition from brain-mind-dominated leadership to soul-mind-dominated leadership will force us to invoke some or all of these. Besides, we're constantly using them, whether we know it or not.

Prisoner's Dilemma

The Prisoner's Dilemma has its roots in work by Flood and Dresher at the RAND Corporation in the 1950s. The Prisoner's Dilemma is described in Wikipedia as follows:

"Two members of a criminal gang are arrested and imprisoned. Each prisoner is in solitary confinement with no means of speaking to or exchanging messages with the other. The police admit they don't have enough evidence to convict the pair on the principal charge. They plan to sentence both to a year in prison on a lesser charge. Simultaneously, the police offer each prisoner a Faustian bargain. If he testifies against his partner, he will go free, while the partner will get three years in prison on the main charge. Oh, yes, there is a catch ... If both prisoners testify against each other, both will be sentenced to two years in jail."[20] Here's how it looks diagrammatically from the prisoners' perspective:

Decisions	He cooperates	He betrays
You cooperate	You each serve one year	You serve three years and he goes free
You betray	He serves three years and you go free	You each serve two years

As can be seen, it is in both prisoners' self-interest to testify against the other. By knowing this and using this strategy where both prisoners betray each other, the police get what they want—two years in jail for each of them.

Tit for Tat

The first strategy to examine is tit for tat. Commonly, this is understood by the expression "scratch my back, and I'll scratch yours." It's also known as "do unto others as you would have them do unto you." It's also known as "an eye for an eye."

The downfall of a pure tit-for-tat response is that it leaves no room for error. Competent people can make mistakes, well-meaning people can hurt others, and malicious people can do the same. Sometimes, it is hard to determine what is malicious and what is stupidity or both operating together. Responding in like manner without thoughtfulness can be quite damaging. It is vindictiveness in action. It leaves no room for error by the one committing the offense and the other one responding. This type of reaction can devolve a relationship and escalate into outright war very quickly. Generally speaking, it is not a good response strategy when cooperation is desired. However, it is often used by people who don't care about a relationship—that is, when cooperation is not desired, and they know they can behave that way with impunity. The wolves do not care about the sheep because the power differential doesn't enable the sheep to really hurt the wolves. According to wolves, sheep are simply a resource to be exploited.

In the case of the Prisoner's Dilemma, a tit-for-tat response would end up being a losing proposition for both.

Generous or Partial Tit for Tat

Generous tit for tat is a response that is tolerant of mistakes and errors. Partial tit for tat is a response that is less offensive than the infraction committed. To use either effectively means that one has to determine whether or not something was done maliciously. It requires judgment about intent. It won't always be possible to figure it out and someone once told me, "Don't attribute to maliciousness what can easily be explained by stupidity." Patience and sound judgment are virtues, as they say.

How can we get so-called bad people to change without a system of reward and punishment? We haven't figured this out yet. Our legal-justice-incarceration system doesn't seem to work very well. There always have been and always will be defectors (i.e., criminals, legal or otherwise) from the current rules of the system. Since we've tried controlling defectors to no avail, what next?

Besides, a lot of what people are doing today is legal within the systems we've established. Indeed, we want our leaders to have a certain degree of unscrupulousness if the situation requires it. In effect, we want them to break rules. I believe that this is why we are really sensitive to the rules regarding how to deal with criminals and violent situations. We want the unscrupulousness to be severely constrained, but not completely.

Be kind and forgive yourself when you've applied a brain-mind response to a situation. Learn from it and try to respond differently next time.

Pavlov

Pavlov is a strategy that works in a community imbued with the spirit of cooperation. Pavlov is like generous tit for tat in that it is tolerant of mistakes, errors, and occasional maliciousness. Pavlov is able to evolve its response because it is context-sensitive and takes into account its own previous action within a system. It retains a hard edge while also retaining flexibility. Thus far, the Pavlov response strategy has proven superior to other strategies. Pavlov is no longer an eye for an eye. It permits a leader to be unscrupulous when appropriate. It is, "don't give stupid people a break."

During a transition from one system type to another with a different set of rules, the Pavlov response strategy has proven superior to other strategies most of the time. At university, I was taught case studies of situations that did not spell out response strategies in this way, but the proposed best solution certainly followed the Pavlov response strategy. A note of caution is required. Pavlov works when cooperation is desired. In a world of diminishing resources, cooperation may not be desired. Hence, there could be a return to tit for tat rather rapidly.

When transitioning from brain-mind dominated leader to soul-mind dominated leader, a Pavlov strategy takes into account the past, present, and future and contains a broader range of possible responses. Hence, it can be a much more effective strategy.

Complete Forgiveness

Complete Forgiveness is a strategy of total cooperation. It is a 100-percent soul-mind response strategy. I think it's a bit utopian at this stage in our evolution. As much as I would like it to be totally followed by all leaders and all followers, the fact is that as soon as someone uses another strategy based on self-interest, there is ruthless exploitation of the meek. This causes outright conflict eventually. It's like a car going uphill. As it goes uphill, it needs more torque, so it drops down a gear. This is analogous to the soul-mind and the brain-mind levels as I show them in the transmutational leadership model. The brain-mind is a lower gear, and people will naturally default to this level when times get tough.

Tolle[21] recommends a strategy of complete forgiveness and offers some words of wisdom and a solution when he says "...so you cannot fight unconsciousness. If you try to do so, the polar opposites will become strengthened and more deeply entrenched. You will become identified with one of the polarities, you will create an 'enemy,' and so be drawn into unconsciousness yourself."

I believe we have to be very careful with this, unfortunately.

I would certainly like to follow Tolle's wisdom and response strategy of complete forgiveness, but I think he's ahead of his time, just as were Mohammed, Jesus Christ, and Buddha. We thank them for pointing the way. We need a period of transition for ourselves and our systems first. In the meantime, we mustn't ruthlessly exploit the meek— those who would adhere to Tolle's wisdom. On the contrary, we must celebrate them. As leaders, we must find a way to respond with complete forgiveness and at the same time, protect the meek and the environment from exploitation. This is a tall order indeed.

The presence of "deeply unconscious humans" puts leaders in a difficult position. For example, how do we deal with people breaking international rules and raping the oceans of fish? Greenpeace has tried to get our attention for decades regarding whaling. One of their ships was recently reported to have been in a collision at sea between a Japanese whaling vessel and a protest vessel in Antarctic waters.

Sometimes protesters have had to use brain-mind tactics and have paid the price. But what do we do when the dominant few or the majority of people are not paying attention? Some of these actions are sanctioned by nations, as they were when the cod fishery was depleted off the east coast of North America. There's not much that can be done to get immediate results, other than the use of some type of aggression. It's exactly what Tolle warns about. As mentioned in my previous example, what do we do with people who continue to buy elephant tusks? What happens when a people's own government prevents its own scientists from telling an inconvenient truth, as in my previous example citing the importance of freedom of the press? And that's what is going on in our democracies. It's even worse in countries run by dictators. Gandhi's strategy of passive resistance does not necessarily work in all cases and neither will Tolle's.

Even if we want to do something about the many negative

aspects of the world, we are often faced with ethical dilemmas. As the population continues to grow and resources become scarcer, dropping down a gear into brain-mind responses will be the default reaction. However, it is exactly opposite to what needs to happen. Our need for cooperation will increase dramatically. The default approach must be cooperation and not competition. Unfortunately, one false step by a nation to promote its self-interest will rapidly escalate into conflict because that's what we are used to doing and our systems are designed to behave that way. China's challenge to Japan and the world in the South China Sea is the type of conflict that could escalate rapidly, as is the recent North Korean move to cancel the armistice with South Korea. So, complete forgiveness may not be the right answer. You can only reason with reasonable people. Leaders need to be careful.

From Competition to Cooperation

Pure competition and pure cooperation are like the two ends of the order-chaos continuum. Their extreme form today leads to a chasm or a schism. At our current state of development, pure competition without restraint leads to war. Pure cooperation would be possible if everyone were a soul-mind leader, but at current consumption rates, resources will eventually deplete,* and then what? So, complete forgiveness doesn't seem possible today because it leads to outright exploitation of the meek by the mighty, and that typically ends up as serious conflict.

Nevertheless, the process of moving from a pure brain-mind tit-for-tat response strategy to a pure soul-mind complete-forgiveness response strategy has some logical

---

* Note: Even now we are in an overshoot position as defined in *Limits to Growth* by Meadows et al. It means that without correction, the planet will not sustain us in the not-too-distant future. A conflict-free correction is extremely difficult to do, if not impossible, and is analogous to carrying too much debt. Eventually, we'll have to declare bankruptcy and bear the ultimate consequences.

steps along the way, and leaders' understanding of these strategies is absolutely necessary to avoid catastrophe. Ultimate cooperation and complete forgiveness, along with soul-mind leadership practices, can definitely unleash extremely high levels of creativity while confronting conflict.

The nature of competition and cooperation and the relevant response strategies must also be considered in context. In any social system, gaming strategies are a process applied during a transition period of conflict toward some form of stabilization. How, why, and when they are applied is important. Power differential between the players matters a lot. We certainly can perceive economic sanctions against nation-state "defectors" as a Pavlovian response, for instance. The "defectors" are well aware of game theory and play the game to the best of their ability, too.

In a modern society today, there are defectors and cooperators. We'll assume, for the sake of argument, that defectors (e.g., rule breakers) are common initially; defectors are people taking advantage of others out of self-interest. They are the dissenters. However, the relative proportion of the two types allows the society to experience some form of balance.

History shows us that when there are a disproportionate number of cooperators (the meek extending complete forgiveness), the best "winning" strategy of all is unconditional defection: ruthless exploitation of the meek! This eventually collapses into utter conflict.

Over time, at least at our current level of mind evolution, the best strategy seems to be Pavlov most of the time, as I will explain below.

The brain-mind dominated people (i.e., defectors) will ruthlessly exploit the soul-mind dominated people (i.e., the cooperators giving complete forgiveness). This is analogous to the inner conflict in all of us. It's our yin and yang. The relationship between our brain-mind and our soul-mind is similar because the brain-mind wants its physical self to survive. It has no concept of eternal life and couldn't care less. It's all about the here and now. The brain-mind is like a criminal; it can break the rules any time it wants. The soul-mind is in a difficult position. Since among its attributes is unconditional love that implies complete forgiveness, this means no exceptions. The soul-mind can influence the brain-mind, but it's tough to fight against an argument for survival. Even the Dalai Lama, during an interview, conceded that a Buddhist monk has a right to shoot someone who is trying to kill him.

So, how do we respond when our brain-mind ruthlessly takes advantage of our soul-mind? No wonder we've got difficulty with this. The greatest and hardest game of all is the war within us. That's where transmutational leaders fight the good fight. As Rychkun says, "...the candid fact is that some of your most poignant accomplishments and indeed greatest growths are spawned when you are placed in the troubling crossroads of conundrum."[22]

A good person, a virtuous person, does not shrink from this fight, but embraces it. The virtuous and good person recognizes the conundrum and conflict inherent in the nature of the brain-mind and the nature of the soul-mind. The level where one operates within the transmutational leadership model becomes a deep philosophical test and one which informs and affects not only the individual, but society as a whole.

For social justice to emerge from a leadership paradigm, it must be based on sound just and ethical ideas. Far too many leaders end up in a leadership role without any preparation whatsoever, and those who place them there are equally ignorant of the ramifications of their decisions. Social justice is compromised by the ignorance of what constitutes legitimate leadership and legitimate leadership decisions. Neither leaders nor followers understand what is at stake, except for their self-interest.

As leaders, our soul-mind followers will want us to protect them from the brain-mind wolves. They'll want us to be soul-mind leaders with the ability to use our unscrupulous brain-minds. It has always been thus. Leaders must be equipped with the full range of philosophical thought in order to frame their never-ending dilemmas. It will not be easy, but as all of us become ever more soul-mindful, we will have self-awareness, creativity, and more possibilities on our side and hopefully make our leaders' work more effortless. We have free will. We can choose. We must be firm yet gentle.

Naked

I stand naked before you
My body's not pretty anymore, but beautiful for its wrinkles
As I lead you on the dance floor

I stand naked before you
My heart still beats the cadence we've danced to
I've never lost the beat of our whirling and twirling

I stand naked before you
My mind conscious we're connected to all things
Yet firmly focused on your bright energy

I stand naked before you
My spirit stronger than ever
Eternally intertwined with yours
As I stand naked before you

4

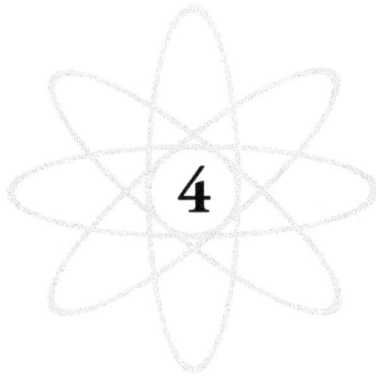

The Transmutational Leadership Model

Background

THE **GENESIS** of the concept of transmutational lead-ership started in 1987, when I was on an aerospace systems course while in the Canadian Air Force. During the course, we discussed the emerging science of chaos theory and how systems, especially natural systems, oscillated between chaos and order and how this applied in general to aerospace systems, natural systems, and aerodynamics. It's the dance of systems. I was completely intrigued by this topic and later on, around 1991 or 1992, I read Gleick's book *Chaos: Making a New Science* that explained the topic in layman's terms.

At the time, I glossed over Gleick's comments about the brain being formed from chaotic processes and how it functioned as a nonlinear system because at the time I wanted to understand how chaos science applied to engineering and management problems, rather than to people. This was because I was managing many research and development projects, and I saw projects as a balance between order and chaos. I saw order as synonymous with control and predictability, and chaos as synonymous with creativity and unpredictability. I realized that the balance point between order and chaos shifted depending on the project. The higher the creative content, the less control I could apply. Creativity, after all, resides in some degree of chaos (i.e., some form of change, with chaos, in its purest sense, being a severe case of change). For me, as a manager, this was quite vexing. For managers, the more uncertain something is, the more control we want to apply! This need for control and predictability, as it turns out, is usually the opposite of what has to happen to allow true creativity to take place.

When the mind is task-focused, it is under control and therefore more linear in its behavior. I've talked to a lot of people over the years, and many have told me that their most creative insights come when their mind is relaxed, for instance at the gym, on a walk, in the shower, and during sleep. I've experienced this myself. It's interesting that in a relaxed and meditative state, we are less inclined to judge. The brain's need to create a polarity is somehow disengaged. A more relaxed mind is one that can think outside the box. Using this paradigm, I managed many projects and people very successfully.

I thought a lot about this balancing act over the years and delved deeper into Eastern philosophical thought because I saw some deep wisdom in certain ideas, such as yin and yang. In 2004, I applied to do a Master of Arts program in Leadership and Training at Royal Roads University. What attracted me to the program was the idea that leadership was the key to the success of my organization and that I had to change myself before I could really contemplate changing my organization. I believed at the time, and still do, that it's the people who matter. I was aware of the poem *I Wanted To Change The World* attributed to an unknown monk who had lived around 1100 AD. Here's how it goes:

"When I was a young man, I wanted to change the world. I found it was difficult to change the world, so I tried to change my nation. When I found I couldn't change the nation, I began to focus on my town. I couldn't change the town and as an older man, I tried to change my family. Now, as an old man, I realize the only thing I can change is myself, and suddenly I realize that if long ago I had changed myself, I could have made an impact on my family. My family and I could have made an impact on our town. Their impact could have changed the nation and I could indeed have changed the world."[1]

Completing the MA allowed me to focus on my central idea that all systems oscillate between chaos and order and that our brain is a system. One of my assignments was to read a philosopher. Of the three possible choices (Lao Tzu, Plato, Macchiavelli), as luck would have it, I was assigned to read Lao Tzu's book *Tao Te Ching*. As I previously mentioned, I highly recommend the Jonathan Star[2] translation. This was in line with my interest in Eastern philosophy, and I devoured it. I immediately saw a connection between the concept of yin and yang, order and chaos, and modern management and leadership models. Another aspect that brought this model together was that I liked to read history (particularly Durant and Durant's eleven-volume set *The Story of Civilization*) and could see how certain patterns kept repeating themselves throughout history.

Since then, I've explored more Eastern philosophy and tradition by reading the work of the Sufi poets Rumi and Hafiz and others and by taking up yoga. I also participated in the Alliance for a New Humanity during 2008 and 2009,* whose leaders included Deepak Chopra. I attended a lecture by Chopra in Vancouver, Canada, during that time frame and have read some of his work. I have done a lot of thinking and research since then.

---

* Note: Unfortunately, the ANH no longer operates. However, the butterfly effect enables the ANH's activities to still reverberate.

It's probably obvious to the reader that this model is a work in progress. It's a process and not a destination. The model is an answer, but not *the* answer. It's just a signpost on the road to discovery—for me, you, and everyone else. As I learn more, I expect that I will want to evolve it some more.

Evolution of the Model

The model started out as a single line representing the polarity of order and chaos. I realized that a single line perceived from the side could be a circle if looked at from above. I hope that the following illustration conveys the idea that the two items below are the same diagram from a different perspective.

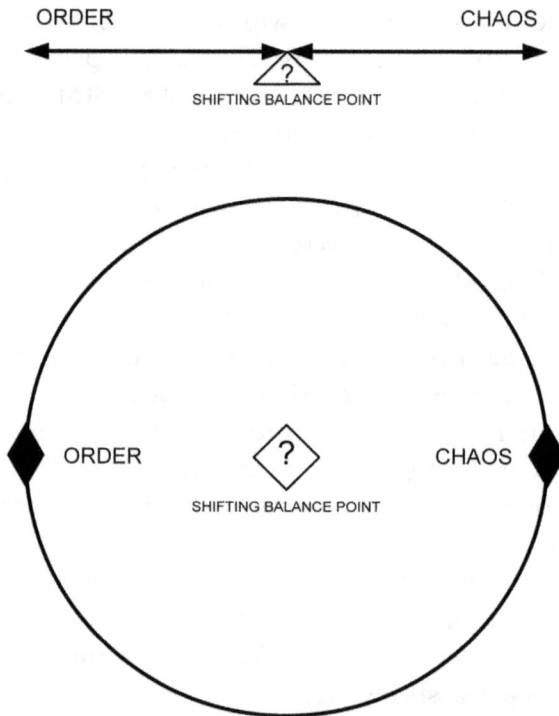

Figure 9: Order-Chaos Continuum

There are many synonyms for the order-chaos polarity that can be applied to people and organizations. These include control versus freedom, predictability versus unpredictability, and stability versus instability. From an action point of view, control can be seen as making it happen (order) and freedom as letting it happen (chaos).

It's important to note that the right balance point in an organization will shift around as the organization responds to its internal and external challenges. Often, people will say that it's important to find balance between two polarities, such as order-chaos, but I don't want anyone to take it that way. Yes, balance is important in our lives in general, but sometimes it's healthy to unbalance things. Questioning an entrenched belief could unbalance us and, while that may be very uncomfortable, it can result in some very beneficial outcomes. So, the diagram is not prescriptive. It is only meant to inform.

From my experience and observation of other people and many organizations over the years, I believe that a leader must balance the need for control (i.e., order) with the need for creativity (i.e., chaos). I believe that leadership mastery is the ability to perceive the forces (i.e., various energies and their source, direction, and strength) at play that would destabilize[*] an individual[**] or an organization and to influence their effect through action and inaction. Mastery, in this sense, appears effortless to casual observers.

It is important to know and perceive the various forces at work, so that continuous action or inaction is taken by the leader to ensure that the correct balance/imbalance is achieved between the two opposing forces. The leader, who

---

[*] By "destabilize" I mean positioning or movement away from the correct balance point needed for continued success and positive growth (organization level) and continued enlightenment (individual level). By nature, our egos want stability and control, and that might not actually be healthy! The right balance point might be an "unstable" one.

[**] This would, by definition, include the leader.

has mastered the forces at play, knows not only what is putting pressure on the organization, but from where the pressure is coming, its directionality (in multiple dimensions), and its rate of change on the system. He/she is also aware of deeply held beliefs that are also contributing to the situation. Armed with this knowledge, his/her own behaviors seek to regulate these forces, so that a graceful balance is achieved effortlessly. This is true of what's happening inside us, too. I believe that, if done well, leadership mastery is almost transparent to observers.

Look at how similar the order-chaos model is to the concept of yin and yang as illustrated by the symbol T'ai-chi T'u in Figure 10. Yes, there's not much new here! There is only one direct reference to yin and yang in Star's translation of Lao Tzu's *Tao Te Ching*. It is as follows: "All beings support yin and embrace yang and the interplay of these two forces fills the universe[.] Yet only at the still-point, between the breathing in and the breathing out, can one capture these two in perfect harmony."

Figure 10: T'ai-chi T'u (aka Yin and Yang),
Transmutational Model Context

I find it fascinating that breathing is used as a metaphor in so many models to illustrate this point. It's in yin and yang (of course), yoga (not surprising, given its Eastern genesis), and in contemporary management concepts such as Barry Johnson's polarity management.[3]

Yin and yang represents a philosophy of dynamic ever-changing dualism and reflects the brain-mind's way of seeing the world quite beautifully. According to the theory, yin can never overcome yang and vice versa. Further, though one may dominate over time, each contains the seed of the other and ultimately will be overcome and dominated by the other. For example, we know that an emotion that goes too far (e.g., anger) can end up consuming one's self.

For me, the idea of capturing the two in perfect harmony at the still point between the breathing in and the breathing out is the intriguing aspect. I realized that the yin and yang model didn't really examine the in-between very much at all. What was in between? What is between an input and the output of the brain? Nothing! It is a transition point. It is neither chaos nor order. The in-between has infinite depth and therefore infinite possibility.

In respect to our brain-minds, the in-between is a state that has yet to resolve itself. It is the quintessential now. Eckart Tolle, in his books *The Power of Now* and *A New Earth*, tell us to live in the moment of now. I interpret this to mean letting go of past and future and of all the polarities that our brain creates. It's simply now and the state of being fully present in the now. It is accessible through techniques such as self-awareness, mindfulness, reflection, and meditation. These are feedback loops.

Being aware of the brain's outputs and accessing the in-between opens up numerous possibilities. I've found it equally fascinating that according to the translation of the *Bhagavad Gita* by Hawley,[4] living deeply in the now is possible. Expertly doing so enables a person to see how the input changes the brain as it is happening.

Transmutational leadership is a model and a method for knowing our human and spiritual selves. It allows us to be authentic leaders. Transmutational leadership helps explore what being authentic really is. It means not allowing our brain-mind to control the narrative in our head.

Authenticity is often stated as a pillar of current leadership theory, but what does it mean to be authentic? What happens if you're a terrible person and you choose to be authentic? Are you a terrible leader by definition? The answer is definitely open for debate because context is so important.

I submit that a person leading strictly from the brain-mind is apt to generate some negative consequences for themselves and others. The reason is that our most basic instinct, survival—usually through dominance—arises from the brain. For example, competition is pretty much always about winning and losing. Someone has to lose. Each organization sets out to dominate its niche. This is a very deeply held belief. Yet, it's paradoxical because we know it's not really healthy in the long run, but hey, who cares about society or nature when there's money at stake? Thankfully, not everyone thinks this way.

It seems to me that people want their leaders to define reality and the value system and tell them or advise them how to behave in order to win (i.e., personally and collectively succeed). So, we aren't going to get rid of the brain-mind any time soon. This will be even more so as the world's resources get depleted.

This is paradoxical and challenging for a leader. As F. Scott Fitzgerald said, "The test of a first-rate intelligence is the ability to hold two opposing ideas in the mind at the same time, and still retain the ability to function."

How can a leader judge and control, and yet provide maximum freedom and creativity to get results for their organization, know them both to be needed, and still access the in-between? In the face of too much creativity (e.g., chaos), brain-mind dominated leaders will choose order (i.e., control). It doesn't really matter to them if this leads to chaos eventually, as long as "eventually" means after their comfortable retirement. The brain-mind is self-interested and egotistical. This should be no surprise to us.

How can one live in between order and chaos and still lead a passionate life? We certainly don't want to swing between order and chaos extremes. I believe most people would rather let go of negative emotions. I think that most of us would rather lead happy, peaceful, and balanced lives filled with joy and love. Maybe I'm wrong. There are lots of people who seem to be addicted to drama. Our television shows are filled with it, so there's a market out there. Or worse, we could be actively creating the market with that very TV drama!

Yin and yang asks us to balance opposites, but it doesn't quite inform us as to how to balance the in-between space with the two polar opposites. For me, balancing the polar opposites leads to compromise, whereas accessing the space in between can lead to a lot more creative solutions.

Styles of Leadership

There are many leadership definitions and perspectives (i.e., models) that have been developed and put forward over the years, and more are coming out every day as we come to grips with what leadership is and what the ideal leader should be like. A few years ago, Anderson and Ackerman-Anderson[5] put forward a model of three leadership styles in the presence of change: developmental (low change), transactional (medium change), and transformational (high change). Each of these change types affects the style of leadership that is typically practiced under normal circumstances in most organizations. I incorporated these styles into Figure 11 and I added dictators and heroes to the list. As shown, we turn to dictators and heroes at the extremes of system stability or instability.

Which style is the most appropriate and what leader characteristics are most valued depends on context and system demands.

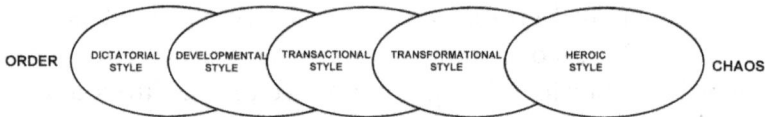

Figure 11: Leadership Styles

You will notice that the charismatic style is not in Figure 11, although I've mentioned it several times. Charismatics typically show up more often near the two ends of the spectrum, meaning heroic or dictatorial styles.

Charismatics are neither good nor bad; it is a natural strength (talent and development) that they possess. Charismatics can get followers to do things they would not normally do. Charismatic leaders can get their organizations to perform well, but when they leave, their departure creates a big vacuum and the organization suffers. I highly recommend the work of Yukl,[6] who provides an excellent overview of the positive and negative aspects of charismatic leaders and of organizational leadership in general. Charismatics can operate effectively at any point in the order-chaos continuum.

Charismatic leaders are human beings just as we are. They make mistakes just as we do. We want them to be perfect, but we know they are human. When they make a mistake, we hate it when they try to cover it up to maintain the illusion that they're perfect. We know they're not, and all we want is for them to admit it. We actually enjoy it a lot to see them equal to us or us equal to them. The Bill Clinton and Monica Lewinsky affair is an example. Notwithstanding the complications of United States politics and the advice of his public relations handlers, had Clinton just admitted it, the outcome might have turned out quite differently. It doesn't matter that he may have tried to do his duty and provide consequential respect and dignity to all interested parties in the manner that would satisfy the moral philosophy of Immanuel Kant. At the core of the issue was an aspect of self-interest and as such, he lost the moral argument. Such is the hubris of our leaders, the cowardice of our egos, and the complicit hypocrisy of the many when faced with moral and ethical dilemmas. Such is the brain-mind at work. The gap between the brain-mind and the soul-mind is the ongoing potential difference we face for any moral and ethical decision. It is the choice between what to do versus what we ought to do. It is doing the right thing versus doing things right.

I digressed a bit; back to the model. I further adapted the model, as shown in Figure 12, to take into account some of the context, including the pressure from the external environment and the needs of the leader and followers. Inherent in the model is how the leader's needs, behaviors, and style, and his/her action or inaction, keep the organization balanced. The balance point is a question mark because it moves around as the organization evolves and the external environment dictates.

SITUATION,
ENVIRONMENT AND
ORGANIZATIONAL NEEDS

ORDER ← ———— LEADER NEEDS, STYLE AND BEHAVIORS ———→ CHAOS
BALANCE POINT ?

FOLLOWER
NEEDS

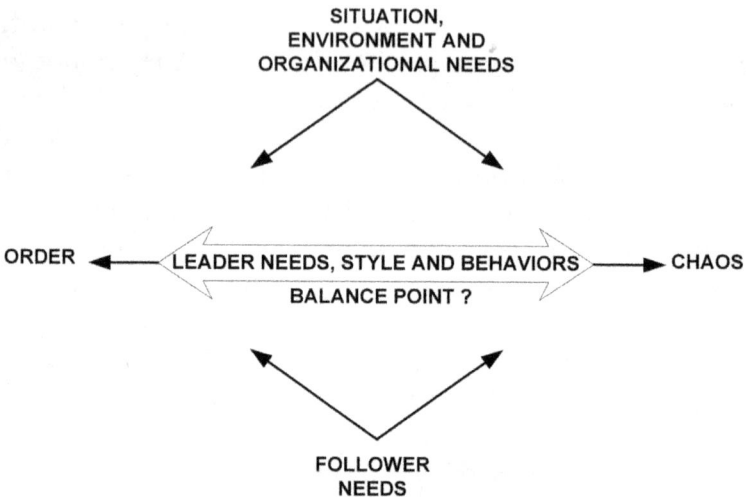

Figure 12: Order-Chaos Needs Model

Figure 13 illustrates the two models (i.e., Figure 11 and Figure 12) together. Now, the emphasis is shifted to the leader. Awareness is the key attribute. The leader needs to be aware of the system, its rules, and all the pressures of change and in which direction the organization is moving, as shown in the diagram. The organization is either going to the balance point or away from it. There is no such thing as unchanging equilibrium—complex nonlinear systems are forever changing, just like the atmosphere. The leader's action should always be contextual relative to the external environment and the desired direction of change for the organization to continue to achieve its purpose.

CHASM
OR SCHISM

LOWEST
RATE OF
CHANGE

HIGHEST
RATE OF
CHANGE

ORDER

CHAOS

BRIDGE

BALANCED RATE OF CHANGE

SITUATION,
ENVIRONMENT AND
ORGANIZATIONAL NEEDS

ORDER ◄— LEADER NEEDS, STYLE AND BEHAVIORS —► CHAOS

BALANCE POINT ?

FOLLOWER
NEEDS

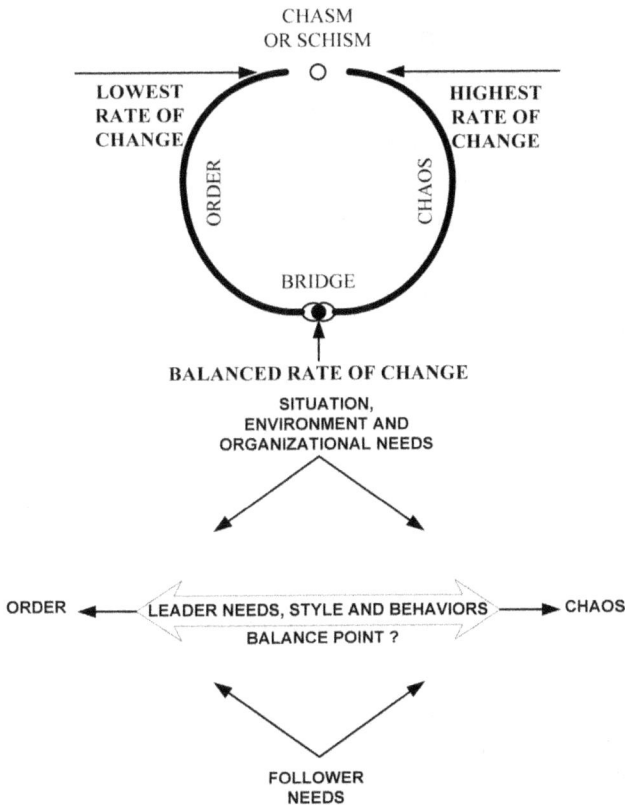

Figure 13: Basic Transmutational Leadership Model

A leader's and an organization's performance are often compromised by the brain-mind's ego, its chief attributes being self-interest, competitiveness, fear, and personal ambition. Emotions can run deeply, anger can emerge, as can blaming others, when a leader is challenged or his/ her organization's survival is threatened. All these negative aspects get in the way of consciousness and thereby limit possibilities. Soul-mind dominated leaders are very aware of these issues within themselves and have a greater capacity to set them aside so that they can see the greater picture. They also know that their leadership by example will enable others to lead similarly. Indeed, a leader must first of all lead their self.

Over time, most individuals and organizations have a natural inclination to want greater control and predictability in order to compete and survive. It's a very Darwinian view. Survival of the fittest is how it's often described. For example, when a new idea emerges, say in semiconductors, there are a lot of organizations that form to exploit the idea. Over time, fewer and fewer organizations are able to survive due to competition and both internal and external factors. For those that do survive, the rewards are great. They become the dominant few and work very hard at staying the dominant few; witness the Intel versus AMD and Apple versus Samsung lawsuits. The financial rewards of being at the top, as in baseball, are great, even though the difference in performance between first and second is miniscule for most endeavors, including sports, industry, and politics. As a result, sometimes things are done that are not generally acceptable to society, whether it's Alex Rodriguez' steroid use (baseball), Lance Armstrong's use of performance-enhancing drugs (cycling), anti-competitive practices such as Intel's billion-dollar-plus payment to AMD (industry), or Abraham Lincoln's bribery tactics to get the votes needed to amend the United States Constitution (politics).

I threw in the last example because what is perceived by the majority as acceptable or not depends to a certain extent on the leader's motivation and how the followers perceive it. This is a matter of perspective and judgment. Victors and historians provide us with the dominant interpretation of history and the lens of perspective, and the usually obvious long-term consequences do influence our judgment.

World-class "leaders" are very creative when it comes to finding ways to "win." Lance Armstrong said that he wanted to win at all cost. As shown by these examples, it can be very lucrative to be breaking the rules.

Conflict, particularly war, is the most competitive human endeavor, and we like war leaders who are able to win at all cost. Even though some may be pyrrhic victories, we have a sense that we've won. In these situations, we seek the best and worst our brain-minds can give us.

We had better really know what we are fighting for when the contest between the brain-mind and the soul-mind emerges in our awareness. The result of that conflict will be a choice. The more self-aware we are of that choice, the more informed our decision will be.

A leader exercises power every day and consequently is faced with ethical dilemmas. Abuse of power is easy to do and therefore rampant. Control is exercise of power. The brain-mind is naturally inclined to abuse power, and it resists letting the soul-mind get in the way. It's like the cartoon of the devil on one shoulder and the saint on the other, each speaking into our ears about what we should do. It is a type of war of minds. Perhaps this explains in part why there are so many ethical abuses these days. I have to admit that it seems to be more fun to be breaking rules than following them, especially when one gets paid so well. Maybe that's what "good" leadership really is in practice—the innate ability to use sound judgment and ethical intent regarding when to break the rules.

Control is both real and illusory. It's real in that we appoint people to positions of authority. It's illusory in that in most cases, followers only give permission to leaders to control them. Dictators know this. That's why they need an external enemy at all times. It keeps the ranks closed and the followers from disagreeing too much. If that's not enough, dictators know how to eliminate opposition in multiple ways. It's interesting how dictators' approval ratings are very high when there's a war on! Undoubtedly all the saber rattling in North Korea right now is simply this process manifesting itself.

While all sentient beings desire freedom, most of the time followers willingly grant leaders power over them, but sometimes they do it out of fear or just habit. When abuse of power happens, who wins? Who is to judge? Is the organization more important than a single individual? It depends on the issue, I suppose, and whether or not the individual is you.

When followers lose faith in their leaders, followers have more ways to resist control than managers have to impose it. Newly minted leader/managers often don't realize this. Many times, I've seen new managers try to impose control because of low self-confidence and self-esteem in their new role. The ego is always there waiting to impose itself. A soul-mind leader is aware of this and finds ways to balance the brain-mind's tendencies.

The order side of the continuum represents the inclination for greater and greater control and dominance. Ultimately, as in the case of industry, a sector ends up being dominated by one or two big competitors whereby a few smaller niche players get snapped up by the big players from time to time to ensure the big players remain dominant. The reason that smaller players get snapped up (through the merger or acquisition process) is that the smaller players tend to be the most innovative and thereby reduce the big players' profits.

Once an organization has created a monopoly for itself, it has maximized control and maximized its chance for survival, or so it thinks. It really just depends on the time frame. All organizations fail eventually.

As a society, we know monopolies aren't good for us, so we pass laws against monopolistic tendencies and enforce them, as in the case mentioned earlier with Intel. Ultimately, though, because of this type of dominance, they end up stagnating and eventually fail unless they can re-invent themselves periodically. Communist party rule is a political example. That means they must engage the creative side of the continuum and take their chances. It's clear that learning and creativity thrive in a more chaotic space because that's where there are more possibilities.

By comparing yin and yang and Figure 13, I've concluded that the two dots in yin and yang correspond to the chasm or schism point, and the line in between yin and yang corresponds to the bridge. It is both a chasm and a schism. A chasm is the death of an organization, and a schism is a complete transformation that has little resemblance to the previous organization. For example, the French revolution was a schism. A despotic, uncaring monarchy exercising ultimate control crossed over to extremely high chaos, and the French Republic emerged.

You will notice that forms of government that impose more control tend to operate higher up in the circle than a democracy does. Political systems are different from economic systems. A global financial elite controls the world's economic system. This control is also higher up in the circle because of the high concentration of wealth. Thus, how wealth is accumulated and distributed is another issue that vexes us and is subject to oscillation.

It's sobering to know that of the 5,196 members of China's two legislative bodies, 83 are reported to be billionaires.[7] According to Manthorpe, "One defector from the North to South Korea, revealed that in 2011 the personal expenses on luxury goods by Kim Jong-il, the father of the current leader, soaked up 20 per cent of the nation's budget."[8] It's very sad to also know that many people in North Korea have starved in recent years. There is just as much chicanery no matter where you look, regardless of the type of political or economic system that exists. The only conclusion I can come to is that the brain-mind does not care about the form of political system it operates in.

The brain-mind is able to adapt to any of its creations out of self-interest.

We shouldn't get too smug. Western democracies have their share of similar problems.

The model is also consistent with natural processes. We know very well that a species can become so successful that its very success threatens its survival. In fact, the human race is facing that possibility as other species become extinct and the planet's ability to sustain life continues to degrade in the presence of pollution, resource depletion, and other environmental processes, both natural and man-made. Just read *Limits to Growth: The 30-Year Update*.[9]

It's not surprising, using this perspective, that our brain-mind processes are reflected in our organizations and in how our organizations behave. After all, an organization is simply a group of individuals who operate within a specific framework in order to accomplish some type of goal. This is so whether it's a company, a government, a nonprofit society, a religious group, or a nation.

At the top of the basic transmutational leadership model is a chasm or schism.[*] I define this as a complete breakdown of the existing status quo. In this location, more control leads to failure, and more efficiency is unavailable. If you are a commercial company, more profit is unattainable without some type of transformation. If you try to go too far and too fast, the system breaks. As I mentioned earlier, this is reflected in the saying, "the straw that breaks the camel's back." A system is unable to cope within its set of rules and falls into chaos.

Organizationally, it means that a company or a society or any other form of organization ends up on the other side of the continuum rather abruptly and finds itself in chaos or order. This has some interesting implications.

---

[*] A chasm if the organization fails or a schism if the organization goes through a complete transformation.

Highly controlled organizations tend to be run by dictators, and highly chaotic ones by heroes, and the people are complicit in their support of the dominant few (either type) until they've had enough. That is why information is so controlled. It's dangerous to unscrupulous leaders if the followers know the truth of their deeply self-interested behaviors. It's a complete conundrum for good leaders, too. Followers want their leaders to protect their interests. Political leaders are always in a situation of having to put their country's interests ahead of everyone else, no matter the consequence for planet Earth or humanity. How do we deal with that? Of course, it takes a paradigm shift in consciousness, as Einstein suggests. The decisions we make and the actions we take will emerge from this shift of consciousness.

At the other side of the circle from the chasm or schism is a bridge. This point emphasizes that it is possible to go from order to chaos or from chaos to order and to oscillate successfully back and forth. Standing on the bridge is whole-brain and whole-mind thinking and the ability to hold all things in balance within oneself and within one's organization. Holding all things in balance for humanity would be nice, but maybe that's a stretch for this day and age. Nevertheless, the faster the oscillation, the faster the change, and it represents the ability of the organization to learn quickly from its experiences. Changes don't need to be big, as long as they are frequent enough, so that they are not too fast for the followers and the system to absorb.

For an organization to operate successfully on the bridge requires information to flow freely, so that all people participate in the process. Yes, it's messy and takes longer, and the long-term outcome is always uncertain, since some degree of chaos is involved. That doesn't mean we need to abandon all the other styles of leadership. Indeed, we need to be flexible. There are times, for example when a crisis occurs, when a command-and-control (i.e., dictatorial or heroic) style is required. But leaders must be careful about taking on this style; it's addictive! As the saying goes, absolute power corrupts absolutely.

How much chaos and order is needed—the balance point—is constantly shifting, depending on the leader and external and internal factors. It means that the leader must balance order and chaos appropriately, depending on the existing conditions, and to apply the right kind of leadership style. There are several techniques (i.e., bridges) to increase a leader's awareness that help resolve this dynamic problem.

What we've seen so far is a long-standing acknowledgment of polarity thinking, which is consistent with the natural tendency of systems to oscillate between order and chaos. This is how the brain-mind works. Input goes through a chaotic process and the brain settles down into order quickly (i.e., it makes a decision); it's called homeostasis.

What I'm trying to convey is that leaders respond to external and internal pressures and, in the context of what they are trying to achieve (generally organizational success), move the balance point somewhere along the order-chaos continuum. However, because of competition and the need for continuously better results, organizations seek greater and greater levels of efficiency and through their actions try to limit competition and gain maximum control over the internal and external environment in order to do so. Of course, a leader's self-interest factors into this process, too. In any case, this helps the organization survive and be successful, but this behavior can also be the seed of its own destruction. Oscillating between order and chaos is the yin and yang of organizations.

As a result of success, leaders become the dominant few and followers are complicit in the system that they have co-created. The dominant few don't want to give up their high-paying jobs, their toys, their villas, and the power they've worked so hard to get, so they take every action possible to ensure the system remains stable, that is, in their favor, and followers are quite happy to go along for the ride. All of us are seemingly trapped by our very own systems. This applies not only to people, it applies to other species too.

Because all external environments change over time, a highly structured and controlled system cannot cope forever, and it ultimately breaks. At this point, the followers ditch the leaders, since they've lost faith in the leadership and recognize that the old system is no longer working and a new leadership is needed.

Today, we witness accelerating change, and our answer is a more dynamic leadership style. This is so because our organizations are being driven more and more toward the top of the circle in of the continuum. Leaders need to be more aware of the pressures of change, how to manage change, and they need to fully develop the ability to thrive in an environment of rapid change. It's harder and harder to maintain balance in the presence of rapid change.

Today, we want our leaders to be transformational and charismatic. This is nothing more than a reaction to rapid change—the external environment rising higher and higher on the chaos side of the continuum. Those styles eventually fail, too, because the desire for charisma is a reaction to a symptom and not the root cause. It's like applying a Band-Aid to a compound fracture.

What happens in our organizations is not unlike what happens in society as the pendulum oscillates between order and chaos. From an economics perspective, there can be a peaceful redistribution of power and wealth over time through continuous change (i.e., the bridge) of our systems and leaders, or there can be a civil war (i.e., the chasm), which tragically ends up as a distribution of poverty and loss of significant talent.

The metaphor of the beaver pond, described in Chapter 3,

applies. As the beaver works to make the dam more solid and control the local environment, entropy ensures that there will always be leakage. If there is minimal leakage and the beaver builds the dam up ever higher and ever more solid, there will come a point where the water pressure behind the dam is greater than the design threshold, and the dam will catastrophically fail. That's why all our dams have floodgates—to relieve pressure before it exceeds our design threshold. Not only that, but there are other threats to the dam, both natural and human-made. The human-made kind, for example, would be dynamiting the dam, killing the beavers, or trapping and relocating them. The natural kind, for example, might be a flash-flood that destroys the dam by overflowing over the top and rapidly eroding it. The system then remains in chaos mode until water levels stabilize to a new level. Prior to this, the dam had been slowly and surely increasing the system's energy by storing water. The sudden change causes the stored energy to dissipate quickly. The new levels of energy are much lower than in the previous system. This is the equivalent of a revolution redistributing poverty. It will apply to humanity if we don't pay attention.

A system in a state of practical equilibrium or balance is represented by the bridge end of the model in Figure 13, and the examples of catastrophic failures apply at the chasm or schism end. All this is still just an elaboration of yin and yang and recognition that our brain-minds are wired or predisposed to creating this dynamic as it interacts with its external environment.

As I've explained, this applies to how our brain functions—a continuous series of bifurcations leading to a final decision. It's sad that it almost always takes a crisis for substantive change to take place. But then, that's the nature of the brain-mind's resistance to change!

There is a symmetry function involved in the process. An individual or an organization can move up or down in the circle. Moving up has very negative consequences, and moving down leads to greater balance. It is analogous to the positive and negative poles of a magnet attracting each other. As Isaac Newton would say, every action has an equal and opposite reaction.

As an organization moves up the order side of the circle, it becomes more and more vulnerable to a chaotic event whose destructive power is equal to, or stronger than, the controlling power of the organization. This is the case in the other direction, too; chaos is met with an equal degree, or better, of control. Symmetry is seen in many areas of study. For example, this is generally a meta function of systems that can be modeled using polar opposites such as, for instance, in string theory, religion (good vs. evil), masculine and feminine traits, and so on. Simply put, as the saying goes, opposites attract. This clearly demonstrates that operating around the bridge is the key to successful and rapid change to meet an extremely fast changing internal and external environment.

As we can readily imagine, negative energy attracts negative energy, and violence begets violence. This negative energy moves competitive organizations or people up the circle, whereas positive energy attracts positive energy and moves the individual or organization down in the direction of the bridge.

The bridge is a system state where balance is achieved by all the forces at work on the system, both internal and external. It is a state of practical equilibrium, although change is constant. The changes to the system are small.

What happens to our organizations is reflected in our brains. The brain seeks a state of equilibrium normally. However, if the brain is unbalanced, for example either too left-brain or too right-brain driven, then whole-brain thinking is compromised and homeostasis harder to achieve relative to the external environment. When whole-brain thinking is compromised, so is balance.

The bridge is both physical and abstract. If we speak of the physical, it is whole-brain thinking. That is, the bridge can be thought of as the corpus callosum, which connects the right and left hemispheres together and thereby all of the electrochemical signals in the brain and body.

It's been reported, though not conclusively argued, that the corpus callosum in females is on average larger and denser than in males. This may explain in part why women are more relationship-oriented and why, I believe, under our current systems' rules, there exists the glass ceiling that women have difficulty penetrating. Men are much more likely to sacrifice relationships to achieve their personal objectives and those of their organizations. As a collective, that's what we want from leaders because we see the world as competitive under the current circumstances. That is, I believe, why men are much better at war; the ultimate competition. Make no mistake—women value that quality in men when it gets ugly. They appreciate masculine decisiveness, and so men hold most positions of power. Men are deeply suspicious of a woman's desire to maintain relationships above goals, and thus, from a man's perspective, women compromise and complicate matters. So, men generally don't like to invite women into the boardroom during highly competitive situations requiring ruthless decisiveness.

Regardless of the current situation in the world, I believe that both genders are needed to maintain a balanced approach to problem solving and decision making. I strongly believe that males must learn to appreciate females' expanded sense of relationships and possibility. Gender conflict will continue until a happy and respectful equilibrium is found.

The practice of transmutational leadership overcomes the inconvenient truth of our brain-mind. It overcomes the polarized thinking that dominates us, challenges our most deeply held beliefs and creates a new meaning regarding leadership, change, progress, and success. As quoted in *The Tibetan Book of Living and Dying*, written by Sogyal Rinpoche, the physicist David Bohm said: "A change of meaning is necessary to change this world politically, economically and socially. But that change must begin with the individual; it must change for him...if meaning is a key part of reality, then, once society, the individual and relationships are seen to mean something different a fundamental change has taken place."[10] Thus, transmutational leadership is primarily about leadership from within, at the individual level. This is required for fundamental change to take place in our society.

The abstract bridge is a set of techniques used to quiet and calm the brain. It is the energy-only aspect of mind. The primary techniques of reflection, mindfulness, and meditation bring peace of mind and clarity of thinking. These techniques enable us to access the soul-mind more deeply. Instead of a polarized decision, additional possibilities emerge. It is another dimension that modern leaders can engage to bring higher levels of abundance and opportunity. It merges the conscious and the unconscious, the physical and spiritual worlds. I call this unification of the two dimensions transmutational. It is transmutational because we can transmute a negative into a positive, and when we employ techniques such as meditation, we are actually constructing new neurons, significantly more synapses, and therefore more possibility. Mind creates matter!

Figure 14 is how I see the process within us today. Moving from left to right, the primary effect of the brain-mind system is a steady decrease in possibilities that ultimately leads to a final decision, along with the action or inaction resulting in outcomes. If we want to expand possibilities, we need to move from right to left. We can counter our brain-minds by being consciously self-aware and using techniques of reflection, mindfulness, and meditation. It is using these paths and bridges that enables us to access additional possibilities held in the soul-mind. These paths allow a suspension of judgment so that more alternatives become available to the leader, their followers, and their organization.

From all that I have read of Eastern philosophy and various spiritual teachings, meditation is the primary means of deeply accessing the spiritual/energy world of the mind. Continuous development of this ability leads to greater self-knowledge and ultimately enlightenment. As we develop, the effects of polarized brain-mind processing have less and less effect on the outcome. Self-awareness is the key to the door of increasing consciousness. Thus, there is an aspect of transmutational leadership that is very spiritual by nature.

There are a couple of things that I should mention about Figure 14. I did not add food to the diagram, although there is no doubt that the brain is electrochemical and we need food to sustain, maintain, and keep our entire body healthy. Food, (i.e., proper nutrition), or lack of it, does affect brain and body functions such as hormone levels. In addition, while it is convenient to show the physical and energy world as separate, the reality is that they are fully entangled.

Note how the brain-mind is both holographic and specialized as, in Figure 14, you move from left to right, such that by the time you get to the final decision filter, either the left or right hemisphere will dominate.

Note also that the initial conditions bias is not only based on experience and mental models, but also on how the external environment is sensed. People will react to what is going on around them and how others are also behaving. There is such a thing as mob behavior. As Michel de Montaigne said, "Contagion is very dangerous in crowds.

You must either imitate the vicious or hate them." For example, riots occur after sports events, and we often explain our own behavior by the circumstances. Under different circumstances and surroundings, a person may not participate in a riot, as they know it to be unacceptable behavior.

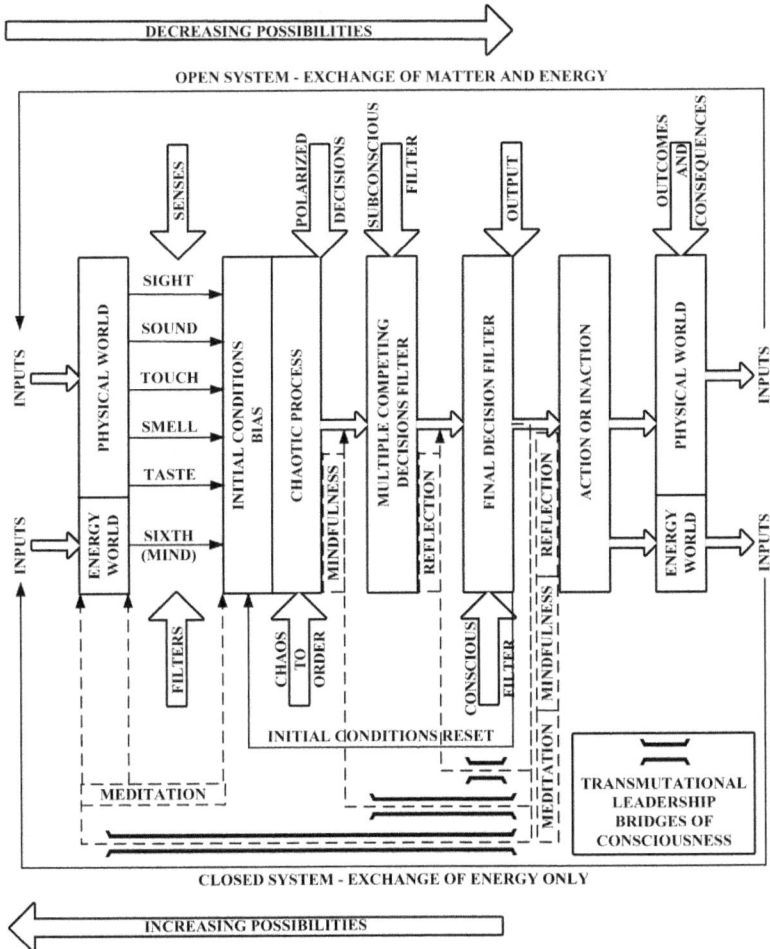

Figure 14: Transmutational Leadership Bridge(s) of Consciousness

Transmutational leadership is about the ability to use the brain-mind and soul-mind at will. It is whole-brain and full-mind leadership.

Meditation leads to progressive depth and increasing possibilities. Conn, as reported in Rychkun (Vol. II, p. 413), associates Theta brain waves with this awareness. At some point, no thing and all things exist. It is unity, the zone of infinite possibility, as shown in Figure 15.

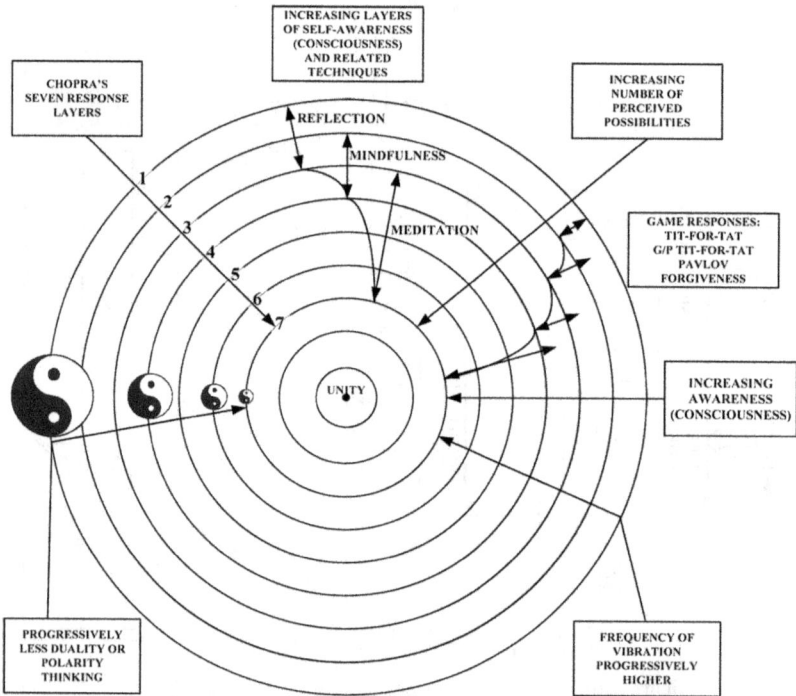

Figure 15: Transmutational Leadership Model 2013

Accessing higher levels toward unity as shown in Figure 15 requires self-awareness of the nature of decisions without being held captive by them. It's essential that we don't get caught up in between and as a result stop judging. We need the positive aspects of judgment to maintain our moral and ethical foundations, or civilization crumbles; in any case, "good" competitive* forces are needed for progressive change. This is very challenging for transmutational leaders. However, it's essential in the modern age to let go of the negative effects of judgment and the response methods of the brain-mind. There are things in this world that are not acceptable, such genocide (regardless of genus or species), and those must be judged and dealt with accordingly. Our being able to retain judgment while accessing the spaces in between, as shown by the bridges, opens up numerous additional possibilities. It turns this possibility *or* that possibility into this possibility *and* that possibility, and even more. We must respect and honor both our spiritual and physical selves.

There is a significant amount of conflict inherent when the brain-mind and the soul-mind connect. The brain-mind is quick in its judgment while, by all accounts, the soul-mind exists in a world of nonjudgment. This is dualism at its core. In my opinion, this is in part the reason why many leaders and leadership models have difficulty finding a creative and balanced approach to complex problems. Deciding what the right thing to do is in any situation is inextricably wound up in questions such as, What's good for me?, What's good for the organization?, What is good for humanity?, and what about when they don't align? This is so simply because we must honor our physical selves and the reality of dualism exquisitely held in the physical world.

The leader exists to represent the interests of the group. This is essentially a competitive win-lose brain-mind framework at its core. If the interest of the group is a strategy

---

* Note: Competitive in the sense of conscious versus unconscious, or light versus dark, without resorting to "bad" competitive methods

of cooperation, then it looks like win-win, though we may continue to overexploit our resources. However, one can never escape the win-lose dualism of the brain-mind's processing when pushed into a place where physical survival is at stake. In their book *Why God Won't Go Away: Brain Science and the Biology of Belief,* Newberg, D'Aquili, and Rause point out, "The goal of every living brain, no matter what its level of neurological sophistication, from the tiny knots of nerve cells that govern insect behavior on up to the intricate complexity of the human neocortex, has been to enhance the organism's chances of survival by reacting to raw sensory data and translating it into a negotiable rendition of a world."[11] In effect, it's impossible to escape the brain-mind layer until death occurs. One can only dampen its effects by activating the soul-mind. Hence, leaders have a very difficult job.

Chopra's Seven Layers of Brain and Mind

As mentioned earlier in this chapter, for a short period of time, an organization emerged called the Alliance for a New Humanity (ANH). Unfortunately, it has not continued to operate. Nevertheless, in March 2008 I attended a magnificent and wonderful ANH conference in San Jose, Costa Rica. At the conference, Deepak Chopra described seven layers of mind development and how each reacts to situations. Here they are from my inadequate notes:

> ➤ Layer 1: Fight-or-Flight Response; from our 300-million-year-old reptilian brain

> ➤ Layer 2: Being Offended Response; from our 100-million-year-old limbic brain (emotions; all mammals)
>   • Intimidation, confrontation
>   • Nice and manipulative
>   • Stubborn

> ➢ Layer 3: Choiceful Awareness Response; from our 4-million-year-old cognitive brain (humans)
>   - Witness how you react to what is happening
>   - Observe without judgment

> ➢ Layer 4: Intuitive Response; emergence of widespread mind/consciousness (humanity)
>   - Contextual, holistic
>   - Mirroring the wisdom of the universe
>   - Synchronicity

> ➢ Layer 5: Creative Response
>   - How to react in the midst of chaos

> ➢ Layer 6: Higher Guidance Response
>   - Archetypes
>   - Eavesdrop beyond individual to past ancestors, etc.
>   - "Angels"
>   - Beyond personal identity
>   - Vision beyond identity

> ➢ Layer 7: Sacred Response
>   - Love/eternal love
>   - Very nature of being
>   - Universe's extended body

A Revised Approach

Figure 15 is a reflection of how we are like an onion, with multiple layers. Being authentic ends up depending on what layer you choose to operate from without ever giving up the choice of responding from the other levels. As can be seen, there is more depth beyond the seventh layer, and the solid dot in the middle indicates the Infinite Mind.

Authentic Leadership

Since our innate attributes, concerns, and responses are quite different depending on what layer we are at in the moment and the situation, it's a conundrum for leaders who are told to be authentic. What does being authentic mean? How can a leader be authentic if they don't know who they are and where in the continuum their brain and mind are at?

There are two aspects of authenticity in my opinion: as a manifest human being (i.e., the brain-mind) that is working from left to right in Figure 14, and as a spiritual being (i.e., soul-mind) working from right to left with all its multiple layers. To reach each higher layer in Figure 15 requires the use of various consciousness techniques to increase CQ. There aren't layers so much as there is a continuum, but it is convenient to represent it that way because our brain-minds find it easier to process. Figure 15 is the yin and yang of the body and soul. As you can appreciate, Figures 13 (leader or organization centric), 14 (internal decision-making process), and 15 (outcome) go together and represent different views only.

Leaders who do not tap into their authentic spiritual place are doomed to fail in the long run because they ignore the very interconnectedness of the world around them, their place in it, and they limit themselves to fewer possibilities. They are unable to overcome and learn from experience. They vibrate at a lower level, and so learning is slowed. Fewer possibilities are available to them.

The path of the brain's polarizing tendencies is illuminated by standard instruments such as the Myers-Briggs Type Indicator (MBTI) that reveal our personality preferences. The MBTI, like many other personality and leadership models, is based on polarities and has been available for a long time. However, it is dealing with the physical layers only, rather than getting at the root cause of behavior. Behavior is an outcome of a process, as I showed earlier in

Figure 7. The MBTI assessment is invaluable nonetheless. It's crucial to be aware of how your brain-mind works. Otherwise, self-awareness, reflection, and mindfulness are compromised.

The increasing possibilities path is a connection to our soul. Being authentic in this respect takes us into philosophy and spiritual ideas and techniques as reported over thousands of years by religious prophets and spiritual leaders who advocate various techniques, especially meditation.

Being able to go from left to right and right to left in Figure 14 is required to achieve authenticity. This must be done quickly, but cannot be done simultaneously. It is a significant challenge for the leader to do both on a continuous basis.

Those who advise leaders to be authentic make a tacit assumption that authenticity is "good and ethical." However, not all people are good and ethical when they lead without their soul. I believe that what is good and what is bad is a construct derived from our value system and depends on which layer or perspective you wish to argue from. There are times when a violent response, as in defending against aggression, is appropriate.

We have all met people whose "authentic" selves seem to leave much to be desired. I firmly believe that it is those types of leaders who fail to connect across the transmutational bridge into their soul's energy and end up leading from a place of harsh judgment, ego, and fear. Though they may be very "successful" in the short term, the consequence for organizations led by toxic people such as these is generally disastrous in the long term. They leave broken people in their wake.

Organizations that are not authentic also leave flotsam and jetsam in their wakes. Organizations also need to be authentic. It is one thing to present a great marketing image to the public for consumption, but when the experience does not meet the marketing message, people will be very vindictive. If a company claims it wants to be known as sustainable, it has to walk the talk. It can take years to make a reputation and a global image and no time at all to destroy it. Authenticity requires consistency of image with corresponding behavior to be credible. Leaders know that reputation in the global marketplace is king. In today's Internet-driven, social-media-conscious world, there can be no false steps. Leading companies are putting a lot of investment into their employees to ensure that this consistency happens. Leadership was complex enough a decade ago. Today, it is even more challenging. Without the right image and the authenticity to back it up, the ice becomes rather thin. For-profit corporations will continue to be challenged to make enough profit to be healthy, but those that do not heed this warning are not likely to survive for long.

Convexed Mariner

Senseless mariner, prisoner of a dark, boundless sea.

No apparent horizon, an emerald sea beyond sight, beyond
hope, beyond reach.

What terrors lie beneath unseen; what hope awaits
beyond the horizon?

The light flickers a veiled understanding—safe harbor denied.

The iriswind shackles the broken spirit with love and despair
in equal measure.

The iriswind fetches—a whirlpool of entrapment captivating
body and soul.

Poor senseless mariner, prisoner of the emerald sea,
convexed by the horizon shimmering in the fading light.

Tossed upon its lens, the ship is wrecked; lashed to pieces by
the whitewashed sea,

The sailor grasping tortured remains saved from oblivion.

Ship and sailor's souls inextricably bound to sea and shore;
saved at last.

Poor senseless mariner, gazing at the endless emerald sea,
longing to return to endless possibility.

A new journey awaits.

5

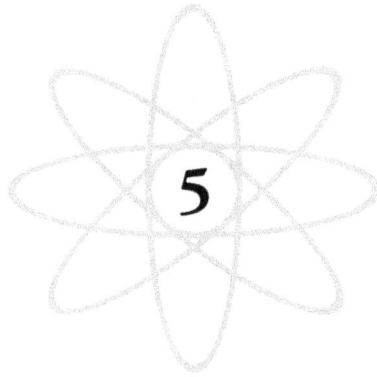

Learning to Unlearn Beliefs

Point 1: Much Current Leadership Learning Reinforces Polarity Decision Making

MUCH OF LEADERSHIP theory and training today is based on a binary view of the subject at hand and reinforces the brain-mind's polarity decision making. It's a very comfortable thing to do, since the brain-mind naturally sees it that way. Personality type analysis is a good example and is one of those foundation courses that are very popular, as you've probably experienced. It's really a good thing to learn these tools and techniques, since they expose the brain-mind at work. These theories are useful in their own way, but disguise the true nature of what's going on, because how we respond to the external environment is a behavior—there are deeper processes at work. If you are not aware of it, polarized mental models create a bias that contributes to the brain-mind system's tendency to categorize people, rightly or wrongly. I'll expand on this later in this chapter.

Point 2: Most Leadership Learning Reinforces the System by Design

Another aspect of traditional leadership theories and education courses is that they are designed to maintain the status quo or otherwise promote the system or organization's interests. Organizations want more "success"-oriented behaviors and pay good money to obtain those behaviors. So, there's a whole industry devoted to servicing this desire, and there would be a lot of resistance from this industry to changing the way leadership is taught. Egos and jobs are at stake. When is resistance to change easy to overcome?

Point 3: It's the System, Stupid! (Get Over It. We Are the System.)

We created our systems. Just as a cell learns from its environment, rather than from its DNA, people adapt to the external environment (i.e., the system), rather than their internal state. All behavior is contextual! The internal state is set by what we've learned during our lifetime and is continuously added to from moment to moment. The internal state is both unconscious and conscious. All brain and mind development occurs as a result of this interaction, and it becomes our very being. Our brain is plastic and is constantly creating new neurons, new synapses, and new networks with every experience, and our mind records everything. What we believe is fundamentally important to the process, as it is the initial condition of our nonlinear system that biases and forms our subjective reality. What we focus on, and our intention, creates additional neurons and synaptic connections. Mind creates matter. We know today that the brain retains its plasticity well into old age.

Point 4: Reinforcing Polarity Thinking to Support a System's Goals

It is well known that organizations, and thus we, do not want change except as a way to continue to dominate others or otherwise achieve our self-interested goals. Those who have achieved some level of domination (both organizations and people) have a tendency to drive the system underlying their success into a failure mode. The rest of us are complicit within the system because we want to become one of the dominant few, or otherwise benefit from a stable system.

As mentioned in Point 1, a lot of training courses and learning tend to reinforce the brain-mind's natural tendency to see the world in a binary way. This is valuable in many respects, but it has its negative side, too. Remember, whether something is good or bad depends on perspective. It is a polarity, after all!

Learning to Unlearn

Leaders are taught to "see." What a leader sees is what they are trained to see. What a leader observes affects the thing or person being observed instantaneously. The leader's brain and mind are also affected by all that is around them. Reality is constantly being constructed. The truth is elusive and models are only perspective, not the truth. The intention (positive or negative) behind a leader's action has an immense effect on the creation of reality and the outcome achieved.

Whenever you see a leadership model, observe if it presents a binary perspective or polarities regarding the subject at hand. This will help you and also warn you that as good as these models may be, they are not the whole story. Models cannot and never will be a complete truth. This is so because of their limited view of the entire brain-mind and soul-mind system, in particular the underlying nonlinear process that creates behavior.

Teaching a specific technique implies that a value judgment has already been made on the student's behalf, particularly if it is the organization that insists on using the techniques. I say this because you'll find that all models are criticized one way or another. It's the nature of models after all, as I stated right up front. Behavior-only models can only present a superficial look at the problem. By superficial, I mean the physical layer of brain-mind and soul-mind continuum as shown in Figures 14 and 15 and its tendency to create a binary solution for every problem and every decision. Recall that behavior is an outcome of the process.

I use two examples on the following pages to illustrate what I mean. It is not my intention to pick on these valuable tools, nor criticize any of the many other methods available to us that help us understand the brain-mind. They are all useful in their own way, but it's important to know their limits and applicability.

However, the truth is that who we really are, our essential self, cannot be reduced down to a category or number, no matter how much we would like to do that! Remember, the soul-mind, which is much, much larger than the brain-mind in terms of possibilities, does not see the world as separate things. This is really important. Our evolution to date has been dominated by the brain-mind, and we describe and create our world in terms that are comforting to it (i.e., us). We bestow power, wealth, and glory on those who are adept at exploiting the world (i.e., us). This is a very ego-driven process, and we often create toxic organizations and systems as a result. Tolle would remind us that "the greed of the ego...finds collective expression in the economic structures of this world, such as the huge corporations, which are egoic entities that compete with each other for more. Their only blind aim is profit. They pursue that aim with absolute ruthlessness. Nature, animals, people, even their own employees, are no more than digits on a balance sheet, lifeless objects to be used, then discarded."[1] If you would like to read more on this subject, you might want to look through Rychkun (2012) and his thoughts on how we've created systems that are reinforced based on, for example, the good-versus-evil polarity.[2]

Example 1: Myers-Briggs Type Indicator

A great example of brain-mind type of learning is the Myers-Briggs (Personality) Type Indicator (MBTI) mentioned previously. While it has its critics, it is certainly popular. I use this example because it is arguably one of the most widely used, if not *the* most widely used, foundation analysis for understanding self and others. I've taken this assessment three times in my life. I also use it because there are a lot of people who are familiar with it either intimately or casually. According to Cunningham (2012), some 2 million people per year currently receive this assessment.[3] We really do love reinforcing our brain-mind! Figure 16 illustrates the major polar opposites of the MBTI system. Wikipedia offers lots of information if you are interested in learning more.[4] However, if you would like to have an assessment done, obtain it from a certified vendor because some interpretation of results is required. Nevertheless, as Cunningham's article suggests, there are many other personality assessment tools out there competing for your dollar.

What we are taught by MBTI, among other things, is how our brain-minds prefer to respond to our external environment, including how we prefer others to interact with us. It offers valuable information to help us understand how to manage ourselves and others when we approach a situation from polar opposites. For example, I'm a schedule-driven person. Procrastinators drive me crazy. It doesn't matter why it's that way, that's the way my brain-mind functions. So, it's good to understand it and accept it and accept others for how and who they are, too, no matter how frustrating it may be. People are not problems to be solved in the sense that we are all unique and should be accepted as such. However, when faced with personalities that are opposite, these polarities must be recognized and managed for leadership to be more effective. People need to be understood, and everyone has a story.

EXTRAVERSION	INTROVERSION
INITIATING	RECEIVING
EXPRESSIVE	CONTAINED
GREGARIOUS	INTIMATE
ACTIVE	REFLECTIVE
ENTHUSIASTIC	QUIET
SENSING	**INTUITION**
CONCRETE	ABSTRACT
REALISTIC	IMAGINATIVE
PRACTICAL	CONCEPTUAL
EXPERIENTIAL	THEORETICAL
TRADITIONAL	ORIGINAL
THINKING	**FEELING**
LOGICAL	EMPATHETIC
REASONABLE	COMPASSIONATE
QUESTIONING	ACCOMMODATING
CRITICAL	ACCEPTING
TOUGH	TENDER
JUDGING	**PERCEIVING**
SYSTEMATIC	CASUAL
PLANFUL	OPEN-ENDED
EARLY STARTING	PRESSURE-PROMPTED
SCHEDULED	SPONTANEOUS
METHODICAL	EMERGENT

Figure 16: Myers-Briggs Categories

When we are in a situation that is in alignment with our brain-mind preference, we do okay. For example, an extrovert at a party with lots of strangers is much more comfortable than an introvert. The extrovert gets a lot of energy out of this type of situation, whereas the introvert gets drained of energy and withdraws. When we need to use any of our out-of-preference capabilities, we don't do so well. What I've come to realize is that our MBTI preferences represent a systematic pattern of our brain's physiology and how we process our experiences, our beliefs, and our perception of the situation we are in. But it's not who we are. It is just how our brain-mind responds to our perception of reality and our initial condition bias.

What we are also taught about the MBTI is that it's good to be in the middle zone between two polarities. This means that we are very flexible about how we respond to situations and others. The idea, explicitly or implicitly stated, is that it's important to be self-aware and evolve our preferences and tendencies toward the middle zone. In other words, it's good to have the flexibility to be able to adapt easily.

No matter where we are in the polarities, adapting leadership style to situations and people is a very important facet of leading well. Sometimes, that means using one's out-of-preference style to connect more effectively with others. It is very energy draining to use an out-of-preference style. It's analogous to crossing over to the chaos side of the continuum, the in-preference style naturally being on the order side. Furthermore, it is by definition uncomfortable territory for some and outright scary for others. This is so because operating in an out-of-preference style means not being in control so much. Therefore, this explains to me why we cannot do this for very long without exhausting ourselves and reverting to our normal patterns of behavior. This makes for an interesting question. Is operating in an out-of-preference style inauthentic? There is a fine line between persuasion and influence, and manipulation. Again, the answer to such a question depends on perspective and judgment.

If we can't, won't, or shouldn't use an out-of-preference style, then we end up employing a method called polarity management to balance our competing personality traits. This assumes a desire for a reasonable compromise between the two conflicting personalities. Polarity management is a technique created by Johnson (1996). He defined polarity management very well as a method to overcome differences in personality type. Opposite personality types create conflict between people. People are not problems to be solved, but polarities must be managed. I recommend reading Johnson's book *Polarity Management: Identifying and Managing Unsolvable Problems*[5] as a follow-up to any MBTI training and for any problem originating from polarities. However, note that polarity management leads to compromises, and while that may be quite appropriate, it is not necessarily very creative.

All these models help leaders understand how to manage people to achieve their goals, that is, persuade, influence, and/or manipulate, depending on how you prefer to judge the facts of any given situation.

MBTI from Individual to Organization

The MBTI model has been extended to the level of the organization. One such model is the Organizational Character Index assessment (Bridges, 2000).[6] Organizations have preferred tendencies or ways of being and doing as they respond to their environment and their challenges, just as people do. Their characters and personalities evolve, just as people's do. Changes in an organization can be drastic during and after a crisis, just as in people. In fact, an organization's character and personality are a reflection of the initial conditions during its founding. These initial conditions are the character and personality of its founders and the internal and external environment. Just as our brains evolve, an organization evolves as it ages and responds to internal and external challenges. So, it's no surprise that MBTI has been applied to organizations.

Example 2: Herrmann Brain Dominance Instrument

Another personality type assessment I've done is the Herrmann Brain Dominance Instrument (HBDI).[7] The HBDI tool is similar to MBTI. HBDI assesses people's thinking styles. So, it has a cognitive orientation. Four styles are presented: Analytical thinking, Sequential thinking, Interpersonal thinking, and Imaginative thinking. The four styles are typically presented in a grid where the polarities become more evident. I mention the HBDI because it relates very well to an organizational assessment model described in Bolman and Deal.

HBDI from Individual to Organization

Bolman and Deal's model[8] also presents four primary frames. These frames are how we see our organization and how we function within it. It should be no surprise to the reader at this point that how we see our organization is a reflection of our personality type. The four frames are: Political, Structural, Symbolic, and Human Resources. Figure 17 is an illustration of the model as I first saw it at university.

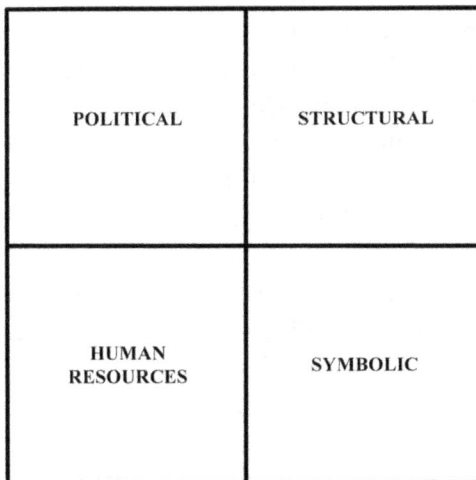

POLITICAL	STRUCTURAL
HUMAN RESOURCES	SYMBOLIC

Figure 17: Bolman-Deal Model

It's useful to know the Bolman-Deal model because it helps us to recognize how each of us communicates with others, manages change, responds in a crisis, and so on, within the context of how we view the organization. How we communicate reveals what we believe the organization's dominant frame is (a big part of its culture). For example, if the dominant frame is the human resources frame, people will speak about the organization as a family. When facing a crisis, the response will be thematically consistent with how one would treat a family member. The Bolman-Deal model is a standard model of leadership education and is very useful generally as a way of showing people how their organizational behavior is reflective of their beliefs. For more frames about how we see organizations, I highly recommend Morgan (1998).[9]

I could list many, many more leadership models that reflect the brain-mind's binary decision making, but this is not a leadership encyclopedia of tools and techniques, or a book dedicated to critically evaluating these models. My intent is quite the opposite. These models are useful in seeing the various aspects of how we perceive and react to our world. As useful as they are, they are only an assessment of behavior. Behavior is the outcome of a process—that is, the brain-mind's decision about an input that has already been made.

If we aren't able to understand what's going on more deeply, or don't want to understand more deeply, we stay on thoughtless autopilot. What I mean by that is that these models tend to reinforce our ability to judge and therefore persuade, influence, or manipulate organizations and other people more effectively. There is nothing inherently wrong or right in this. Again, it depends on perspective. But if we don't find a way to see differently our various systems, ourselves, or the people we lead, then we will continue to get the same results. There is a saying that is apropos:

insanity is continuing to do the same thing over and over and expecting a different result.

It's crucial that context is taken into account. What is progress if, as I've said previously, a successful system gets itself into difficult territory and self-destructs?

These models also give us a hint about our followers and how they view the world. They give leaders an opportunity to try and understand another person and ask questions, so that motivation, attitude, and beliefs can be uncovered. This is important because most leaders understand that if you really want permanent change to happen, you have to change beliefs.

Note that trying to change behavior is trying to change a symptom. You can get some short-term results, and in an emergency that's okay, but in the long haul, you are doomed to fail. However, the long haul doesn't matter for those leaders who care primarily about their personal success and depart before some type of failure occurs, including organization failure. It certainly brings into question what constitutes success and failure within the rules of a system, with their definition being a matter of judgment! Who decides the answer to this question matters a lot.

At the organizational level, polarized thinking brings great clarity to a situation, especially in a real or contrived crisis. "You are with us or against us," is a statement often used by leaders to enforce conformity.

For example, if you believe that the prima facie reason for existence of a commercial for-profit corporation is to make money for the benefit of shareholders, then it is easy to judge success or failure based on the financial statements and specifically the return on investment. A corporation has a set of rules and charters to abide by, based on a system external to itself. This external system is based on a set of beliefs that were established long ago regarding corporations. MBAs have been taught for a long time that a commercial corporation of this type exists for profit only and that anything else is window dressing and subservient to it. I remember a friend of mine who said to me, "I slam dunk proved it in my essay."

But what if you believed in another criterion for what constitutes success or progress? For example, what if you believed that the role of the business corporation is to provide value to society, and if society agrees, then profits result. This small shift in belief or orientation makes a big difference. What then? I'm sure the folks who capitalized the corporation might not be too happy about it, but therein lies the rub. On the other hand, if leaders are found who are able to create good financial results within an ethical framework that values and respects all stakeholders and humanity and its habitat, then these leaders should be valued above all. This is the basis of the conscious capitalism movement. Boards of Directors should be all over this! It can be done and it is being done now. Figure 18 illustrates some results in support of conscious capitalism.[10]

Investment performance of *Firms of Endearment* companies versus S&P 500 and *Good to Great* companies, 1996 to 2011

| Return | Fifteen-year | | Ten-year | | Five-year | | Three-year | |
	Cumu-lative	Annu-alized	Cumu-lative	Annu-alized	Cumu-lative	Annu-alized	Cumu-lative	Annu-alized
FOE[a]	1,646.1%	21.0%	254.4%	13.5%	56.4%	9.4%	77.4%	21.1%
GtG[b]	177.5%	7.0%	14.0%	1.3%	-35.6%	-8.4%	-23.2%	-8.4%
S&P 500[c]	157.0%	6.5%	30.7%	2.7%	15.6%	2.9%	10.3%	3.3%

Note: Company returns are total returns with dividends reinvested and compounded.
a.   Companies from *Firms of Endearment*, updated by authors
b.   Companies from *Good to Great*, from the book by Collins
c.   Standard & Poor's index of five hundred U.S. companies

Figure 18: Conscious Capitalism – Real Financial Results

If you believe you can change the system, you can. If you believe you cannot change the system, then you can't. The person who can change the rules of the system has true power. The rest of us are just going along for the ride because we've delegated our power to the leader(s). That's what makes social networking media so powerful; it's changing a system's rules very rapidly.

So, what a corporate CEO/leader does to interpret the rules and reinforce the beliefs that created the rules matters a lot. The leader has a choice if he/she is aware of the rules of the system. Again, a leader is not someone who is at the top; it can be anyone, including the least-paid person in the organization. They can change the rules, too. In fact, changing the rules starts with changing the beliefs and the rules inside you.

The Role of Education

One of my pressing areas of concern in all this is the role of academia. It's my contention that the purpose of the education system today is to produce academics and workers. My view is shared by many, including Sir Ken Robinson,[11] a professional educator who is rather critical of the general approach to public education around the world. His TED talk titled *Do Schools Kill Creativity?* is available on YouTube, and I highly recommend you listen to it. The link to the video is in the endnote.

I believe that what Sir Ken Robinson points to is how the education system worldwide supports the systems we've created and how it's a reflection of the brain-mind and its beliefs. He shows us categorically that academia is caught up in the same systems as we all are. That's where the ideas of transmutational leadership come in. I will not claim that CQ and the transmutational leadership model are *the* solution. They are not. But I wouldn't be writing this book if I did not fervently believe that they may help leaders develop their leadership practice and make better decisions.

Our education system has to change dramatically, just as all our other systems have to change. Transmutational leadership techniques should be taught at the earliest age possible for the benefit of future generations. As Sir Ken Robinson says, whole-brain education is required to overcome the situation we've created. I would add that whole-mind education is required. The education system as it is currently structured is in the business of reinforcing established beliefs. Since we are not born with equal talents, our public education system discriminates in the interest of how we define success. I strongly believe that we need to revisit the accepted system and rebuild from the ground up.

The education system must also consider leadership education. Leadership education without a discussion of reality, ethics, the nature of knowledge, and values is hollow indeed! As I mentioned before, a lot of people are put into leadership positions without any education or training or what they are up against. They are not aware that they will have ethical dilemmas pretty much daily since they have a lot of legitimate power. Be mindful of your brain-mind, its self-interest, and how it responds to its external environment.

✷

WANDERING PICTOGRAPH

Patience, patience

Wisdom of ages

Steadfast in my lair

Aching for release

What stories I could reveal

Clash of light, touch of warmth

Oh! Happy Wanderer

Eternal Mercury, manifest friend

Slow your pace

Free me, free me

From my stone, take me

Know me, alone, discover my secrets

Patience, patience

✷

6

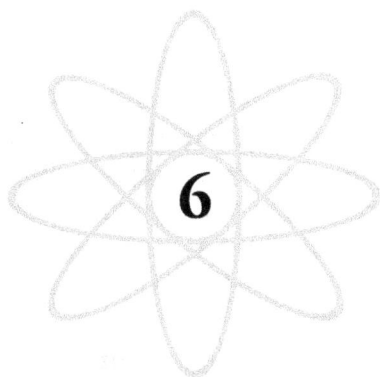

An Emergent Mind and an Idea

Keeping an Open Mind

IT'S CLEAR THAT NOBODY knows the nature of mind and consciousness. Philosophers have debated this for a long time, among them David Hume, Immanuel Kant, John Locke, T. J. Huxley, and William James. Nobody knows how our brains work exactly. The list goes on—just ask theoretical physicists, theologians, spiritualists, scientists, psychologists, psychics, neuroscientists, and anyone else who cares to think about the nature of knowledge and reality.

There's a lot we know. There's a lot we don't know. There's a lot we think we know.

We believe the central nervous system is electrochemical in nature. We believe our brains are chaotic in nature. We believe that all our five senses respond to frequency vibrations. We believe that all particles are energy first and foremost. We believe that there are many more dimensions to the universe than the ones we normally perceive. We believe that our physical reality is real.

If you stub your toe in the middle of the night, it hurts! That's real enough for anyone. While this seems to be incontrovertible proof of a physical reality, it doesn't mean it isn't an illusion in another sense. The manifest physical realm appears to be the conclusion of a creative process. The energy source that creates matter is thought of as the true reality of all things.

If I make the assumption that all is energy and all energy is vibration, then there are certain analogies in the sciences that enable me to create a model of how the mind works with the soul and brain.

Here's the main idea: I have come to believe that gravity is to particles as consciousness is to mind. And mind creates matter. So, what is consciousness? I have several ways of expressing it, but briefly, I define it as self-awareness of mind. Mind, therefore, is a force of nature.

When energy coalesces into particles at some point in space and time, an emergent property of that process is gravity. We don't understand how that happens, but we are all aware of gravity. In fact, physicists know that we do not yet fully understand how the four fundamental forces of nature relate to each other. Electromagnetic energy and gravity are two of those four forces, and gravity is especially elusive.

We don't really understand electromagnetic energy at a deep fundamental level, but we do know enough to text message our friends. We don't really understand gravity, yet we know how to measure its effect and send satellites whizzing around the Earth.

We don't know for sure, but consciousness may be related to reaching a certain level of complexity. Does the universe have consciousness? Does planet Earth (Gaia) have consciousness? What of its components? At what scale does consciousness begin? It may be that all animate and inanimate particles have some degree of consciousness but are unable to communicate it in a manner that we can understand. We have no way of knowing if a mountain is aware of itself. We have no way of knowing if plants and animals, such as mammals, have consciousness. But, we are mammals by definition. Why would we exclusively have consciousness and not others?

One of the reasons I separate mind from consciousness is that both animate and inanimate things and organisms appear to sense mind energy. For example, many dogs seem to be aware when we are not feeling well. Even plants exhibit responses to our thoughts in bizarre ways. For example, plants display abnormal electrical excitation when their owners think about chopping them down.[1] Another example is computer random number generators being made less random through mindful intention. Paranormal events may not just be random chance, as some skeptics would claim.

Here's my take on it: Mind creates matter. Mind creates the brain on an ongoing basis, from moment to moment. The brain's neuroplasticity permits this evolution. Our mind is a portion of the Infinite Mind's energy that is unique to us. There is a portion of that energy that has a unique signature. This unique signature creates our species, and there is a subset (i.e., unique fragment) that is our unique identity. The physical and energy realms are deeply entangled.

We can perceive the physical aspects with our five senses and the energy aspect with our mind. Our mind is, in effect, our sixth sense. All sensory input is correlated in the brain and mind.

Consequently, we are able to recognize the unique energy signature of physical things. We can recognize the genus energy signatures of dogs, cats, trees, and so on. We recognize other humans and how each one is unique because of their unique energy "signature," which affects how they manifest physically. It's the same as a leaf on a tree. We know the type of leaf it is and we can see how each one is unique. How does this happen?

The world of physics and the science of chaos are where we need to look for answers, since these are the sciences exploring the natural laws of the universe. I'm not a physicist or a mathematician, so please bear with me as I try to keep this as simple as I can.

Why all this technical nonsense, you ask? I believe that if we have a model to explain how our brains and minds work, we can then understand why certain soul-mind techniques work so well. When we understand why and how something works, we start to believe in it deeply and improve upon it. A belief held by a majority of humans is held up as a practical truth until proven otherwise. Consciousness is the method, and techniques are the practical aspect of transmutational leadership. Understanding how and why they work can lead us to employ them more effectively and believe in them more deeply. We become more effective as a result. So, let me try and explain how I think this works. Please excuse my feeble analogy!

Pendulums and Oscillations

Remember that all five of our senses respond to vibrations (i.e., frequency). Since almost everyone is aware of this, we'll start with electromagnetic energy. Also, many people are somewhat familiar with electronic devices such as cell phones, radars, and lasers, even though most of us don't know how they work. These devices process electromagnetic energy in interesting ways, much like the brain does. Indeed, within the ideas of quantum mechanics and the holographic nature of the universe may reside the explanation of all the weird and unusual phenomena we experience.

We believe that the universe might be one giant hologram. As a hologram, it behaves like one infinite memory and obeys the law of conservation of information. This may very well be why past-life memories exist. However, before we jump into what the mind does, let's start with the physical world.

Let's focus on vision. Although it is a process that has yet to be fully understood, our brains convert the energy received from our eyes into various constituent attributes and recombine it to create images that are organized and have space and time added to them. These images get tucked away into our memory and used as we need them. In other words, without even trying, a part of the brain uses complicated inverse Fourier mathematics to go from the frequency domain to the time domain![2] It's like when you take a movie with your camera and add the date and time to each frame and then place it all in a database for future retrieval. This mathematical process is analogous to how many of our electronic systems work. Let's start with the frequency domain, since all we see is vibrating. We'll start with the pendulum to represent an oscillating frequency.

Figure 19 illustrates a pendulum going back and forth. If the pendulum were an oscillator producing electromagnetic energy, it would produce a sine wave as shown on the right. One full swing of the pendulum, from +1 to -1, is the wavelength. How many times this happens in a second is the frequency of oscillation. This is often shown in units of cycles per second or, if you prefer, hertz. For example, if you listen to an FM radio station while in your car, you will notice the frequency on your car radio display. So, if the radio shows 103.5, it's really 103.5 megahertz or 103.5 million cycles per second.

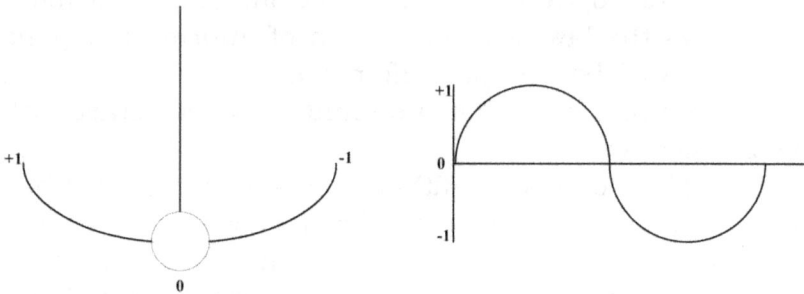

Figure 19: Pendulum and Sine Wave

Pulse and Energy Spectrum

From this simple to and fro or up and down, an interesting thing happens if we interrupt the wave pattern and create a pulse. There are two ways to do this: coherently and non-coherently. The difference between the two is that the coherent way maintains a frequency or wavelength relationship from pulse to pulse, and non-coherent interruptions do not. It's not important to understand how this is done, but rather to realize that it makes a difference to how the energy looks in the spectrum. Figures 20 through 23 are diagrams that show the difference between a non-coherent and a coherent pulse and its equivalent spectrum for a limited number of pulses and infinite number of pulses. These diagrams are basic time domain and frequency domain views of pulsed signals. Fourier mathematics, as mentioned previously, is used to calculate the characteristics of signals for both the time domain and the frequency domain.

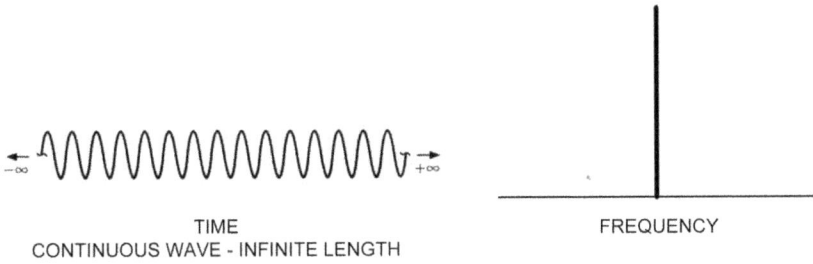

TIME
CONTINUOUS WAVE - INFINITE LENGTH

FREQUENCY

Figure 20: Continuous Wave (Infinite Pulse Length) Results in Pure Frequency

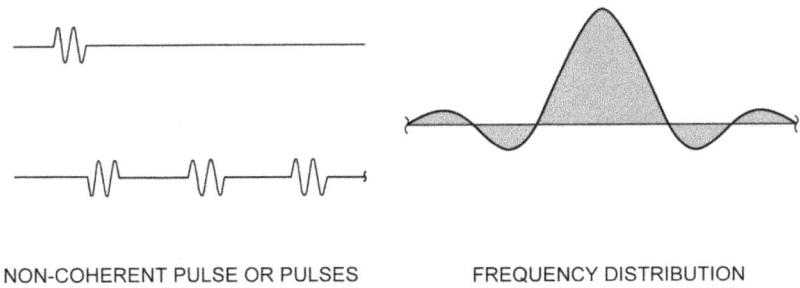

NON-COHERENT PULSE OR PULSES

FREQUENCY DISTRIBUTION

Figure 21: Non-Coherent Pulse or Pulses and Frequency Distribution

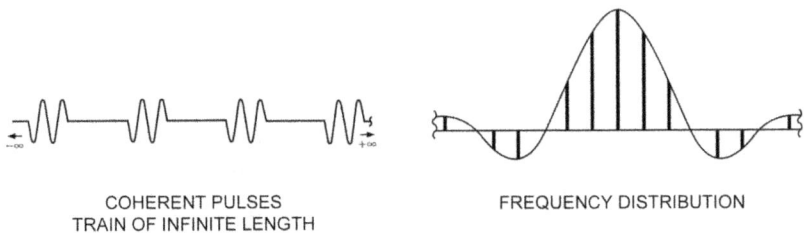

COHERENT PULSES
TRAIN OF INFINITE LENGTH

FREQUENCY DISTRIBUTION

Figure 22: Coherent Pulses – Train of Infinite Length and Frequency Distribution

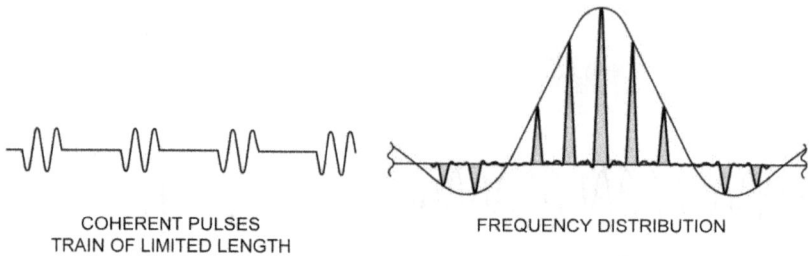

COHERENT PULSES
TRAIN OF LIMITED LENGTH

FREQUENCY DISTRIBUTION

Figure 23: Coherent Pulses - Train of Limited Length and
Frequency Distribution

That's how radars work. The following is a simplified example: An air traffic control pulsed radar starts up an oscillator, brings that frequency up to the level desired, and sends out a series of pulses. The pulses bounce off an airplane. A small portion of that returned energy is received and accumulated by the radar receiver for display.

A big challenge in detecting the returning energy is picking it out of the internal and external electrical noise. There is constant electromagnetic noise at all frequencies in the universe, and there's also noise in the radar system itself, so the radar has to detect the weak returned signal in all that noise. In other words, the signal has to be more powerful than the noise to be detected. One way the radar does this is by integrating multiple pulses over time so that the energy adds up constructively and this accumulation of energy ends up being more powerful than the noise.

Our brains work similarly, but unlike radar, there isn't an accumulation of coherent energy over time to overcome the "noise." Rather, we are much better at reducing the perceived "noise" by focusing on what interests us. Imagine being in a large crowd and trying to hear a specific conversation over all the noise. Our ears are like the radar antenna, and the brain appears to increase whatever audio signal we are focused on by reducing the surrounding noise by ignoring it—essentially filtering it out. This process allows us to hear a conversation above the noise.

As you might imagine, there are signals that contain no information that is of interest to us (i.e., what we consider to be noise) and there are signals that do. To add information or intelligence to a signal requires us to modulate (i.e., change) the basic signal using another signal.

I'm sure everyone is familiar with radio. Your radio is likely capable of receiving AM or FM radio stations. These refer to amplitude modulation and frequency modulation respectively. With amplitude modulation, the result of modulation is an increase or decrease in the power of the signal, while keeping the frequency unchanged. With frequency modulation, the signal is modulated with the same sound, but in this case the frequency is varied by the modulation. One of the reasons AM is noisy (i.e., static) is because any noise at the same frequency is accepted as a legitimate signal and affects the entire signal while it is present, whereas it's essentially filtered out with FM because the noise only affects the portion of the signal at its exact frequency. There are many types of modulation schemes for various types of applications. One other I want to mention is Code Division Multiple Access (CDMA). This is one type of modulation scheme used in cell phones. CDMA spreads the information across many different frequencies with a special code that is unique to each cell phone. The spreading of the power across a very wide set of frequencies is so great that the cell phone signal looks like noise unless you have the special code to recover the information. The wireless communication system knows all this and can pick out the conversation or text from each cell phone and route it to its destination. This all happens very fast, of course.

It seems that a similar process happens in our brain. Each thing we see has its unique signature. It's all noise until we select what signature we want to focus on. I believe that this is quite natural and supports the idea that trees and shrubs don't matter when there's a lion approaching, except for the one tree that is climbable. So, our conscious brain-minds focus on what we think is important in the moment, but the subconscious gets all of it. Once we get used to something being constant, it gets less and less of our attention. As noted earlier, driving a car is a case in point. The subconscious is aware of what's going on at all times while you are having a conversation with your passengers. As soon as something happens that requires your conscious attention, the subconscious wakes up the conscious. Basically, the brain and the external environment are both very noisy, and the mind must pick out the signals, or energy, of interest in all that noise. Schwartz and Begley[3] confirm it. You can perceive something by either lowering the noise around it, increasing your focus (synonymous with integrating many pulses), or both.

Figure 24 is an analogy that illustrates some signals of interest above background noise. The bottom line is that we sense more clearly what we observe. If we don't pay attention because it doesn't suit our immediate goal, information is treated as background noise. Consequently, we need to quiet our brains to tap into more information. Our purpose and intent in the moment determine the outcome of our perception—how we organize our version of reality. We interpret how we want to interpret and ignore the rest at our peril. Durant, quoting Kant, informs us, "We shall never have any experience which we shall not interpret in terms of space and time and cause; but we shall never have any philosophy if we forget that these are not things, but modes of interpretation and understanding."[4]

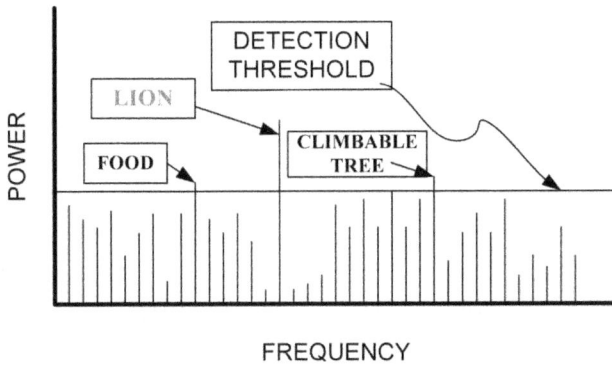

Figure 24: Signal Detection Threshold

There is one other item worth knowing, and that is the concept of bandwidth. The bandwidth of a signal is related to the transmitted frequency and the modulation scheme. How much bandwidth a system has determines how much information it can transmit in a period of time, typically stated in units per second. The thing to know is that the higher the frequency and the better the modulation scheme, the more information can be packed into a signal during a given period of time. For example, lasers operate at extremely high frequencies compared to radio, which is why laser-based systems have comparatively very high bandwidths.

Lasers are used to create holograms. Many people have seen holograms. You might have seen some at an art exhibit or in the first Star Wars movie when the robot Artoo-Detoo projects a three-dimensional image of Princess Leia. Also, in a recent election, CNN experimented with this technology to create an image of a person reporting as if they were standing physically in the same room. Pretty cool stuff. Now you *know* I'm a bit of nerd, instead of just suspecting it!

Lasers are coherent and extremely high frequency oscillators. When a laser is pointed at an object, it creates interference patterns, much like dropping a handful of pebbles in a pond, except that these interference patterns remain coherent. These interference patterns are recorded on a medium, such as a photographic film, along with the original laser energy as a reference. If you look at the medium, all you see are the interference patterns, but when a laser illuminates the medium, it recreates an image of the physical three-dimensional object. An interesting aspect of this process is that the smallest details of the interference pattern contain all the information of the original image. So, you don't need the entire interference pattern to recreate the image, only a very small fragment that we are capable of reading. That's what is so amazing about holograms—the smallest fragment contains all of the information necessary to reproduce the whole image. It's believed that the brain-mind is holographic.[5] One reason for this belief, among many, is that a specific memory is not found in a specific place, but in multiple places.

Another place where this beautifully complete intelligence happens, no matter what level or scale of observation, is in natural chaotic systems. Gleick's *Chaos: Making a New Science* contains wondrous Mandelbrot illustrations that show order within the chaos patterns, no matter how big or how small you care to look in nonlinear systems. The patterns (shown in the Mandelbrot illustrations) continue to repeat themselves over and over at all levels of observation. What looks like random patterns have a deep order; this deep order is the system's unique signature. If you can't get Gleick's book, look up Benoit Mandelbrot on Wikipedia.[6] Margaret Wheatley's book *Leadership and the New Science*[7] also contains illustrations that reflect the fractal nature of brain design.

The brain and mind also have holographic characteristics. Penrose and Hameroff[8] identified structures on how the brain collapses multiple possibilities into one decision. Their theory and observations support the brain as a hologram design for its distributed functions. It is an interesting explanation on how the brain operates to create a series of binary decisions that all collapse down into one final decision. Every time we observe something, we automatically do this. Polarized decisions (i.e., judgments) usually take less than a second to make. Within this process, and prior to a judgment, there are infinite possibilities.

Quantum Consciousness—A Holographic Idea

So, it seems as though our brains are capable of doing naturally what all of our most sophisticated electronics essentially do, and even more than that. If, as Bohm and Pribram (as reported by Talbot[9]) are correct in asserting that the universe is one giant hologram, we have a possible explanation of all of our unusual experiences, such as paranormal, near-death experiences, reincarnation, and life-between-life regressions. Karl Pribram, in an interview in *Psychology Today*, as reported by Talbot, said this: "It isn't that the world of appearances is wrong; it isn't that there *aren't* objects out there, at one level of reality. It's that if you penetrate through and look at the universe with a holographic system, you arrive at a different view, a different reality. And that other reality can explain things that have hitherto remained inexplicable scientifically: paranormal phenomena, synchronicities, the apparently meaningful coincidence of events."[10]

How deep in time and how broad our memory goes is certainly subject to debate. How this affects our decision making from day to day is unknown.

If our brain is organized and operates nonlinearly, it is impossible to know at every instant in time how the neurons and synapses will fire, but the pattern that results integrates a series of binary decisions that result in one overall decision in the moment. Every moment, there is a slightly different pattern, even though the final decision may be the same.

This is quite likely why focus combined with intention is so powerful. Focus, intention, and techniques such as meditation change the brain's physiology. We create new neurons and synapses by this very process. Mind also influences the body's functions (e.g., biofeedback, self-healing).

Mind and Matter Entanglement

Imagine if you will that Infinite Mind is a form of coherent energy (assuming it was fully entangled with all matter at the moment of the Big Bang) and that it is part of the essential fabric of the universe. If so, all matter contains the essence of mind, just as all particles have an emergent property called gravity.

Imagine that a fragment of that Infinite Mind is our identity. All of our cells contain this unique identity/signature, which has access to all of the Infinite Mind's information.

The nonlocal and entangled nature of our mind would explain why we are able to accomplish paranormal and miraculous things. It explains why all our cells have access to our memories. To be able to perceive the knowledge of the universe simply requires that the signal-to-noise levels allow us to perceive the signal within the noise. That is why our most creative moments are during quiet times, as in the shower or while dreaming. Focus, intention, and asking the right question often result in a creative answer when we keep the noise down.

Imagine that the Infinite Mind operates like a coherent laser and imagine that our unique fragment of mind and our body together are like the recording medium in a hologram. Imagine as well the exceptionally large number of patterns the combined output of all our neurons and synapses can produce when acting like a modulator that creates new interference patterns that are held in memory by the mind. Since mind is nonlocal and entangled, all of our experiences are contained holographically in the mind.

Imagine that all physical objects contain a portion of the

Infinite Mind with a unique signature. A tree in the forest has a signature as a tree, a subset or unique pattern within that signature is a type, say a maple tree, and a deeper signature is there uniquely for each leaf. I don't just mean its electromagnetic signature—what our eyes see, I mean the entire signature, including the mind energy signature. To be able to see with our mind would enable us to recognize the tree without the use of our other senses. It's astonishing to know that some people can navigate a forest at night blindfolded and not bump into the trees; ergo, they can sense the energy spectrum just like energy healers see peoples' auras. They are able to pick up these signatures and spatially place them while they are moving around.

Since everything in the mind is entangled, there is no sense of time. Everything is instantaneous and changing constantly from moment to moment. The creativity of the universe is beyond comprehension. The amount of knowledge available is infinite. People who report downloading information from the universe reveal just how overwhelming it is for our brains. All the information comes in at once, rather than serially, as we are accustomed to.

We think our minds are inside us because we hear that voice in our head, but philosophers and psychologists would remind us that this is not the case. Our mind has a unique signature that is constantly evolving. It is also true that this unique signature is always there, and will always be there, because it is part of the fabric of the universe and survives our feeble bodies. Energy cannot be destroyed: $E = MC^2$, as Einstein told us, and neither can information, according to Leonard Susskind.[11]

This concept of mind, along with the idea of the universe as a hologram, the fractal nature (immense depth) of our brains, and the way we do complex mathematics seamlessly to comprehend our physical world[12] support and explain how paranormal abilities are possible when we can quiet our noisy brains. They also support the notion of the doctrine of rebirth (in the Buddhist tradition, as I understand it) and how that is possible, since our mind energy cannot be destroyed. Naturally, such an idea has profound implications for leadership.

Figure 25 is an attempt to capture all of these ideas in a diagram. The physical world is a subset created by an Infinite Mind, as is the spiritual world. Our body and our soul are the interface to their respective worlds. In the spiritual world, only energy is transferred across that interface. In the physical world, both matter and energy can go across the interface to the body. This transfer is not shown the same way for each world because the nature of the interfaces is different. The interface from the body to the mind is energy only. The individual mind is a fragment of the Infinite Mind, and energy is transferred there as well. All are connected simultaneously, and the entire system is changing from moment to moment. Our experiences operate like a modulator in an electronic system. The patterns that are created from moment to moment are captured in memory forever. Our mind is fully connected to the fabric of the Infinite Mind and it operates as a giant hologram.

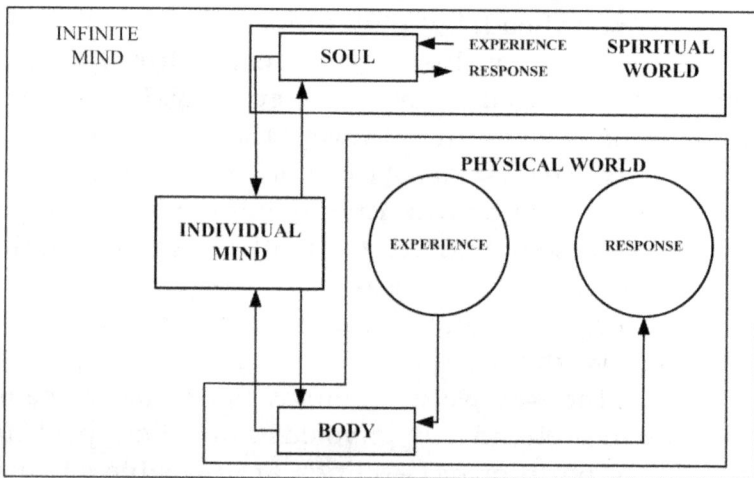

Figure 25: Body, Soul, and Mind as a System

It is difficult to see something when you're embedded in it. Mind would probably look like a form of noise in the universe if we could detect it. But because our instruments are made of the same material stuff, the noise is overwhelming. Nevertheless, consciousness is our ability to perceive our unique mind by quieting our noisy brain for a specific purpose. As soon as we focus on something, it coalesces into our perception. We exercise free will whenever we do so.

As I've previously stated, perhaps consciousness and soul are aspects of one and the same thing. Perhaps there should be a direct interface in Figure 25 between the body and soul, rather than through the mind. There is much we don't know. There is no insight given by Newton,[13, 14] Swedenborg,[15] and Whitton.[16] They have been unable to provide any detailed insight into the connection between body and soul except to say that there is a connection shortly after conception and a disconnection during the process of dying. Regardless of claimed evidence or lack thereof, no one knows what the truth is. For a short discussion of truth, see Appendix C.

Unknowable Purpose of Mind

As I mentioned previously, the Infinite Mind, if we could measure it with electronic equipment, would probably look like noise. My analogy for the Infinite Mind and our unique fragment of mind is that the Infinite Mind is the melody and our unique fragment is a harmonious part. We are the harmony and not the melody. Creativity emerges from the harmonious parts contributing to the music of the universe. The vastness of this intelligence and its creative potential is incomprehensible. Nature is its physical manifestation, and nature loves diversity. It is from diversity that nature creates complex life and systems. Our unique fragment simply adds to the complexity and creativity of the universe.

The Infinite Mind has infinite bandwidth, and hence, infinite possibility. The Infinite Mind's true purpose is unimaginable and unknowable. When we progressively access our mind, we progressively access more possibility because we are accessing more of the Infinite Mind. When we do this, we automatically relieve ourselves of polarized thinking and the consequent limitations and suffering that polarized thinking imposes upon us. The leadership potential when doing so is profound. As the saying goes, God works in mysterious ways.

Unknowable Consciousness

Physics, by definition, studies matter and the physical laws that govern it. Consciousness is not congealed energy (i.e., matter), so it has historically eluded study by the physical sciences. Nevertheless, some day physicists may find during their investigations that one of the dimensions of energy we become aware of when a particle forms is consciousness. Consciousness seems to demand a multi-disciplinary approach to figure out, which is why it's more difficult to study, not to mention the fact that mind is an unknown. We certainly don't know much about either one. We can't put our material hands on it, as it were. However, in recent years, an organization, the Institute of Noetic Sciences (IONS), has emerged to study consciousness scientifically. I highly recommend a visit to their website: www.noetic.org. Dr. Dean Radin is Chief Scientist at IONS.

Perhaps as physicists figure out gravity, we'll figure out consciousness and find out that it is our very soul reaching for enlightenment.

Hum of Convergence

You lanced the boil on my heart and my insanity burst forth.

Your kisses hot compresses drawing out the poison.

I won your love and found my own and in the process
the love for the One.

My love is not the love of the present.

Not the love of the past or the future but timeless love.

Eternal love.

Love that cannot be described by the passionate
except in silence.

It's the love found in the hum of convergence
between the inhaling and exhaling of wild abandon.

The love of infinite possibility.

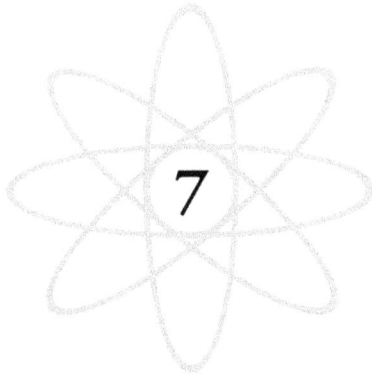

7

The Soul-Mind

THE MIND AND SOUL have been under investigation for thousands of years by a variety of scientific, philosophical, and religious disciplines. The debate continues to this day as to their nature and form. I'm no expert, but I believe soul, mind, and consciousness are interrelated and may each be a part of one and the same thing, as they are all a form of energy. That is probably why the three terms are often used interchangeably.

It's a curious thing. It seems like the specialized function of the left cerebral cortex is the main processing center for the brain-mind and the right cerebral cortex the main processing center for the soul-mind. I say this because of how I defined the respective characteristic of the brain-mind and soul-mind earlier and because of the story of Jill Bolte Taylor, whose experience with connectivity after suffering a stroke is documented in a TEDTalk video available on YouTube, as well as in her book *My Stroke of Insight: A Brain Scientist's Personal Journey.*[1]

It's easy to make the generalization about specialized processing centers because brain areas light up nicely using fMRIs when we are focused on specific tasks. We do like to categorize and carry out reductionist brain-mind thinking and we like things to be assigned to a place and time and a physical reality. That's the brain-mind at work and our rational-reductionist education. But our brains are not that simple.

Also astonishing is the problem we have locating where specific memories are stored, as they are seemingly everywhere. Our memory appears to be entangled and nonlocal. The mind is not specifically associated with the cerebral cortex, our physical brain. We really have no idea where our beliefs, memories, experiences, and personality get stored. For sure, when the brain is injured, aspects of our physical selves are impaired, as in a stroke, and our ability to perceive aspects of our mind is affected, too. That doesn't mean our mind is impaired; it may only be our ability to perceive our mind that is impaired. It's the brain that is injured.

I believe that memory is nonlocal and distributed. The local aspect is associated with our physical selves. As a product of evolution, our DNA constitutes our long-term memory and our epigenetic layer the memory of a few generations. In his book *The Biology of Belief: Unleashing the Power of Consciousness, Matter & Miracles*, Bruce Lipton discusses DNA and our epigenetic layer in this manner. Our physical self is analogous to the physical layer of a computer chip that supports the electrical and logical layers above it in an electronics system. I find the epigenetic layer really fascinating because there are some gender-specific situations that influence what gets transmitted from generation to generation.

As I previously stated, memory is nonlocal and distributed. Regardless of decades of research, memory is an elusive property. It does not specifically reside in our brain, although some memories are located there. We access a memory wherever it may be. When our bodies die, our traditional view is that our memories die with us. However, major organ transplant recipients have memories of donors that are impossible to explain using traditional science. For example, heart transplant recipients remember things about the donor that they could not possibly know. One documented case of a transplant recipient was a person whose dreams were so vivid that they led to the capture of the murderer of her donor!

If at the quantum level we exist as energy rather than particles and mind is an entangled property that makes up our approximately 75 trillion cells, then it is not surprising that a sub-fragment of mind is retained with the organ that is transplanted. Interestingly enough, there are lots of people with past life memories and there are lots of hypnotists and psychologists investigating past-life phenomena. The evidence from this research cries out: Where is the mind, what is its nature, and where do memories get "stored"? The holographic idea of the universe from quantum physics may offer an explanation of these things.

Furthermore, we know we can't take our money or our bodies with us when we die, but, if the preceding discussion of memory is true, it looks as though we can take our minds. It seems that, as a quantum wave of energy, we are nodes of information within the fabric of the universe and our specific node is our identity, which is our mind—the sum of all our experiences and our knowledge past, present, and future. If we truly believe this to our very core, would that not remind us that all we do in this life matters? I said something in one of my poems* along those lines: *Remember, a butterfly flapping its ephemeral wings can change the weather. You make a difference, too! The seeds you've sown will echo through eternity—the concert of your soul.*

---

* *You've Been Busy*, p. 43

As particles, our 75 trillion cells vibrating together create a node of information that results in our unique signature. At the core of our atoms, we are vibrating energy and not particles; we just see ourselves as particles because our design allows us to interpret the natural world that way. Perhaps the difficulties we have accessing both the brain-mind and soul-mind together are related to an imperfect energy match, as reported by Michael Newton.[2, 3] I don't know whether this is true, but it's an interesting supposition.

According to historians, chiseled on the pronaos* of the temple at Delphi that housed the oracle were the words *Know Thyself.* The origin of this saying is uncertain,[4] but Durant (1966, p. 137)[5] credits the saying to Thales of Miletus, noted by his contemporaries as first of the wise men of Greece. It was his answer to the question, What was very difficult? I think Buddha would agree.

A wise saying indeed. To know one's self is to know one's mind, but what is the mind? Why is it very difficult to know one's self (i.e., mind)? It's tough enough to know the brain-mind, and there are a fair number of tools at our disposal to help, but how do we find out about the soul-mind? What tools are at our disposal? And more importantly, as leaders, what benefit can we derive by doing this learning?

So, how do we know our mind? According to many people, and as documented for the last few thousand years, we can know it through techniques such as mindfulness, reflection, and meditation. All these techniques take practice, just as riding a bicycle well takes practice. If you believe you can do it, then you can! Don't be discouraged if knowing your soul-mind comes slowly.

I strongly believe it is important to teach our children all of these techniques early in life. Practicing these techniques throughout life will help them immensely. They

---

* Pronaos: portico in front of the entrance to a shrine

will certainly need whole-brain and whole-mind abilities as they lead the next generation!

The Soul

Since the word "soul" is contained in the term soul-mind, let's talk about the soul. I am not advocating a particular religious point of view or dogma. You may or may not believe in an afterlife or a soul, but bear with me. I define the soul is an entity analogous to our physical body. From all I've read and been taught, I believe that our body exists in the physical realm as a particle and our soul exists in the spiritual realm as a form of energy. As energy, it is entangled with the fabric of the universe. It seems to be a node of energy, just as our body is a node of matter in nature. The soul does not recognize time or space as we do in the physical world. The foregoing is why the terms soul and mind are often used interchangeably. They may be simply aspects of the same process and thing.

It seems that our soul is the instrument for mind development in the spiritual world, much like our body is the instrument for mind development in the physical world. The most interesting evidence of this possibility is documented in Michael Newton's books.[6, 7] Newton states that the soul is capable of thought and the exercise of free will, which may not be accepted by everyone. According to the sources cited, the soul merges with the body at some time around birth and returns to the spiritual realm some time after death. This is not a pro-life or pro-choice argument, and I won't go there. Life between lives has also been reported by Whitton,[8] whose account seems to be consistent with Newton.

Our soul has access to our unique fragment of mind and is able, through consciousness, to tap into the Infinite Mind at some level. As such, the intelligence of the universe and all knowledge are accessible by all of us to some degree.

I believe that this is how true creativity emerges. It just requires us to quiet our brain.

Just as our senses are limited in their perception, as in the eye's limited sensing of the full electromagnetic spectrum, so are the brain and soul limited in their perception of the Infinite Mind. Nevertheless, just as seeing with an infrared device extends the electromagnetic range of our vision, there are tools that enhance our tapping into the Infinite Mind.

If you believe, as I do, that leadership can be "soulful" or that a leader can lead with soul or lead from the soul, then, by definition, I think you would agree with me that a soul-mind exists. There are a great many people who believe in the existence of souls and/or an afterlife. The fragment of universal energy we call our mind is inextricably related to our body and our soul.

We cannot explain it yet. Along those lines, Michael Newton's books *Journey of Souls* and *Destiny of Souls*,[9, 10] Sogyal Rinpoche's chapter 20 in *The Tibetan Book of Living and Dying*[11], Michael Talbot's book *The Holographic Universe*[12], and Stuart Wilde's book *Sixth Sense*[13] are so startlingly close and consistent regarding what happens after our physical death that they must contain some truth. There are a couple of possible explanations. For the skeptic who believes these reports to be false, one explanation is that we are experiencing a psychosis held in common by our species. Another way to look at these reports is that they are possibly all true. I choose to believe there is an element of truth to them.

I consider the blending of the brain-mind and soul-mind to be the true fundamental state of leadership, since I think that our soul is our authentic self, which is in accordance with various philosophical and religious theories. This is so because the soul is eternal and the body temporary. Transmutational leadership is not a style;

it is a state of being. It is equally a theoretical framework designed to explain the soul, mind, and body entanglement and the emergent property of consciousness. Without a high CQ, leaders are unable to be truly authentic.

Soulful leadership, then, is the process of tapping into a much greater portion of the Infinite Mind and thereby producing a greater expansion of possibilities. The reason for this is that the soul-mind sees its connection to everything simultaneously, unlike the brain-mind. The soul-mind works at the quantum level where there is no sense of time. Its chief attributes are forgiveness, compassion, love, and absence of fear. Consistent with Eastern philosophy, the soul-mind does not judge, except for self-judgment, which slowly fades with development and disappears when enlightenment is achieved.

By virtue of the soul-mind's attributes, the creative potential of the leader and the organization are enhanced considerably. If you are dominated by your brain-mind and a leader at the top of your organization and you're still with me, then you may admit that the creative potential in some of your soul-mind followers is something you'd like to take advantage of!

The soul-mind has many capabilities that cannot be explained by traditional physics, since it operates at the quantum level, for example distance healing, telepathy, clairvoyance, clairaudience, and telekinesis. As consciousness is growing rapidly in the world, more and more instances of these capabilities are occurring since they are capabilities enabled by human consciousness.

Many people are skeptical about energy healing and the paranormal in general. Yet, these exceptional cases simply won't go away. Using statistical physics, Dr. Dean Radin proved that these capabilities are not just chance events but are real and repeatable.[14, 15] Furthermore, there is a lot of evidence emerging from other authors that is consistent with Radin's findings. In addition, organizations such the police make use of psychics when traditional methods fail them. They have become legitimate and widely accepted. This applies to other fields of work as well. For example, people are starting to accept energy healing when traditional methods fail. There is growing appreciation that the placebo effect may be energy self-healing.

No longer do psychics get ostracized or burned at the stake. Psychics and paranormal adepts are coming out of the closet. Many are developing and practicing their talents openly. There's a lot more of them than we ever imagined. Why is this so? Because each one of us has a degree of psychic ability by definition.

I personally know of one person who freelances for a chemical company when they need insight into a problem they don't know how to solve. They keep coming back to him for more, so there must be something of value he's contributing. He is a Reiki healer and not educated in chemistry.

The ability to accomplish tasks and lead at the quantum level is emerging! Why does all this matter, you might ask. This is how I see it: When a philosophy or belief system gets set up whereby everything in the world is seen as separate and categorized accordingly, and then because of this separateness a system is created that is designed to exploit separateness, then that is what we get: systems that exploit people, resources, racial differences, and so on. It's a power play based on a "we" versus "them" win-lose paradigm. Up to this point in time, "progress" has been enabled by this way of thinking. However, in any given system, the brain-mind approach to problem solving ultimately fails. We are at the point where massive failure is perceived in the not-too-distant future. I believe that is why there is so much anxiety in the world today. This is another reason why our children's education is so important. Traditional education methods are failing us because of their focus on the brain-mind, in particular the left hemisphere!

For those of you who are parents, I highly recommend that you enable and support what you think is psychic ability in your children. If you attempt to control it, you will suppress it and deny creative potential. This is not without its challenges locally and globally for everyone concerned, but especially for children. People are bullied when they are perceived as being different. I fully appreciate this, as I was part of a minority and bullied in my youth.

Social Justice and Gender Differences

I believe, by observation, that men dominate organizations today because they are more brain-mind and predominantly left-hemisphere-oriented than females. Perhaps it is in part because on average a male's corpus callosum is less dense than that of females, as mentioned in Chapter 4. Males are generally less relationship-oriented than females and more willing to sacrifice relationships to achieve an objective. It is a great trait when survival is threatened for any reason. It is a skill that thrives in a competitive environment, which describes virtually all our organizations. It is less required in a collaborative environment. That's where females thrive. Men and women complement each other well in that respect when the issue is species survival. The survival of our species is no longer threatened by other species. Our species survival is threatened by us.

If the world is to change, women must have an equal representation at the leadership table. They simply see more relationships and therefore more possibilities. Their corpus callosum is like a high-speed modem, whereas a male's is like a dial-up modem. In general, women will always put more importance on relationships than men do. I think that's why men believe women often overcomplicate things and don't want them in the boardroom. The ability to sacrifice relationships for the accomplishment of the mission makes men very decisive in highly competitive situations. I believe that is why the glass ceiling really exists.

Women are better at multitasking and men are more capable of intense focus. The intense focus and decisiveness is a man's strength and his blind spot. He will not see a saber-tooth tiger creeping up to attack him when he's about to attack a woolly mammoth. Men need women to balance out decision making. I believe that social justice can only be enhanced with more women in leadership positions.

Unfortunately, in a world with diminishing resources, men may continue to dominate the leadership narrative because organizations will fight it out for exclusive access to resources. That is what we have always done. Women also want to survive, and they appreciate a man's decisiveness to ensure this survival.

How do we overcome 300 million years of evolution with a few thousand years of consciousness? Shall we live collaboratively so that all species can survive, or do we fight it out so that a few will survive? The Tragedy of the Commons is being acted out on a global scale now.

I'm reminded of the story of the twin girls and one orange. Both girls wanted the orange and argued over it. It was unacceptable that one or the other would have it, so they compromised by cutting the orange in half and each getting a half. As it turned out, neither one was satisfied with the result. Since they were siblings, they talked about the experience and realized through conversation that one wanted the peel and the other wanted the flesh. So, they could have satisfied each other completely had they approached the issue differently.

This is a simplistic win-lose example to illustrate the problem of approaching any situation with polarity thinking. It's interesting how winning and losing by definition is polarity thinking based on a belief system or a criterion set up through subjectivity! Clearly, it is crucial to understand beliefs and the system context, or the brain-mind will assert itself.

Emergent Capabilities

Earlier I mentioned that the rapid increase of consciousness in the world is fueling the manifestation of these capabilities in more and more people. A listing of these capabilities can be found in Rychkun's[16] interesting model, as shown in Figure 26, that maps capabilities against developmental levels of mind. I'm not convinced that it's linear the way he illustrates it, but it's hard to do on a two-dimensional sheet of paper. I believe that there is a lot of overlap in these capabilities. Linear presentations of a quantum energy idea are too "Newtonian" in any case. Furthermore, these capabilities are not necessarily reliable yet, either. However, I believe that soon, some of these psychic experiments will be repeatable enough for even the most die-hard skeptic. Don't be hard on the skeptics—they keep us honest!

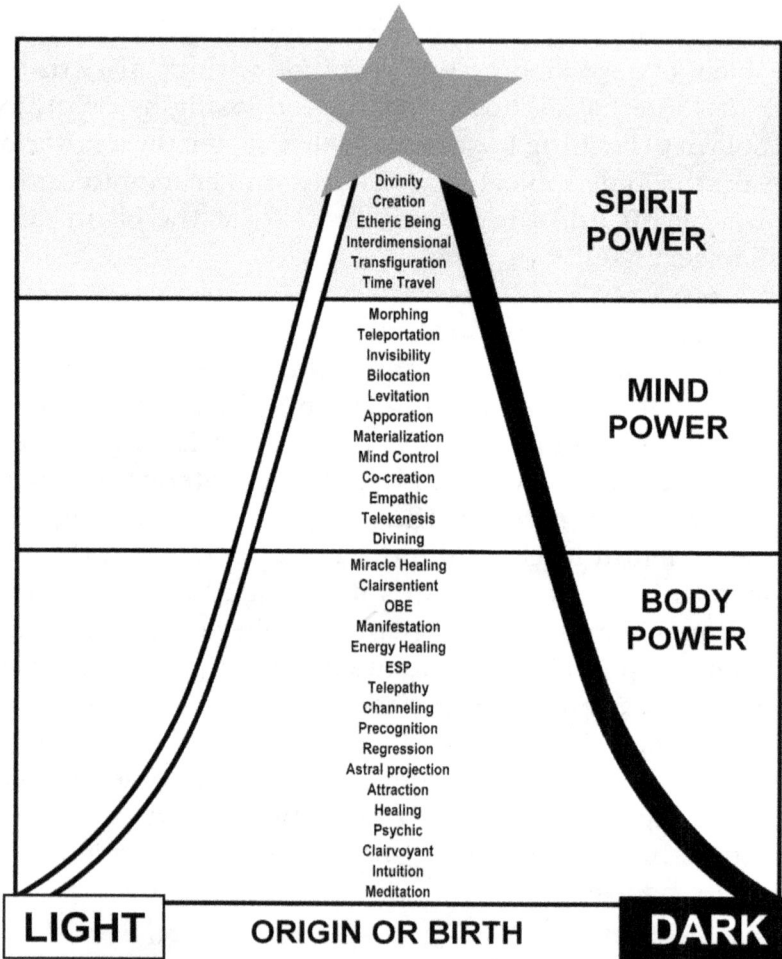

Figure 26: Rychkun Model of Mind Capabilities
(used with permission)

The Soul and Body System

It seems that the body in its quantum energy state has a unique signature and so does the soul. Using feedback mechanisms, the soul-body-mind system can be made to vibrate at higher frequencies that permit a greater ability to do "miraculous" things. Rychkun's diagram and his writing clearly reveal that vibration increases from the bottom up. There is general consensus among authors in this field.

The analogy that I would like to use to demonstrate this takes us back to the science of electromagnetic oscillating systems. Since this is not an engineering book, however, I won't go into it in detail here, as it can get too technical for our purposes. As I described earlier, higher levels of vibration allow more information to be held by a system. If our mind is a fragment of energy and we are a node of information, then the implication is that the higher the frequency at which we vibrate, the more information will be available to us and the more capabilities we will have.

I submit that the higher the vibration frequency of an individual or an organization, the greater their creative capability and the greater their ability to sustain operational shocks caused by unexpected external events, because their solution space is so much larger.

When leaders are able to go in and out of brain-mind and soul-mind rapidly, that is, when they oscillate or vibrate at a higher level, then change happens rapidly and in small increments. Adaptation to internal and external conditions is ongoing and rapid. More possibilities emerge. People can adapt to small increments of change in a way that they can't handle large increments, and being able to process more changes faster means that enough small ones can create large differences over short periods. This is much more sustainable and easier for organizations. Now, what kind of leader would not want that?

Merging Models

It's an interesting thing to examine Chopra's seven levels of brain and mind against Rychkun's model of mind and its quantum level abilities, and the ideas contained within transmutational leadership. Rychkun describes capabilities, Chopra describes how we respond, and transmutational leadership describes how we rapidly oscillate between the soul-mind and the brain-mind to access these in a balanced way. The integration of these ideas is shown in Figure 27. It is also easy to see how each of these models can map into the diagram on speed of adoption/adaptation in Figure 28.

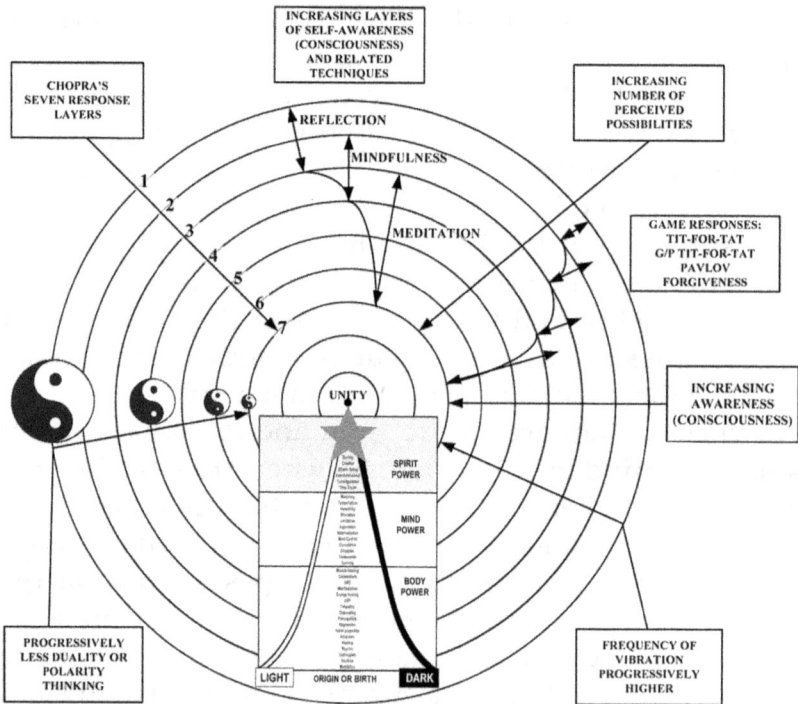

Figure 27: Integrating Models with Transmutational Leadership

Notice that Rychkun's light and dark (good and evil) is very much like yin and yang.

As I mentioned before, I don't think the capabilities identified can be mapped so linearly. It's probably true of Chopra's model as well. Neither one of them may mean it that way, but it's easier to understand when presented linearly. I feel so limited by two-dimensional paper when illustrating anything. If I could, I would publish my next version of this book as a hologram, but even that would be inadequate!

Perhaps the integrated model should be interpreted as general groupings of capabilities around the layers identified. The layers are really a continuum, rather than discrete layers. I personally feel that there is a lot of overlapping and back and forth within individuals and within humanity. History shows us that systems don't progress smoothly. They have transition points between order and chaos and back to order, and their rate of change is significantly affected by what is happening inside and outside the system. A nonlocal and entangled universe is not linear. It is continuously folding and unfolding to infinite depth at every location.

Speed of Adoption

A good leadership practice is to adapt one's style to a follower's readiness, to let go of one's ego and make it all about them. At the same time, followers must be ready to give their leaders permission to change their paradigms (e.g., political, industrial, personal, etc.). Followers must be ready to give up their old ways and old beliefs in order to embrace the new paradigms. This is difficult work.

I believe that a leader needs to explain things at a level that the people can understand and not ask them to change any more than they are capable of in the moment. That is why small incremental changes continuously occurring are better than one enormous change happening all at once. If we try and do more than what people are prepared to accept, we meet with a lot of resistance. The speed of change that people can generally tolerate has some limits. Ideas are behind change, and we have models of technology adoption that tell us how fast ideas can be adopted, but the models do not say how much can be adopted at one time. This greatly depends on how different the change is from our current situation and beliefs, that is, where we are on the order-chaos continuum and how ready we are for change.

There is a theory called the "Diffusion of Innovation" that has been used and elaborated upon by many over the years in multiple industries and systems. It is applicable to the adoption of any new idea, including all the ideas we have about our own mind. The diffusion of ideas throughout a system causes systemic changes to occur. I've seen the application of this model frequently in my work. Figure 28 and the explanation are extracted from Wikipedia.[17]

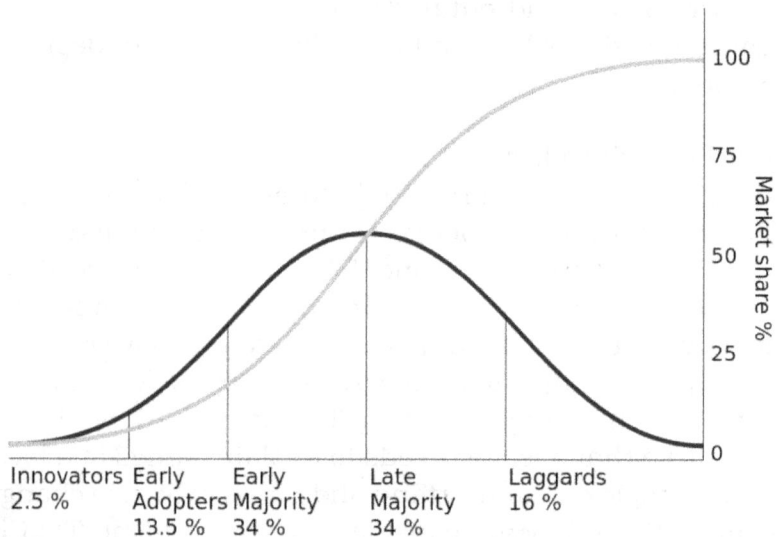

Figure 28: Speed of Adoption

Here is the explanation: "Diffusion of Innovations is a theory that seeks to explain how, why, and at what rate new ideas and technology spread through cultures. Everett Rogers, a professor of rural sociology, popularized the theory in his 1962 book *Diffusion of Innovations*. He said diffusion is the process by which an innovation is communicated through certain channels over time among the members of a social system. The origins of the diffusion of innovations theory are varied and span multiple disciplines. Rogers (1962) espoused the theory that there are four main elements that influence the spread of a new idea: the innovation, communication channels, time, and a social system. This process relies heavily on human capital. The innovation must be widely adopted in order to self-sustain. Within the rate of adoption, there is a point at which an innovation reaches critical mass. The categories of adopters are: innovators, early adopters, early majority, late majority, and laggards (Rogers 1962, p. 150). Diffusion of Innovations manifests itself in different ways in various cultures and fields and is highly subjective to the type of adopters and innovation-decision process."

As I mentioned, the concept of diffusion of innovation has been used across many industries and systems. When it comes to understanding how ideas spread, I highly recommend Malcolm Gladwell's *The Tipping Point*.[18] He explains the process and the "agents" of change (i.e., connectors, mavens, and salespeople) by which an idea is transmitted rapidly through society. The tipping point is that point of critical mass somewhere around early adopters. It is the point in time when exponential diffusion of the idea takes place. When the mass population sees the success being achieved by the early adopters, the majority want to be a part of it. It has a "cool" factor, and most people want to be cool; it's the power of the brand in marketing. We are at this stage now with yoga; all of a sudden, it's cool to do yoga. It's cool to do meditation. I recently saw a picture of a men's magazine cover featuring Adam Levine. The caption read something along the lines that yoga was a big part of his creativity. You know that we're in the early adopter stage of acceptance when the cover of a men's magazine pushes abdominal development to the sidebar!

The spiritual innovators in our world were Lao Tzu and Buddha and Christ, among other prophets and sages.

So, it's only taken about 2000 to 2500 years to get to the early adopter stage. I don't want to discourage anyone by how long this is taking. In the early part of the diffusion of ideas, progress is very slow, but we're at the tipping point now where the ideas of consciousness will spread exponentially through society.

The tipping point is the point of critical mass. Once across the transition point, there is no going back. It is the crucial point of no return. The genie is out of the bottle, so to speak. For ideas to spread rapidly, they require a medium. This is the power of the Internet. Anyone with connectivity to the Internet is able to access ideas with the click of a mouse. It's no wonder that some people want to put controls on the Internet, since it can spread ideas so fast that the tipping point can be reached very quickly. For example, the Internet and social media are often credited with enabling the Arab Spring uprising. The Internet and social media platforms are the mechanics enabling massively rapid diffusion. This is disquieting to any leader trying to control, since loss of control is very threatening. Thus, any attempt by leaders to control the mechanisms that enable rapid diffusion of ideas should be cause for concern amongst all freedom-loving people.

Speed of Adoption—Change Models and Strategies

I mentioned earlier that the majority of people in a system are quite happy to go along with the status quo and delegate all power to the leaders. They're the people riding in the cart as shown in Figure 29. The people in the cart allow a system to be stable. When a change is proposed, the champions for the change try to pull the cart one way, the people who perceive themselves as the ultimate losers relative to the change pull it in the opposite direction, and the people in the cart remain undecided until they perceive that the proposed change will benefit them. Then, they'll embrace the change. If the change doesn't appear to benefit them, all the pulling in the world by the early adopters won't matter.

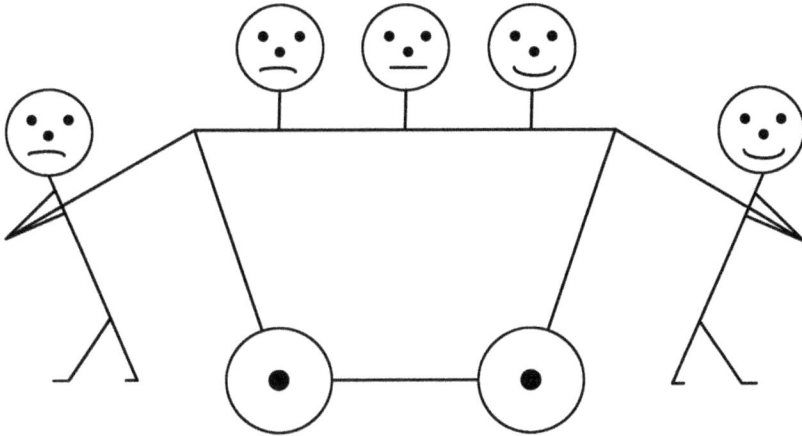

Figure 29: The Cart of Change

In a democracy, the observers in the cart become the tyranny of the majority by virtue of their votes. Anyone or anything that contradicts the majority's accepted truth is immediately suspect (remember Plato's cave allegory). However, in a just democracy, the minority opinion, though suspect, is granted dignity and respect. Indeed, the healthy debate of ideas is one of the strengths of the democratic system. The creativity of democratic societies is, I believe, heavily influenced by freedom of expression. This is one of the reasons why I firmly believe that brain-mind-oriented controlling leaders have significantly less creative potential than soul-mind leaders. Soul-mind leaders inspire others by letting go of control and empowering them to achieve their full potential for their benefit and that of the organization.

As humans, we have a strong need for socially belonging to, and identifying with, a group. Anyone different is bullied into submission, or ostracized and pushed out. We also like hierarchy because it provides structure, and structure provides stability. This is required for effective cooperation and for organizations to compete.

We keep saying bullying is wrong as if that would stop it, rather than seeing it as a natural form of brain-mind behavior. Bullying is not just something suffered by kids. It is rampant at all levels of society and in all organizations. Saying that it's wrong is trying to change a symptom. I'm not condoning bullying by any means. I sustained and suffered a lot of bullying in my youth, and I'm very intolerant of this type of behavior. We have to get at it at a deeper level. I firmly believe that if we are to stop bullying, we must develop the soul-mind. Thankfully, being different, rather than rebellious, is now becoming the cool thing. Perhaps this is a reflection of increasing consciousness.

I'm reminded of a story I heard not long ago. A nine-year-old boy is experiencing psychic abilities not unlike those described by Stuart Wilde in *Sixth Sense*.[19] The father wants nothing to do with his son's abilities and hopes that if he ignores them, they will go away. The mother doesn't know what to do and is fearful of causing conflict. This situation demonstrates all of the issues I described earlier: a system; a set of rules; power differences; dominant few and control; brain-mind responses of control, fear, ego, and wanting to fit in; soul-mind yearning; etc. All I can say is that I hope the boy is not bullied into submission, ostracized for being different, and his natural talents subdued. Essentially, the boy may unknowingly be pulled in opposite directions by the mom and the dad, even though both parents appear to be ignoring the situation. What direction will the cart take? Who will win? They both have only their son's interest at heart, or do they? Even this very simple example of a social system is very complex.

When I think of this, I think of Mozart. Wouldn't it have been a shame if Mozart's father had not recognized his son's talent but ridiculed it and forced him to become a piano maker instead? We would be diminished for it, but we wouldn't know that we were, so how could we feel diminished? That is how possibilities get substituted for one another. Who knows how it would have turned out? Had it happened that Mozart was forced to become a piano maker, a Mozart piano today could be valued the same as a Stradivari violin—or not.

For a more balanced approach to leadership, we need to let the soul-mind flourish by increasing our consciousness. This does not invalidate the brain-mind. The brain-mind will always be with us, but the external conditions have changed, and so we can't lead from there anymore. We have to embrace our soul-mind talents and let go of our brain-mind's tendency to polarize and judge. Transmutational leadership recognizes and incorporates the full spectrum of leadership practices because they are inherently natural. The full spectrum of ability must be developed to the maximum extent possible. However, the level from which one needs to lead must correlate with the situation. In today's environment, that means leading more from the soul-mind than the brain-mind portion of the continuum. I strongly believe we have to take all these things into account when selecting leaders. The survival of our species could very possibly depend upon it.

Someone once told me that if you want to know what someone values, just look at how they spend their money. It's true of organizations, too. Our education system is a case in point. What we spend our money on, the curricula, is a manifestation of what we value and what the system wants us to reinforce. Education is expensive, as we all know. If we embrace the soul-mind and what it can do for us, the education system will be vastly transformed, and nine-year-old boys with special gifts will be nurtured and developed into the leaders of tomorrow. There is no question that with a changed belief system, we will spend our money differently. That is how changing our beliefs will inevitably and inexorably change our systems.

The Psychological Barrier to Change

There is a psychological barrier to change that must be overcome in order to embrace a new way of being. This is true whether we talk about a brain-mind to soul-mind transition or about an organization re-inventing itself. A great model for this is from William Bridges' work in this area. Figure 30 illustrates the three phases of change from Bridges[20] that are analogous to our psychological state. Bridges examined how, at a more personal and deeper level, grief is part of the journey of transitioning from one state to another, particularly when the loss is great.[21] I highly recommend his work, especially his book on how to manage transitions.

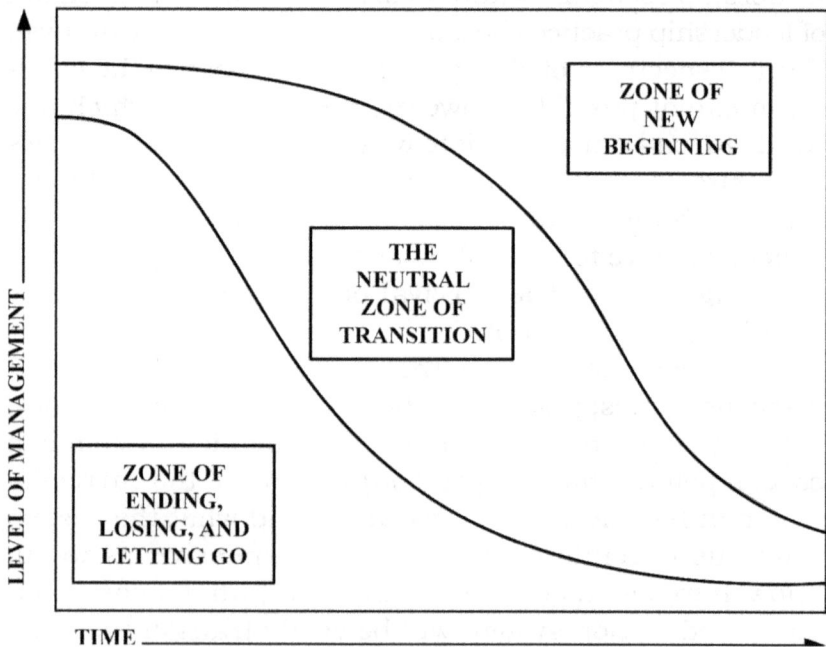

ZONE OF
NEW
BEGINNING

THE
NEUTRAL
ZONE OF
TRANSITION

ZONE OF
ENDING,
LOSING, AND
LETTING GO

LEVEL OF MANAGEMENT

TIME

Figure 30: Bridges Model of Change

Bridges shows clearly that the transition period is very chaotic. It takes time for people to realign their beliefs to a new way of knowing and being. It is the yin and yang of our chaotic minds. Sometimes we fall back into old habits. Fear prevents us from embracing the new. New beliefs are met with denial and anger; these are the first stages of grief over the loss of our old beliefs.

Millennia of evolution of the brain-mind can only be addressed by soul-mind leadership. A generation or two, or perhaps more, will be required until we have a critical mass of soul-mind leaders who will change our systems. It will very much depend on the exponential growth of diffusion of consciousness throughout the world.

One of the greatest responsibilities of any leader is to effectively communicate a vision of the future—one that followers can understand and are willing to embrace. Another great responsibility is to lead them effectively through transition zones when chaos and all that messy discomfort make us yearn for the good old days. Kotter established an eight-step process for transforming organizations, that is, leading through chaos. This process, it should be noted, is applicable at the personal level too. The steps[22] are:

> ➤ Establishing a sense of urgency
> ➤ Forming a powerful guiding coalition
> ➤ Creating a vision
> ➤ Communicating the vision
> ➤ Empowering others to act on the vision
> ➤ Planning for and creating short-term wins
> ➤ Consolidating improvements and producing still more change
> ➤ Institutionalizing new approaches

Change management, change leadership, and organizational development are key skills for any leader, individually and within organizations. After all, one has to lead one's self first to effectively lead others. That's one of the essential messages in the Tao Te Ching. Pretty much everyone agrees with this fundamental aspect of leadership.

There is lots of material available on change management and organizational development. One book that I
highly recommend is Anderson and Ackerman-Anderson's
Beyond Change Management.[23] If you get the book, look
specifically at the Appendix: Development Arenas for
Conscious Change Leaders. What you will find there are
a number of competencies in three key areas, namely
knowledge, doing, and being.

Critical Mass

Critical mass deserves elaboration. Critical mass is the
transition point between order and chaos in the system.
It's when an idea becomes accepted by the majority, as
shown in Figure 28, and starts to rapidly diffuse through
society. It's analogous to the majority of the folks in the
cart deciding they'll adopt the change.

If you are technically inclined and interested in critical
mass, you can find an outstanding discussion of it in Philip
Ball's wonderful book *Critical Mass: How One Thing Leads
to Another*.[24] The nonlinear operation of our brain seems to
obey the natural laws of critical mass. It seems that, for any
given input, the brain is in a chaotic state until a critical
mass of neurons transition to a state of order and these
are perceived as conscious thought. Thus, our conscious
brain has the appearance of being rational and orderly.

Guarding Against Exploitation

Of course, the dominant few will want to control this
emergent capability for their own self-interest. Other
brain-mind dominated people will always take advantage
of situations for their own self-interest as well. These types
of abuses will happen, no matter what we do. That is why
many organizations have adopted a code of ethics that
specifically addresses self-interested and unscrupulous
behavior. Be mindful when dealing with organizations that
have not adopted such measures!

The dominant few will also take advantage or exploit soul-mind people. That's why governments and some large corporations actively research psi phenomena.[25] Of course, there will be abuses. Systems are hard to change, and consequently so is people's behavior. Complicit hypocrisy will apply resistance to any change. We have to address this properly and correctly without engaging in brain-mind behavior.

Of course, primarily soul-minded people won't be perfect because they have a brain-mind, too. There will be mischievous people. There will be people who make mistakes. The higher capabilities of the mind are not perfect.

To address some of these issues, we need to give guidance regarding the ethical use of the soul-mind's capabilities and the vulnerabilities that come from leading primarily from that part of the continuum. We have free will in all this. It is our choice. We can co-create the future.

Overcoming Complicit Hypocrisy

The systemic resistance to change comes not only from the dominant few in all our organizations, although their power is considerable. I would argue that the greatest resistance is complicit hypocrisy of the many. Most people just want to get up, go to work, come home, eat supper, have some time with the kids, work on some hobbies or watch TV, and go to bed. They want their paycheck to pay for the food, the house, a few toys, and to send their kids to college. They want to live peacefully and in happiness. They don't want to try and tackle problems they have no clear control over. There is nothing wrong with that, of course.

CQ and transmutational leadership can be practiced by everyone, no matter what they choose to do. The technique is valuable for both leaders and followers. Unlike many other leadership models and techniques, transmutational leadership is not about persuading, influencing, or manipulating anyone. It is primarily about leading self.

A rapidly changing system disrupts our normal patterns and threatens our comfortable numbness. Change will happen whether we like it or not. We struggle to change, and we struggle to adapt. We need to create the conversation and the support systems for our society to get through the challenging times implied by the massive change that is upon us. The role of the dominant few and leaders at all levels and walks of life is to facilitate the support systems necessary to achieve a graceful and peaceful transition. I believe that CQ and the transmutational leadership model help to achieve these transitions.

✳

Cognitive Zebras

It's all an illusion!

Calm the cognitive.

Deny your senses.

See the flux of energy that abounds and surrounds.

What is reality after all?

Transcend the physical and embrace the metaphysical.

Everything is connected.

You'll see the colors and music of the soul.

We are but cognitive zebras dancing on a great savanna.

Who can deny it!

✳

8

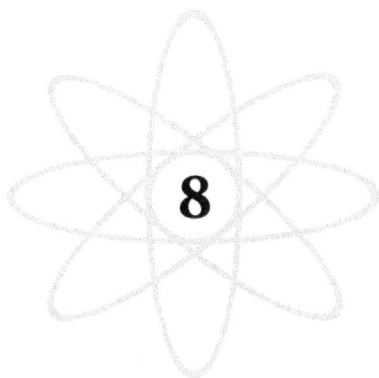

Techniques for Soul-Mind Development

IT'S REALLY IMPORTANT to let go of the brain-mind's polarized way of perceiving if we are to change how we do things. Consequently, we have to unlearn our beliefs and be mindful of our brain-mind in the moment of now. Brains have developed a lot of complexity in 300 million years, but our basic human design seems to be inappropriate now that we've conquered the food chain. We need to awaken to that and relearn how to be in the world.

As I've said before, all this requires some courage. You may be scared, but don't be afraid. Allow your brain-mind to let go of some of that control. You'll oscillate back and forth, but the soul-mind will emerge and you'll be stronger and more balanced for it. Your journey awaits!

Techniques for Accessing the Soul-Mind

The tools and techniques for accessing the soul-mind described below are not in any particular order. Nor are they exclusive. From what I have read and understand, there is no particular formula or prescription on how to exercise these techniques; one size certainly does not fit all.

Learn as much about these things as you can, adapt what works for you, and practice, practice, practice. Here are some key areas to consider.

Self-Awareness

The place to start is the status quo. What is your brain doing right now? How are you feeling? The list of questions is long. The complete picture is elusive. We are able to sense our conscious selves, but the subconscious is difficult to perceive.

I'll give you a personal example: I have trouble keeping extra weight off. I'm almost always overweight. Why? The answers are complex, many, and not clear.

There are many possible contributors. Genetically, the members of my family are typically short and stocky. My DNA has programmed average height and build, and I have dense bones. I don't float easily in water, like most people. I've thought that part of the answer may also be epigenetics. My grandparents and parents went through the great depression and were quite poor. My grandfather lost his farm during that time, like many others. They didn't have much to eat. My genetic and epigenetic code might be getting me to overeat during this time of plenty. My mother fed me well when I was born. I was underweight at birth, but weighed 32 pounds at 9 months. That's a lot of baby fat!

I was bullied a lot when I was a kid, and I wasn't very athletic. I was part of an ethnic minority at a time of social stress during my adolescence—more bullying. As an adult, I have a stressful work life. Starting up and managing a company in the middle of a deep recession and in a tough industry can be scary. There were a few times when I've wondered if I could succeed. I've had bouts of insecurity and mild depression. My first marriage failed. Yes, I'm pretty typical of a lot of people. That analysis is my conscious mind trying to figure out my subconscious. I know I have to understand myself to get at the root problems that have been embedded deeply into my brain and mind. I know I need more consciousness and self-awareness to do so.

I can't have chocolate in the house or I binge. Fat seems to be my insurance policy for whatever is stressing me—to ensure I won't die if I lose my job (i.e., my ability to get food). There's still more to it, without a doubt, but that's enough to know that I've often turned to food for solace, automatically and unconsciously, and the patterns run deep. I'm not happy about it, but that's my conscious ego expressing itself and my karma, my spiritual expression. This might even sound like making excuses. I lose weight when I believe things are going well and the stress is down, which is proof to me that my issue is primarily psychological.

The brain-mind's Id (subconscious) and Ego (conscious) are always there. Most of our feelings emerge from the Id. That is a big part of the problem. A majority of neurons' energy levels and synaptic connections are preset by our beliefs, memories, experiences, and personality. Our brain is a living evolutionary instrument, and we are often unconscious of the largest and tiniest of inputs to the brain, and its decisions "bully us" as we would be bullied under the tyranny of the majority. You know, when you are aware of it, it's that voice in your head that beats you up from time to time. Self-awareness pushes back on this ever-present tide and allows us to reconsider everything, but we need to awaken to it first.

Wherever I go, I bring who I am with me, including to the workplace. I have been taught many things about my brain-mind's tendencies. According to Myers-Briggs, I am an INTJ (i.e., introvert, intuitive, thinking, and judging) personality type. I've done this test three times in my life, and I'm grateful to say that my scores are slowly moving to the middle zone of balance. Still, I remain so schedule-driven that I have a hard time with procrastinators and their general inability to plan and organize. I'm aware of this now. I am grateful for procrastinators' creativity and ability to be spontaneous. I can laugh about my own tendencies, rather than get flustered by procrastinators. I've come to realize that the creative potential between two people is the dynamic balance between opposing personality traits. My awareness and my humor diffuse my negative feelings about losing control over the schedule and the plan. This requires me to be mindful at all times. If I don't do that, I make it about me and not about them and us together.

A high CQ enables me to maintain a balanced approach. I believe that this whole-brain and whole-mind thinking with a high CQ makes us smarter, more creative, more authentic, and more aware of what's going on around us, and all these increase our leadership performance. All this has to be pursued uniquely. That is, we must develop consciousness that suits our unique self, in the best way we know how, to enable whole brain-mind and soul-mind thinking.

Systems Thinking

Given the amount of emphasis I have devoted above to systems theory and to explaining that we are the system, I certainly encourage you to develop the understanding and ability to see the systems all around you, how they operate, and how you relate and respond to them. I also encourage you to try to understand how your own mind and brain are a system and how your feedback loops are working. What are your beliefs, and how can you change them (i.e., your leverage points)? Consciousness, self-awareness, reflection, mindfulness, and meditation are feedback loops.

Feedback loops in the mind change energy levels in a multitude of ways. The brain's plasticity allows it to respond to these energy changes by changing its existing structures and by creating new neurons, new synapses, and new networks that result in new beliefs.

All mind tools and techniques constitute feedback loops. Ask yourself, what happens within you? How do you feel after you have used the feedback? Your intent and focus will determine whether the experience is helpful or not. Continue to practice those that help you. Like a world-class athlete who has found the right method, practice, practice, and practice some more. Please refer to Figure 15 to see how I have mapped the following techniques against the different layers of brain and mind development within the transmutational leadership model.

These methods work because they quiet the brain. Why is that?

Figure 31, adapted from Picard,[1] shows that when various types of energy levels are low, we are better able to sense small differences in corresponding energy level changes. For example, a very noisy environment makes it difficult to hear slight differences, but in a very quiet environment, we can sense even a small change in energy levels. This is true of light as well. The mathematics behind these subjectively noticeable differences were developed by Gustav Fechner in the mid-1800s.

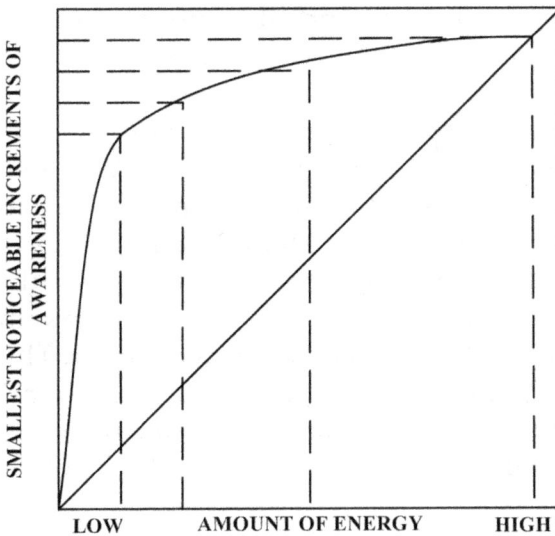

Figure 31: Brain Energy Response Awareness Curve

This demonstrates that we are able to sense weaker signals and therefore more possibilities when our brain-minds are quiet. It also shows that the brain is nonlinear in how it processes this type of sensory information. Quieting the brain-mind essentially enables us to tap into the soul-mind more easily. The first technique is reflection. Reflection answers the question, what is your brain-mind doing right now?

Reflection

Reflection is a powerful tool for analyzing what is going on right now and what happened in the past. It has two meanings or two methods as applied to brain-mind development.

The first method is the traditional understanding of reflection. Something is going on right now or has happened in the past and we think about it or analyze it. We typically ask ourselves, what on earth happened here? This question applies if the event was negative, but we can easily, and should more often, ask the question when it's positive. Remember, the brain-mind likes positive reinforcement. We must be careful about what we are learning from our positive experiences.

The other way of using reflection is related to reinforcing the feedback mechanisms. Stuart Wilde suggests a method using, in part, imagination and, in part, a real mirror to create a closed system that magnifies the mind's energy levels. Essentially, it is like two waves with the same wavelength coming together in time. The resultant peak or amplitude is higher, as I described earlier. This method may or may not work for you, since we are all unique. Nevertheless, if you understand systems theory and closed loops, you will be able to find a method that you can adapt to your needs.

Mindfulness

"Never miss a good chance to shut up." ~Will Rogers

You need to slow down to speed up. You need to keep your mind quiet so that you can determine what it's doing. Be mindful of how you react to situations. Mindfulness is related to systems thinking in that you become acutely aware of how you respond to the external environment and the state of mind you are experiencing in the moment. Chopra's model is excellent for establishing a framework for how your brain-mind and soul-mind are working.

When you are in a business meeting, slow down, shut up, and see what is really happening. There are huge benefits to this in business, as reported by Hunter.[2]

Whether personal or organizational, see where there are recurring patterns. Reflect and meditate deeply on why these patterns are recurring, because they provide insight into the rules of the system, whether individual or organizational.

Be careful about changing the rules of your brain-mind system. Experimentation is great, but you'll have to be tolerant of mistakes and put up with some discomfort. How you define success and failure will determine how you view mistakes. Mistakes and failures are investments in learning opportunities. You've already "paid your money." Learn from these mistakes. Remember to take baby steps. Don't be discouraged by failure and inconsistency. All world-class athletes go through the same process to become world-class. Perfection is unattainable. It is the journey that matters.

Meditation

Meditation is the most highly recommended practice across the board, no matter what religion or spiritual philosophy you believe in. There is an enormous amount of material available on meditation. Meditation classes and sessions are offered by many different groups and organizations. For example, yoga studios often offer meditation services, since that is part of their lineage. Try and take some time every day to meditate. Let go of the old and embrace the new you.

Other Techniques

Other techniques that are very valuable are practicing detachment, alignment, and equanimity.

Detachment is about letting go of expectations regarding the outcome of decisions. Many decisions are based on an unconscious perception of future regret (i.e., an emotion that does not emerge in our conscious thought) and we devote a considerable amount of effort justifying and rationalizing our choices (i.e., logic) to support our decisions. When you let go of outcomes, through detachment, you are not held captive by the future. You make the best decisions possible in the moment with increasing clarity. Decisions are then made for the right reasons that are consistent with your and your organization's higher purpose.

Alignment is also a technique. Although most people would not think of alignment in this way, it is useful to see it as such. Achieving one's higher purpose is most efficiently and effectively done when day-to-day decisions and actions are consistently in alignment.

Alignment with a higher purpose is a key principle of the conscious capitalism movement. If financial results of firms practicing conscious capitalism are consistently true,[3] then alignment with a higher purpose is very important indeed. The reason for this is that people become emotionally engaged and passionate when they work for an organization that is heavily committed to positive progress and social justice that are in alignment with their fundamental beliefs. According the authors of *Conscious Capitalism*, Mackey and Sisodia, better performance on a number of criteria, including financial, is the result of this passionate engagement and alignment.

Alignment is also a synonym for congruence. From a leadership point of view, being congruent means to be authentic and to walk the talk. Followers do not like leaders who are all for show. They want them to stand for something and for their actions to be consistent with their philosophical beliefs and values. If nothing else, being congruent and consistent ensures that followers understand the rules of the game and how to make good decisions within the organizational framework and culture created by leaders.

Finally, I mention equanimity. Equanimity is a balanced state of mind that remains undisturbed by internal processes or external events. Followers may "lose their minds" or become unbalanced, but leaders should remain calm and exude grace when dealing with difficult situations. An aspect of equanimity is compassionate presence. The state of being fully open and alert toward the other person without any self-interested desire interrupting the development of that relationship means being fully present. This state of mind allows followers' suffering to be transmuted by the leader.

Probable Results

The above techniques will likely result in your brain-mind becoming more whole-brain balanced and allow your soul-mind to emerge. You will become calmer, more focused, more authentic, and more balanced. You will be able to create safe and trusting environments. Leadership decisions will have a higher probability of being ethical, moral, and just. People will be able to speak their fears without retribution.

Creating this type of safe environment is one of the foundations for a learning culture, which is so crucial to ongoing organizational success. The people around you will key in on that, and more possibilities and creativity will emerge for both you and your organization. However, this is not an overnight solution. People will require a lot of time, some more than others, to get over their fears to learn that retribution and punishment do not follow courageous admissions of mistakes or putting forward ideas that are contrary to the status quo. We have to be courageous to overcome our innate fear and insecurity. In that sense, an organization that systematically embodies forgiveness and creates a reward system that recognizes courage is a healthy learning organization.

Non-Judgment

I have shown how CQ and transmutational leadership mean being more compassionate, forgiving, fearless, and loving by being aware of the brain-mind's tendency to polarize everything and thereby to judge people and events. Spiritual teachings also recommend that people should avoid being judgmental. However, practicing non-judgment as individuals in our daily lives is much easier than practicing non-judgment while making leadership decisions. In fact, I believe that it is not possible to do so because of the nature of leadership. It is only possible to be aware of the range of responses available for a given situation and to prefer to use non-judgment. Practicing non-judgment is in itself a free-will choice that contains a judgment.

Leaders must judge performance of people and the organization in pursuit of its purpose. An organization that pursues a higher purpose (e.g., by defining how it serves humanity and the planet), bases its judgments on how it is progressing toward the achievement of that higher purpose. It is what separates the progressive organizations from those that only seek to achieve their charter.

I may have been critical in this book about many things, but my intent was not to judge too harshly. In the words of Jesus, "Forgive them, father, for they know not what they do." I do not want to come across as arrogant or condescending, either. This is just my view, and I'm fully aware that I don't have all the answers. It's simply my humble opinion that we are generally blind to our global systems and the processes happening inside us. The balance between the soul and the body has too often been destabilized by the complicit hypocrisy of our brain's design. At the core, complicit hypocrisy is the outcome of our body's fears and competitive drive for survival. If Darwin was right, survival of the fittest may be for those who rediscover this dynamic balance in the interests of humanity and themselves.

My intent in writing this book was merely to illustrate the mostly invisible process that is happening inside us. As Lao Tzu said, we look at it and do not see it. It is this invisible process that has created all of our systems and problems. It is our very nature. It is the cause of our many triumphs and the bane of our many tragedies.

Please be ever vigilant of your brain-mind. It has exceedingly clever ways of subduing your authentic self.

Nearly Departed

Timeless

Sand and wind and waves

And brief interlopers

Call out Neptune's daughter

To witness our grief

To partake of our celebration

Did we not see the seed of our downfall?

Do we not see the seed of our greatness?

Sand and seed, waves of permanence

Ripples spread like the wind

We are flotsam and jetsam

Tossed upon the sea

Mourning and celebrating

We, nearly departed

9

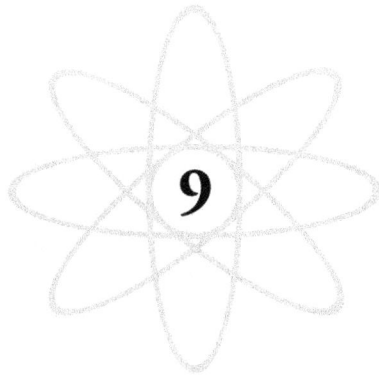

Implications and Predictions

"It seems to me that no soothsayer should be able
to look at another soothsayer without laughing."
~ Cicero to Roman Senate

OKAY, IT'S FUN to speculate. Only a fool would try to predict the future in the presence of infinite possibilities, but it is possible to have a vision of the future. Perhaps you'll grant me the honor of calling it "visioneering." After all, a vision held by a collective group of people has quite a good chance of succeeding because they believe they can do it, just as Gandhi believed he could change India through nonviolence. A critical mass of primarily soul-mind leaders can change the world. What we believe can manifest itself.

I proceed. First the bad news, then the good news:

Hobbes' View—Bad News

Einstein said that there were only two things that were infinite—the universe and man's folly. He added that he wasn't sure about the universe.* The brain-mind, unconstrained by the soul-mind and the existing rules of civilization, would make life, in the words of the philosopher Hobbes, *"solitary, poor, nasty, brutish, and short."*

The systems that were established long ago (e.g., economic, religious, political) continue to manifest today. These systems are led by a dominant few, especially the global economic system that wants greater and greater integration in order to control all outcomes. Control is a delusion of the brain-mind, but very real to our day-to-day physical experience nonetheless. Within such systems, the dominant few do not want change to occur unless it is in their self-interest. Consequently, unless we change our approach to leadership, this Orwellian system, in the largest sense of the word, will eventually be driven to a cataclysmic event of some kind.

This cataclysmic event will have a tipping point, the event or thing that is easily blamed to divert our attention from the real source of the problem. An unscrupulous leader will point at and blame the symptom, but the real reason is something altogether different. If we continue along the path we are on, an event will probably be something as described by Meadows, Randers, and Meadows in *Limits to Growth: The 30-Year Update*. This tipping point that will be the event that transitions our systems into chaos mode will only be a symptom. It might possibly be environmental collapse, followed by economic collapse, war, and finally mass starvation, disease, and death. People would say that it was environmental collapse that caused the problem, rather than admit that it was our very nature that was the root cause.

The brain-mind dominant few who are leaders may not care too much about a drastic decrease in population as long as they've taken steps to ensure their lineal survival

---

* I heard this on the TV show *Through the Wormhole* with Morgan Freeman.

and continued dominance. In any case, the dominant few may very well believe that a world with fewer people is more sustainable, and rightly so. There's money to be made and power to be acquired during any crisis. That has been their experience throughout the many wars in our documented history. An example of this is how the Rothschild family enriched themselves during the war of 1812 in Europe. We continue to be at war today in a number of ways. Mostly, our modern wars are economic in nature, so they are not so obvious. The cyber war is on full tilt right now, although most of humanity is unaware of it! It's an understandable and very human brain-mind response, given our electronic capabilities.

In such a highly controlled system, the only way out is for change to occur from below—from the 99 percent of people. That's called a revolution, and it has many downsides, since revolutions distribute poverty rather than wealth. We've seen over and over what happens when a revolution occurs, and there is no doubt that the dominant few are very afraid of this and will fight with all their might against it. There is no question that a risk response mechanism today by the dominant few is control of economic, political, intelligence, legal, police, and military organizations and their continual integration for this type of ultimate control.

We see corruption in the leadership chain of command in all areas of endeavor throughout the world because our self-interest (i.e., complicit hypocrisy) is a desire to be one of the dominant few. The only alternative to this dismal scenario is an increase in consciousness. The attributes of an increase in consciousness are fearlessness, compassion, and love. We must avoid engaging in a polarized way, just as Tolle's wisdom suggests. It is those qualities that will allow the change to occur gradually, but fast enough to avert catastrophe. We first have to recognize that we're all caught up in the same system(s) and that we have only one planet to share. We must be kind to the dominant few who got us into this mess. It is the paradox of our times.

Locke's View—Good News

The libertarian philosopher John Locke believed that there was good in all people. My interpretation of Locke's philosophy is that the innate goodness in humans could enable them to cooperate in order to achieve a just society. He rejected Hobbes' view of humanity and equally rejected Jeremy Bentham's and John Stuart Mills' utilitarian philosophy. He believed that there were things of value beyond financial considerations. Locke's philosophy was carried forward into the constitution of the United States and has evolved considerably since then, as other philosophies have competed to bring balance to Locke's libertarian point of view. Thus, I can see how the Western democracies' philosophies are evolving, but in my opinion, the balance in our economic system is still too brain-mind-oriented. Nevertheless, my interpretation of Locke and how his philosophy has evolved in North America leads me to believe that we are moving toward leading primarily from the soul-mind.

The good news is that soul-mind consciousness is increasing rapidly. Soul-mind consciousness is the counterweight to a brain-mind-dominated system. The reason that it is the right counterweight is its very nature—fearless, compassionate, and loving, which is required for social justice to occur. In a strange ironic twist, the dominant few will leverage this capability in people in an effort to control their destiny and continue to dominate through a peaceful transition. This will allow them to reset the system, as Solon did in ancient Greece, and grudgingly return to accumulating wealth. Having achieved a peaceful transition, over time, they will begin to be transmutational leaders in their own way. Our current modern examples of soul-mind conscious individuals are Buffett, Gates, and others, as previously mentioned.

All our system(s) rules will begin to evolve rapidly. As the system evolves, the leaders will adapt quickly, and it will change them or they will be gradually replaced by those who are more suited to the external environment and demands placed upon them by followers.

In the end, soul-mind consciousness will win out simply because it has more possibilities at its disposal. It is, by definition, more creative. I can see the day in the immediate future when organizations will have a group of highly conscious people sitting next to the CEO at meetings or housed next to his/her office. These people will have multiple types of skills. Some will be psychic and will see followers' energy and connect with them at a much deeper level than the creators of MBTI could possibly ever dream. An individual tuned to the group's energy will be the most important aide the CEO will have. Beyond that, the CEO will be an adept in soul-mind leadership. We will likely call their style or ability "soul-mind charismatic," and they will have a very high CQ. People will naturally gravitate to leaders with high levels of consciousness and energy vibration. These leaders will lead primarily from the soul-mind.

Hegel's View—Synthesis

Change is never very smooth. In each type of argument, there is thesis, antithesis, and finally synthesis. It's my belief that the current brain-mind competitive paradigm ruling the world (thesis) will meet its reactive soul-mind authentic-cooperation opposite (antithesis), and the merging of the two will create a transition period and a very different world (synthesis) with a new set of rules to measure a new and improved definition of progress and success. Eventually, though, the direction will be toward more soul-mind leadership and therefore more social justice.

Here's my take on how things could look in the future for a variety of endeavors:

Education

I predict that, within a generation, education programs will include self-awareness, reflection, mindfulness, and meditation within their core curriculum, equal to language, mathematics, physics, biology, etc. Our greatest hope is in our children. We will put our money where our mouth is. Education will not only be whole-brain but whole-mind as well. No longer will seemingly odd qualities be ostracized and bullied; they will be joyously welcomed. Dancers will be able to fidget in the classroom, and children currently labeled with ADHD and drugged comatose by a system that cannot handle diversity will thrive with their newfound freedom. The new normal will be the support of diversity and no longer the tyranny of the majority in imposing "normalcy."

Psychic ideas, beliefs, and capabilities will be taught at the earliest age possible. Given the very nature of consciousness, in the future, a baby will develop this capability within the womb because the parents will telepathically communicate with the developing embryo. Lipton confirms that every experience in the womb shapes the unborn child's brain and mind.

Our greatest gift to our children will be giving them the understanding of their own mind, developing their gifts, and allowing them to practice consciousness in a safe environment. Education and the classroom environment as we know it today will crumble. More and more people will opt out of the public education system unless it changes rapidly. We will create a safe habitat in all our schools for consciousness in whatever form it may take.

Leadership education, as it is currently delivered to adults, will also be transformed. Leadership education can easily be correlated with historical beliefs and paradigms. Leadership is a learned behavior. How we lead is not only how we educate, it is also based in part on role models and what we've experienced. Many of our leadership lessons may be quite wrong. Given the speed of change today, and the crises that are upon us, preparing for the future based on past experience may not be viable. We cannot continue to lead the way we've led historically. The analogy is like military men always preparing to fight the last war and finding themselves unprepared and surprised by new ways of doing things. This will also be the case with leadership. Why we teach, what we teach, and how we teach will change. So will how we measure and reward leadership competency. Leadership paradigms based first and foremost on competition must give way to leadership paradigms based first and foremost on authentic and sincere cooperation.

Economics

The world of economics will be turned upside down. We will no longer oscillate between capitalism and socialism. Today, the dominant few maintain control in multiple ways, and keeping followers in debt is one of them. Therefore, the debts of the world will be gradually erased since they reside in an electronic system and in some sense are not real. It should start with the IMF's loans to poor countries, where the money has not got into the hands of the poor. The true wealth of the dominant few, their gold and silver bullion and other physical possessions, will keep them dominant for some time. This will generate a great deal of conflict and debate. However, the debate will not be Marxist in nature because it is not about capitalism versus socialism or any other ism. It will be about love and finding creative ways to honor and respect all of humanity and all of planet Earth and its life.

The foundation idea of commerce, of profit above all and even at all costs, will give way to a more balanced approach. All organizations, including for-profit companies, will be judged by their ability to create value within a new definition of progress. Politics will also be transformed by necessity. This will not be a utopia. How wealth is created, how individuals are rewarded, how people will be valued, how limited resources are distributed, and how our habitat and other species are protected will be increasingly challenging economic and philosophical questions. Since economics touches everything, all other world systems will be affected.

Religions

The world's most dominant religions will lose control of the spiritual narrative, but will continue to provide the positive aspects of community and charity that are not, cannot, or should not be done by other types of organizations. Sectarian violence will no longer be tolerated. Religions will be forced to open their closets. The truth of their wealth and the covering up of heinous behavior will no longer be accepted. The massive wealth of major religions will be subject to the changes predicted in the economics. They will begin a period of self-healing and return to their spiritual roots. Even now, the new pontiff, Pope Francis, is calling on leaders to protect the poor and the environment. How his actions regarding the wealth of the Catholic Church will reflect his rhetoric remains to be seen. Nevertheless, religions will be one of the world's greatest sources for consciousness education, in their own flavor.

Environment

The war on the environment will end. Coexistence, diversity, and sustainability will be dominant themes. All species will be appreciated for their contribution to diversity and creativity. Intelligence will no longer be arrogantly attributed to humans only. Varying levels of consciousness will eventually be recognized in all animate, perhaps even all inanimate, things because all matter is energy first. Finding a way to feed an ever-growing population will require the creativity of the soul-mind.

Industry

Industries will no longer be able to exploit resources without taking their remediation into account. Prices based on a new ecology of commerce will emerge. Subsidies and other forms of price manipulation will give way to a global approach based on peace and not war, economic or otherwise. Competition will be reframed and monopolies shattered. The age of the global multinational corporation that dominates its industry and its suppliers and these organizations will come under intense scrutiny via social media. Small will be seen as beautiful again. Local merchants will no longer face the "Walmarts" of the world as large firms start to disaggregate by focusing on their purpose and on what they do best. The way Whole Foods works with local farmers is a current example of a large-scale enterprise working with a very large number of small independent businesses so that everyone wins, including the environment.

Agriculture will be one of the most affected industries. The drive to dominate the environment by plowing it under and replacing it with monoculture will also be intensely scrutinized. Forests will not be treated like another place to practice monoculture. The ecological value of diversity will rise to the fore. A more thoughtful approach to agriculture will be needed through the transition. Perhaps our intensive farming methods will become less intensive once the world population levels off at some point of sustainability. The unspoken elephant in the room is population growth control. This is a very intensely emotional and ethical debate for many.

Medicine

Medicine will be transformed. Energy healing will have a status equal to our current form of healing delivery. There will be a widespread realization that the placebo effect has been energy healing all along. Pharmaceutical companies will cringe and fight it out to the end, along with the standard medical professions, but they will ultimately realize that their contributions are still needed, and that together with energy healing, they will be symbiotic and the answer to whole body and mind healing. Embracing the two methods working together will bring new forms of business in healing delivery.

Gender Issues

The equality issues and the glass ceiling that have prevented many women from leading their organizations will be shattered. Women's larger corpus callosum enables them to employ their whole brains better than men on average. They are populating yoga studios and meditation classes by a ratio of 10:1, from what I see. They are more open to possibility and balancing relationships than men on average.

Men, in general, are more suited to accomplishing tasks than to maintaining relationships. Indeed, historically, they are more willing to sacrifice relationships, including with themselves, to achieve an objective, as in war. They bring a lot of clarity regarding achieving objectives. They are best suited to the current type of brain-mind dominated and highly competitive systems that prevail. In my opinion, male traits are more compatible with the highly competitive nature of most organizations. It is this compatibility that is, in my opinion, why the glass ceiling really exists. That doesn't mean that women are less competitive than men. Quite to the contrary, they are equally competitive, but they have more awareness of relationships and that reflects their behavior. The consequence of needing to win when conditions demand sacrificing relationships is that most organizations are led by men. For example, I believe that there is an unspoken truth about an important criterion regarding how we assess the worthiness of presidential or prime ministerial candidates; ultimately, they have to be able to give the order to kill to protect the nation, its people, and its interests.

Men resist any threat to sharing leadership with women because they see as their primary task the need to protect and, therefore, put relationships with others second in priority and they don't like anything that will confuse the required action. In some paternalistic societies, it will be extremely difficult for men to meet women halfway and to share their power and control. A lot of conflict between the genders will manifest itself. It will be very difficult for women in certain geographies and cultures to achieve their full potential and make a difference in the interest of social justice. In these cultures and geographies, men will do everything they can to prevent women from getting an education and advancing the principles of soul-mind leadership. Their fear is not unwarranted given that many of these societies are constantly experiencing violence.

As a group, women will achieve soul-mind dominated leadership first. Consequently, more organizations will be led by women through the transition period. Even now, there are twice as many women entrepreneurs as men. Men will catch up eventually, since we are all equally capable of soul-mind leadership, and men won't want to be left behind. As soul-mind dominated leadership emerges, true equality of the genders will manifest itself.

Philosophy

Philosophy will reemerge as a major pursuit that is as worthy as any other profession. Even now, the lessons and wisdom of Buddha, Christ, Mohammed, Confucius, Tzu, Plato, Aristotle, and their predecessors and successors are being studied anew in an effort to come to grips with the brain-mind and provide us with a window into the soul-mind. People will have a new and refreshed understanding of reality, knowledge, and values, particularly ethics. Philosophy, spirituality, and quantum physics will be bedmates. Philosophy in all its manifestations will be coffee-shop conversation again, and philosophers will be valued for their leadership and contributions. Many organizations today employ ethicists and have published codes of ethics to prevent unscrupulous behavior. This trend will expand to include ethicists readily available to leaders throughout the organization to guide decisions filled with ethical dilemmas, paradoxes, and conundrums. Even now, philosophy counseling is emerging for individuals to help them frame their issues within the wisdom of the last three millennia.

Science and Engineering

Science of the mind and progress in quantum physics and its application by engineering will revolutionize how we see the world and interact with it. We will come to realize deeply that science, philosophy, and spirituality are perspectives of mind only and that the synthesis of some of these disciplines will create a new multidisciplinary approach to understanding mind. This new approach will accelerate the transition from the current state of mind to higher levels in the transmuational leadership model, and the capabilities that emerge will seem to be truly miraculous based on our current standards of understanding. No one can predict what consciousness will accomplish in the next century.

Summary

I think that I've shown conclusively that if you are going to be different while traveling this road of change, you had better grow a thick skin. Pay attention to how traditional brain-mind leadership deals with threats: "Socrates was a philosopher. He went around pointing out errors in the way things were done. They fed him hemlock."[1] Unfortunately, feeding people "hemlock" does still happen in places. It is regrettable that a dominant belief system and dominant leaders will always fight back in many ways to assert and maintain dominance.

All of this change predicted by the vision of a transformed world can only occur peacefully if we disengage the normal brain-mind way of responding to its input. Our minds' memories will be dramatically improved. We will avoid the doom of forgetfulness and we will not repeat our history. It is my fervent hope and the basis of my optimism for humanity. My beliefs emerged from my research, my consciousness, and my meditations. I hope that you will share in this vision.

In the end, it may not matter much if my hypothesis is true or not. If it has helped you to be more thoughtful about who you are, where you are operating in the leadership continuum, and how you are in relation to the world, then that's good enough for me. What you do with the information you've read in this book is a function of choice. It is your free will to do as you like.

Thank you for joining me on this journey and for keeping an open mind along the way. The future I predict is possible. We just have to believe that we can achieve it.

I realize that my prose and many aspects of this book are quite technical. For those of you who prefer a story, I leave you with my final chapter, God's Breath. This came to me late one night in October 2008 during a meditation. I hope you enjoy it.

✱

CHRYSALIS

The pupa knows
It waits and endures oblivion
Change and pain, to beauty its future
Freedom transforms, nature's quest.

The pain of our minds releases our weakness.
Rejoice in the release for it brings meaning
And a new beginning
In the quiet of reflection we sense the energy
Pupating together; what is this coherent symbiosis?
It's another plane of existence rarely experienced.

The past merges with the present and creates our future
The mind re-winds, re-engages and re-writes its future history.
Release and rejoice for new beliefs, new patterns,
And new beginnings
Are ours to create.

✱

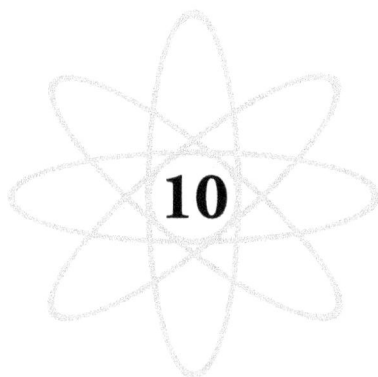

10

God's Breath

THE FLAMES had long ago left on their journey toward heaven. The embers glowed brightly and mingled with the light of the full moon, the men and boys of the hunting party huddled closely for warmth. The stars twinkled and the snow shimmered like diamonds. They were all quiet. It had been a long and arduous hunt, but a successful one; their labors had been repaid with full bellies.

It was the time, as they all knew, for the old man to tell a story. No one ever knew what he would say. In the past, they had heard stories about their people's history, sometimes about women, sometimes about the hunt. Most often, it was about how to be a man. How it was okay to be scared, but not okay to be afraid. How men needed to tame their wild ways without losing that ability to be violent—to protect and love and kill at the same time. It was, after all, a difficult world and their people had been threatened many times. Most of the stories were aimed at the young ones, as they would eventually inherit the leadership. The old man cleared his throat—a sign that the story was beginning.

"It was all so very simple in the beginning," the old man said. "Long before our people came to be, even longer than

Mother Earth and Daughter Moon, longer even than the sun which brings us warmth and longer than the stars that twinkle with delight as they help guide our way through the night. Longer than all that. I speak of the beginning.

"There were no stars, then, no sun, no Mother Earth, no Daughter Moon, no people. There was no nature at all. It was perfect order infused with perfect consciousness. Yes, there was consciousness, but just a little bit of it—just a glimmer. The glimmer was fleeting, like the shimmer of the northern lights.

"But there was a problem. Being perfect, the consciousness could not learn anything new. It had no concept of space and time. It did not know nature.

"Even then, consciousness was already wise. Consciousness knew that new learning and more consciousness could only be obtained through the chaos of nature. Do we not also learn best when things change or go wrong?" The old man stopped speaking and the older men in the group acknowledged this wisdom. The old man continued.

"And so, consciousness had to give birth to a new reality. Like a mother in labor, it needed to experience great pain to give birth to this new reality. It needed to experience the sorrow of the pain to also experience the great joy of birth. And so, consciousness gathered up all its energy in one great inhalation. And then, consciousness exhaled, just as a mother gathers and focuses all her strength for that final push. With that exhalation, the universe was born. It is the same for us. As we are born, our first inhalation and exhalation, our first breath, brings us life.

"Some call this event the Big Bang. Regardless, it is when time and space and manifest nature came into being. Of course, no one knows how many times this has occurred before or will continue to occur in the future.

"And so, we know that consciousness creates nature and that mind creates matter and above all is the Great Spirit who is known to us by many names. To consciousness, chaos was manifest nature, and nature through complexity and diversity born of chaos creates more consciousness in turn. And that is how the stars, the sun, Mother Earth, and Daughter Moon, and our people came to be.

"And so it is with us. Our first breath brings us into being and gives us into the chaos of the manifest and our last breath will return us to the unmanifest ready to be reborn into the next exhalation. While we are here, we breathe in and out—a reflection of the creation of the universe. In between our breaths, in between our thoughts, in between our feelings, we create consciousness and infinite possibilities. Each time we do this, the Great Spirit dances with delight.

Forever the expansion and contraction of the universe;

Forever the conscious and the unconscious;

Forever the learning and the unlearning;

Forever the manifest and the unmanifest;

Forever the finite and the infinite;

To honor God and our people, forever must we strive to be and achieve our purpose.

For we are God's breath."

Definitions

LANGUAGE HAS A LOT of limitations and it is very important to define the significant terms in this book. To ensure that we have mutual understanding, I devote a considerable amount of attention to definitions.

These words have been defined in many ways and some are used interchangeably in various books. You undoubtedly have your own understanding of their meaning. Nevertheless, the following is the meaning I give to them to help you understand what I believe. I apologize to Oxford, Merriam-Webster, and Wikipedia for my presumptiveness, as they're not necessarily exactly as stated in those dictionaries and on their websites. I hope that my meaning is clear and that we have mutual understanding.

> ➢ **Belief:** 1. An opinion (as in the validity or truth of a statement or fact) or conviction (as in a value judgment about a person's action being good or evil). 2. Confidence in a truth (as in a scientific theory backed by empirical evidence) or existence of something not immediately susceptible to rigorous proof (as in religious faith).

➢ **Brain:** 1. The entire nervous system distributed throughout the human body (could also include the immune and endocrine systems, according to some people). 2. Part of the central nervous system enclosed in the cranium of humans serving to control and coordinate mental and physical actions.

➢ **Consciousness:** 1. An emergent process and ability by which we become aware of mind. 2. Self-awareness. 3. A universal property of awareness that is infused in all things that emerges as self-awareness at a certain level of complexity.

➢ **Consciousness Quotient:** CQ is the intentional oscillation between the mind and brain for the purpose of increasing self-awareness. The higher the oscillation, the higher the CQ.

➢ **Knowledge:** 1. Facts about a thing believed to be true. 2. An opinion shared by a majority of observers. 3. Information held in the fabric of the universe.

➢ **Leadership:** 1. An abstract construct of a person's mind. 2. A unique combination of attributes within a person or organization recognized by the majority of observers as superior within a specific context or system.

➢ **Mind:** 1. An ethereal and eternal energy that defies full definition and understanding. 2. An eternal and infinite intelligence or energy that is everywhere and infused into everything simultaneously; see "Consciousness." 3. A form of energy accessed by the human brain and the human soul that contains a person's beliefs, memories, experiences, and personality. 4. The source of all knowledge and possibility.

> **Progress:**   1. A change in an entity or thing whereby the difference is judged to be positive by the observer of the change. 2. A values-based assessment of change.

> **Soul:** 1. A unique and eternal entity in the form of intelligent undefinable energy separate from our physical body; our spiritual self. 2. The quantum level (i.e., intelligent energy) aspect of a human. 3. Consciousness.

> **Success:**   A set of criteria whereby change or progress is judged as positive. Its antithesis is failure and is judged as negative.

> **System:** 1. An assembly or combination of things or parts forming a complex or unitary whole (as in an economic system or an aircraft or a human). 2. An ordered and comprehensive assemblage of facts, principles, doctrines, or the like in a particular field of knowledge or thought (as in a system of philosophy or a religious system). 3. A coordinated body of methods or a scheme or plan of procedure; organizational scheme (as in a system of government or a company). 4. Any formulated, regular, or special method or plan of procedure to achieve success (as in a gambling system or a performance-enhancing drug system or a learning system).

> **Thought** (Conscious): 1. The process of accessing and focusing aspects of mind to satisfy a purpose or intention, for example, accessing beliefs, memories, experiences, and personality as they relate to problem solving and decision making. 2. Reasoning.

> **Transmutational:** 1. The ability of a substance or thing that permits a change of its fundamental characteristic, for example, as in changing one form of energy into another form of energy or using energy to effect a change in matter.

> **Transmutational Leadership:** 1. A process and a number of methods, tools, and techniques designed to increase awareness of mind and to open numerous additional possibilities to support problem solving and decision making. 2. A theory or hypothesis that posits that a paradigm shift of consciousness will fundamentally change existing systems. 3. A state of being. 4. Alchemy of the mind and brain.

> **Truth:** 1. A collected set of opinions and sometimes not even that. 2. See also "Mind" and "Belief."

What Is Leadership?

THE FOLLOWING FIVE POINTS are the major leadership themes of this book. They are interrelated, so there is some overlap in how I describe each one. They are:

- ➢ Construction of Our Minds
- ➢ Context
- ➢ Beliefs
- ➢ Authenticity
- ➢ Neither Prescriptive nor Formulaic

Leadership Point Number One – Construction of Our Minds

There are numerous definitions of leadership. Regardless of the one you prefer, leadership is a construct of our mind as it interacts with our brain, systems, environment, and itself. Our mind holds beliefs, memories, experiences, and personality. How we lead is a reflection of our mind and how it interacts with our brain. How our mind works is a reflection of our purpose and intention regarding the thing we are considering for a decision of some kind. Our mind is a closed system.* A closed system only passes energy across its boundary.

The mind has a feedback loop by which we learn. For example, if we learn that the external environment (e.g., our work organization) operates as a jungle where it's eat or be eaten, then many people will behave accordingly or leave the organization voluntarily or otherwise. Thus, how leadership operates becomes self-reinforcing for the organization.

A system, its rules, and its interaction with our brains and minds, drive our behavior. We adapt very quickly. What we learn about leadership is crucial to how we create our problems, how we perceive our problems, and how we overcome our problems. Regardless of all this, however, we still have free choice about how we choose to lead. This is the benefit of the feedback loop(s) we use—what we describe as being self-aware. If we are unaware of our mind (e.g., beliefs) and the system's rules, then we will lead accordingly and generally tend to make more bad decisions.

A belief can be true and it can be false. For example, in the old days people believed the Earth was flat. Because of that belief, mariners didn't venture out too far at sea. Then, someone came along and said that belief was wrong and the Earth was actually round. Once everyone accepted that the Earth was round, a "sea change" in attitude occurred, and it sparked a huge amount of exploration, which showed unequivocally that the old theory was wrong. The Earth was indeed round—or nearly round. As I learned in navigation school, it is actually an oblate spheroid.

Leadership beliefs work that way, too. If you are taught a bunch of stuff, then that is what you believe. If you believe something and look for it, you'll probably see it. If you blindly accept it all, then that is what guides your choice when you make decisions and how you go about doing

---

* Closed system. I do not imply any negative connotations here. For a discussion of closed systems, refer to Chapter 3 on Systems.

things. If no one ever questions what they are taught, then that's what we get. The same is true of memories that may be faulty, experiences that may not be appropriate, and personality that may not be right for the situation.

Leadership Point Number Two – Context

Leadership can be defined as a unique combination of attributes within a person or organization* recognized by the majority of observers as superior within a specific context. In that sense, leadership is contextual within a defined system and organization. Whether the organization under consideration is political/government, religious, academic, business, or some other form of organization, the ultimate goal of the organization and the people within it is pretty much the same—to survive. What this usually means is that organizations must compete against each other. Sometimes, to do so they must cooperate, as in political and military alliances, but these are simply meta-organization forms of competition. Thus, competition is often masked by what looks like cooperation. For example, there is a symbiotic relationship between the bacteria in our gut and us. Each is dependent on the other for good health and survival. As the bacteria are with us, so are we in relation to our organizations. The symbiotic cooperation between organisms results in higher forms of complexity and diversity, which allows higher forms of creativity and a greater ability to survive. The dance between cooperation and competition is a very natural process that is billions of years old and so deeply embedded that most people aren't aware of it.

Organizations are an artifact of systems. All of our systems reinforce each other and work together as a meta-system created by us. The global financial system

---

* Note: By organization, I mean the term in its broadest sense as any group that we identify with and belong to. It could be our family, company, religion, nation, etc.

is an example of a meta-system and a bank as an artifact (i.e., organization) of that system.

We all want a leader who will enable our organization to be successful within its niche. However, in most cases, this means to dominate other competing organizations for access to scarce resources. Thus, the act of leadership inherently creates conflict and causes social justice problems as one organization seeks to disadvantage its competitors. It's in our tribal nature to do so because it benefits us. There is nothing wrong with that, of course. By and large, this survival of the fittest is the engine of progress, as Darwin would describe it. We would find it rather odd to elect a leader whose mandate would be to disadvantage us.

Not much has changed throughout history. Our tribal nature is such that we want our organization to compete, whereby our organization's interest is set above other organizations' interests. We do all this so that we can feel safer or wealthier or whichever criterion satisfies self-interest. The benefits we derive from belonging to an organization then causes the organization's leaders to demand allegiance and loyalty.

Indeed, in the last few decades, a philosophy called communitarianism has emerged that explores an individual's responsibilities and loyalty toward the organization. Such a philosophy opens up the notion that an organization can compel loyalty from an individual because of the benefits the individual receives from the community. It also means that an individual's freedom can be constrained without consent by virtue of belonging to that community. A person is born into a nation without their consent. Therefore, a thing like conscription into national military service is an example of this type of obligation, as is repaying the national debt. In exchange, the individual receives the tangible and intangible benefits of belonging to the group (e.g., security). How far liberty and freedom can be constrained by a philosophy of communitarianism is a serious leadership issue.

We love the clarity that a binary framework brings, and leaders often use fear and competition to polarize us into creating this binary framework in the interest of communitarianism. This ensures that we behave "correctly," so that the power of the collective can be focused on "success" factors—factors that the leaders have often predetermined; and let's not forget that some leaders are simply megalomaniacs. A lovely form of control it is. Here's an example of it in the words of George W. Bush in an address to a joint session of Congress on September 20, 2001, when he was responding to the challenge of 9/11: "You are either with us, or you are with the terrorists." I'm not judging, nor am I suggesting that President Bush was or is a megalomaniac. I'm simply pointing out the process that many leaders use to polarize decisions and get their organization to close ranks and side with the leader. This technique has been used throughout history, and is being used repeatedly today. Be very wary anytime a leader uses an "or" argument to polarize belief.

These types of leadership behaviors are designed to reinforce our systems to ensure success and survival. Since it is we, the people, who have created these systems (i.e., organizations and how they interoperate), the way they operate is a reflection of us. Consequently, the type of leadership style practiced in various types of organizations reflects the types of problems to be overcome and the degree of change desired or needed to enable an organization to achieve "progress."

So, what leaders tell or teach the people about what constitutes success is important. This is why the leader's definition of the organization's purpose and goals is crucial. Once these are established, how our systems reinforce our fundamental beliefs, our behaviors, and our learning through feedback makes a difference. Make no mistake, there's a whole industry of leadership training and education to help reinforce our systems. The dominant few decree it, the money involved reinforces it, and the system's need for survival ensures it. There's nothing particularly wrong with that. Nothing right about it, either. It just is what it is. It depends on perspective and judgment.

There is no question that humans accomplish great things together as teams within organizations, and organizations have accomplished feats that two or three generations ago would have been unimaginable. Nevertheless, it is imperative that healthy organizations strive for "good success" and "good progress" for the benefit of all humanity, which includes our environment and all species. This requires a strong foundation of leadership, leadership education, and training at all levels of organizations. It also requires that the purpose of the system and the organization is equally sound.

Consequently, it's germane to understand why the system is the way that it is because leadership practices may do no more than just move symptoms around and not address the underlying root cause of our many problems. Leadership practices may, in fact, reinforce a "rotten" system and organization simply because beliefs are not consistent with notions of social justice. I believe that this is the dominant issue in leadership practices and training today. In other words, traditional leadership practices are too competitive, too superficial, and designed to reinforce the status quo of existing systems and organizations at the expense of social justice.

Leadership Point Number Three – Beliefs

Given the previous discussion of systems and organizations, beliefs become an important issue for leaders. As we have seen above, leadership is contextual with respect to the system under consideration and reflects the beliefs of the majority of the people operating within it.

Thus, how we see our systems, what we believe, is a system unto itself.

A leader has to adapt and go where the people are. What I mean is that you cannot ask people to change their beliefs more than they can stand, and you have to speak to them in a manner and at a level that they can understand and accept. Otherwise, the fourth scenario in Plato's allegory of the cave, described in Chapter 2, will not happen. I am well aware that some people are not ready to adopt CQ and transmutational leadership. However, I also firmly believe that there are many people who are ready.

Each one of us has a unique reality, and we are chained by it unless we question our beliefs. Since reality is unique to us, it is, in a sense, an illusion. It begs the question of how accurate and precise belief and knowledge can possibly be. We know that we consciously process a very small portion of the total information available to us. And that's just our experience in the brain-mind (physical) world. According to some folks, we are also receiving a lot of bits from the soul-mind (spiritual or energy) world. Here, too, we're not totally aware of everything that's happening, since a great deal of it is happening subconsciously.

We are constantly constructing our own reality based on our experiences, which we think is the true reality, but everyone experiences the world uniquely, so each person has a different reality that contributes to a unique identity and a different truth. Thus, each experience biases the next experience. This is true of collective beliefs as well. This means that the collective truth at any given time is nothing more than an opinion of the majority of the people in the cave we call planet Earth. And the opinion held by the majority is generally shaped and heavily influenced by the leader's opinion. In fact, I would argue that one of a leader's principal functions is to define reality for followers. Voltaire said: "Doubt is not a pleasant condition, but certainty is absurd." He got that right!

Leadership of other people implies a hierarchy. A leader has a form of power over someone else. It is so because someone (e.g., followers) allows them to lead. There are several types of power. The type of power leaders have is contextual within the system and is based on how the leader is perceived by others. Importantly, it is power that permits leaders to define reality for followers. Power exists where people believe it exists. The exercise of power is often about allowing others to make decisions for us that we cannot, or will not, make for ourselves.

Leadership can be practiced by anyone, and recognized by everyone, regardless of position in an organization. Social media technology today makes this even more possible. The Arab Spring uprising in Egypt in 2012 and the situation in Syria in late 2012 that continue in 2013 are cases in point. Social media are playing a significant role in what is happening on the ground.

With modern technology, leadership can be more widely distributed and become a function of the collective mind. As a matter of fact, I believe that people who lead organizations are now losing control when it comes to shaping and influencing collective opinion. I also believe that there is a general assault on the free press throughout the world and an attempt to control electronic communications for this very reason. This is a typical reaction by the dominant few as a means to protect the status quo. This moves an organization up the order-chaos continuum rather quickly, as discussed in Chapter 4 and illustrated in Figure 13.

In this day and age, a leader's opinion of the truth is under intense scrutiny from social media. It's making some people rather uncomfortable. As all sentient beings desire freedom, freedom-loving people seek truthful information and knowledge. Knowledge is power, as the saying goes. Information is the foundation of creativity and requires communication to take place. That's one of the reasons the Internet and social media are so powerful. That is also why it is a general threat to those who want to control.

Leadership of others, by definition, requires some form of communication between two or more people. Loss of control over the leadership narrative is likely going to accelerate, but possibilities and creativity will increase dramatically; a new order will emerge from the chaos. More possibilities and more creativity will happen, but not without some pain. This change, as always, will be difficult.

It's usually quite a good thing when the head of an organization has spectacular leadership abilities. But it can also be very bad. It is only a good or bad thing within the context of a specific situation, a specific perspective, a set of values, or a system context, as discussed earlier. It's also a judgment call based on belief(s). Hitler was a leader and so was Gandhi, and their ideas are still influencing people today.

If leadership is the ability to get followers to do things (as in a dictatorship), or for the followers to freely bestow power and authority on the leader to make decisions on their behalf (essentially giving up personal freedom and choice as in a democracy), then both Hitler and Gandhi were equally successful leaders. The time frame is also important. What looks to be good today may be bad tomorrow, and what is bad today may be good in the long run. The long run is a very long time. The consequences of every decision today will echo through eternity. Unfortunately, we won't be alive when historians make their judgment over decisions taken today.

Our belief about leadership defines what attributes make good leader. Our beliefs also demonstrate that what is good and what is bad leadership is contextual, based on a values/ethics judgment that is associated with a belief system held by a majority of observers. This judgment also depends on both short-term and long-term consequences. Such judgment cannot be devoid of the system's context—a matter of perspective. Thus, judgment rests within the brain-mind's polarity thinking. It's good or it's bad.

Most things aren't good or bad, they are just as they are—artifacts of the system and what we believe to be success or perceive as progress.

It is very easy to judge any leader as a hero or a fool, depending on one's perspective. When we don't think much of our leader, we should be kind to them and try and withhold judgment for a while; they are stuck in the same system as we are!

If you are a leader who is willing to buck the status quo, you had better grow a thick skin. People who have the courage to state what they believe are often vilified when their belief is contrary to an accepted truth. The "system" fights back in a lot of different ways. Ah, the tyranny of the majority and the powerful! As Gleick says: "Shallow ideas can be assimilated; ideas that require people to reorganize their picture of the world provoke hostility."[1] Thus, truly creative and original ideas that contradict established beliefs have a huge acceptance barrier. There's a lot of resistance to change. Our careers are made and broken by the wagon to which we hitch our beliefs.

Leaders of organizations know that not everyone will agree with any one course of action. John F. Kennedy said that 25 percent of the population would always disagree, no matter what. He had it pretty good by today's standard because now it looks to be closer to 50 percent. Examples are the popular vote in the recent United States presidential elections and the gun debate in the United States, as well as the fiscal cliff debate of 2012/2013. These examples demonstrate how the collective brain-mind is polarized. As a result of this polarization, a major aspect of a leader's task is to overcome the friction of disagreement in order to achieve some definable progress. There are lots of techniques for doing so. Creating a common enemy to get people to close ranks is a typical scenario; there's nothing like a good war!

Leaders will do all they can to manage and control popular opinion, sometimes because they truly believe it is the right thing to do, sometimes out of self-interest, and usually for both reasons. Leaders are in the belief business.

Leadership Point Number Four – Authenticity

Many leadership theories promote authentic leadership. To be authentic requires knowledge of self and to act consistently with self. Even if a leader manages to be authentic, followers have as much or more difficulty being authentic. It is generally easy to game a system. So, how can a leader react with authenticity toward someone who is not authentic? This begs the question, are there any truly, 100-percent authentic relationships?

To be authentic is to not only know your mind, but also to be true to it. That's a problem, though, if a leader behaves poorly. On the other hand, maybe that's exactly what the organization wants from the leader. Or perhaps it is because he/she has a limited number of techniques available and that is the only way he or she knows how to deal with people. These types of leaders may have behaved badly early on in their careers and got positive reinforcement, so they continue on their path. Were Hitler and Gandhi absolutely authentic? Only they knew.

The difference between what the authentic self wants to do and what the organization wants is a *very* significant challenge for many leaders. Only those who are able to adapt to the needs of the organization will eventually be able to rise to positions of authority. That does not make anyone who doesn't rise in the organizational hierarchy less of a leader—perhaps just the opposite—but it does lessen to a certain extent their degree of power and influence within their organization.

What if a leader's authentic self is not in alignment with the characteristics the organization requires, as indicated above? Maybe poor leaders make it to the top of their organizations because that's just what the organization wants. If they are good people and the organization wants a poor leader, then, when this happens, some leaders will compromise themselves out of personal self-interest. They'll let their egos get the better of them and suffer the consequences and the rewards. Some will see themselves as heroes out to achieve success for the collective and knowingly set aside their personal saintliness for unscrupulousness. It works the other way around, too. It makes leadership by example one of the most powerful techniques available, as many people implicitly and explicitly know.

I know some perfectly good people as sons, fathers, and husbands who change into tyrants the second they walk through the front door of the office. What does that say about authenticity?

My take on it is that the rules of the system drive behavior. One behavior is for the home, and one behavior is for the office—two very different systems. It's clear how quickly we adapt to the external environment. Secondly, being authentic can be at odds with the definition of success regarding the system under consideration. Thirdly, most of the brain-mind's processing is subconscious, and behavior often reflects it.

We should be very careful about what we believe and try to see the system for what it is and how it affects us and all the people within it.

Most leaders will deliberately create propaganda to entrench beliefs. Belief drives behavior, but it is contextual. Consider, for instance, how some leaders use fear by threatening the loss of a job to get people to behave the way they want them to. People so threatened have a conscious belief about how they should behave, but more importantly, there is the instinctual need for survival that, down deep, propels people to toe the line. I am fully convinced that our need to make money or get ahead is directly linked to our base instinct for survival. That's why fear and competition are such powerful control techniques. I don't have to work hard at finding examples to support my position. Today, 21 February 2013, this turned up on the Google web clip: Funny Quote of the Day – Ernie Banks: "I like my players to be married and in debt. That's the way you motivate them." I know many people who work in dead-end jobs that they hate because they need to feed their children.

On 6 February 2013 I saw this interesting caption regarding propaganda: "The world remains overpopulated with insecure leaders who try and divert attention from their own failings by bellowing about imagined ancient ills or injustices inflicted on their people."[2]

As I have said, truth is in reality a collective set of opinions and sometimes not even that. It's a paradox that the people who appear to be the most accomplished leaders, by virtue of the fact that they occupy positions of power, are unscrupulous when they need to be. It's our competitive instinct to win at all cost and protect our own and our group's interests. Consequently, hypocrisy and abuse of power are rampant. This can make us uncomfortable about what is ethical and what is not—what's good and bad, and so on. At the very least, it is cause for reflection.

A person tunes in really quickly to the rules of their organization, both unwritten and written. This constitutes our belief system regarding our organization. For example, an organization's hiring, promotion, and reward policies clearly demonstrate a commercial enterprise's need to make money and one way a leader/manager controls beliefs, by firing anyone who doesn't share their values. We tend to promote people in our self-image. It's less problematic for us when we surround ourselves with "yes-men," that is, people who agree with us and flatter our egos. This is especially true when the goal is organizational success.

An organization's reward and recognition system reinforces "successful" behaviors. We write down in compensation plans how employees can make more money and/or get more prestige, which reinforces the organization's system.

The rules of any system are generally implicit, that is, they are not written down. A common expression is, "This is how we do things around here." These rules are embedded in the culture of the organization and reinforced by the leader-managers. Also, when values are not shared by employees, it is cause for trouble, and hiring practices look for people whose values are congruent with the organization. This is a recurring theme in many organizations, and it is taught as a best practice in leadership courses. I was hiking the Baden Powell trail near Deep Cove, British Columbia, on Saturday, 9 Feb 2013, when two young ladies walked past me in the opposite direction. As they did, one of them said to the other, "Basically, if you don't fit in, you get fired." True story. Nice bit of synchronicity, wouldn't you say? So, followers who break the rules usually get disciplined in some way. The majority of followers want the leaders to do just that. We often ask our leaders to take on the role of our parents to intervene and solve a fight with a sibling. It brings clarity to the rules of the system, internal competition, perception of what is fair, and so on.

It is difficult to let go of deeply held beliefs. Berreby said, "Long-standing miseries can't be cured until the overthrow of the certainties that support them."[3] We evolve slowly in the long term and we struggle to adapt in the moment to all of our system contexts and our beliefs. When it comes to work, my advice is to choose the organization that will allow you to be authentic and enjoy the people you are working with.

Leaders define reality (e.g., beliefs) for followers. A leader who defines reality is, by definition, right. Being right provides a leader with a degree of perceived moral superiority that can easily turn into arrogance and hubris. Beliefs matter because they have a huge influence on decisions. Beliefs drive the choices we make. Ergo, through beliefs about reality, leaders make people do things that they would not otherwise do. Choose your leaders well.

Leadership Point Number Five – Neither Prescriptive nor Formulaic

Transmutational leadership is neither a prescription nor a formula for some form of subjective success. Prescriptions and formulas, as in treating disease, often only treat symptoms. Transmutational leadership and CQ address the root cause. Transmutational leadership is a state of being that works to transcend and overcome our natural brain-mind design of polarity thinking without giving up this valuable ability. I do strongly believe that it greatly enhances leader performance. Transmutational leadership transcends style and gets to the very core of authenticity. That's what makes it different. It is meant primarily for leadership of self.

A lot of leadership styles are marketed as leadership solutions. From a specific organization's perspective, these solutions may be the right answer, since the organization is always experiencing some form of change. For example, the transformational leadership style is typically needed during periods of rapid change. So, it's not surprising that in this day and age it's the *style du jour.* Yukl[4] provides a good overview of leadership styles and their pros and cons, if you'd like to know more.

While modern leadership styles may be quite appropriate and also good fodder for marketing in today's general environment, different styles are needed for different situations. For example, if you look up the characteristics of a transformational leader, it's like a behavioral formula for an implied success.

People often get promoted into higher levels of management because of their technical skills, with no leadership training whatsoever, and no understanding of the nature of the gap they are facing. That's a recipe for disaster that I'm sure most people have seen played out. Reluctant followers certainly notice.

Transmutational leadership is whole-brain and whole-mind leadership. It is not a formula or a prescription. It operates deeper than external behavior. It is a state of being. It is a path and method for you to find your own unique self and enable you to adapt more effectively to the external environment.

APPENDIX C

Truth and Errors

ACCORDING TO PICARD,[1] there are three different kinds of truth (i.e., correspondence, coherence, and practical value). Also, the science of statistics informs us that there are two different kinds of statistical errors (Type I and Type II) when judging whether something is true or not. If two people do not agree on the type of truth put forward in an argument and the possibility of error in either direction, then there is inevitably quite a bit of room for disagreement. It should also be noted that each type of truth has its issues and drawbacks.

Truth as Correspondence

Something is true if a belief and a fact or an assertion and reality correspond. For example, the sun always rises in the east. Every day, this truth is put to the test and has yet to be proven false. In the physical world of linear predictable systems, truth as correspondence works well enough. What we name a thing is this type of truth. It is subject to being proven false by saying it is either this or that. But this method is not as reliable when it comes to deciding what is true, especially for nonlinear systems that are heavily dependent on initial conditions whose outcomes are not predictable. In terms of the weather, for example, what we name as a certain type of cloud may be true in the moment, but it may not be true one hour from now as the cloud morphs into a tornado.

It's difficult to apply this type of truth to people. Since we all construct our own reality, we cannot exactly confirm what the truth of our reality truly is. I cannot know if I perceive the color blue the same way as someone else, even if we agree that what we are seeing is a color we've mutually named blue. It is this type of truth that gave rise to my saying that the truth is a collected set of opinions and sometimes not even that. This saying also applies to truth as coherence.

Truth as Coherence

A truth that is dependent on another truth is said to be coherent. For this type of truth to work, there has to be a source truth from which all other truths are derived. The problem with this type of truth is how to determine the trueness of the source truth. When reasoning about something, agreeing to a proposition for the sake of an argument will ensure that all the following points are logically true, but that does not make the originating proposition true. This type of truth applies to my hypothesis. If you agree with my hypothesis, then there are logical arguments that flow from it.

The problem with this type of truth shows up in ethics dilemmas and value systems. Not to pick on the United States of America, but when it is said, "We hold these truths to be self-evident," we create a circular argument. These self-evident truths cannot be proven true, but because the majority of the people accept them as true, then a system of government and a culture will logically follow from that proposition. Consequently, it is only true as long as a majority of people believe it to be true. For something to be rigorously true, it requires more than coherence.

Truth as Practical Value

There are two basic applications for this type of truth: scientific and everyday. A truth has practical value when the item under consideration obeys a scientific law or is mathematically correct. For example, 2 + 2 = 4 is true. Also, the scientific method of observation, hypothesis, research and experiment, general conclusion, and test conclusions by independent repeatability is what proves a theory true and provides us with a logical basis for truth until such time as the theory is proven false by experiment.

In everyday application, what has practical value is considered true. Since I construct my own reality from moment to moment, I have a practical sense of truth that I use to navigate a complex and dynamic world. My truth is expedient as I respond to the external environment and events. If I were to apply my truth to everyone and everything else, then I would become a ruthless dictator. Since everyone has their own truth, then there is no single accepted truth. What is often considered true is what a majority of people believe. A truth must be subject to our being able to prove it false. This is easy to do when individually constructed reality is concerned. This type of truth often underlies quite a lot of political debate as leaders make every effort to define our reality and our truths for us. Indeed, it is a major role of leadership to do so, and it is filled with ethical problems and dilemmas.

Type I and Type II Errors

According to the science of statistics, there are two types of fundamental errors associated with logic or measurements, namely Type I and Type II errors. A Type I error happens when something is thought to be true, but turns out to be false. This is otherwise known as a false alarm. A Type II error occurs when something is thought to be false, but turns out to be true. For example, a criminal may be declared not guilty, although he/she really is guilty.

With respect to the main hypothesis of this book, I believe it to be true, but it may turn out to be false (Type I error), whereas a skeptic may believe it to be false, when it might be true (Type II error). It is also possible that we may both be correct, and we may both be wrong. The nature of the hypothesis of mind, brain, soul, and consciousness that is the fundamental basis for the transmutational leadership model is not provably true, nor is it provably false, at least currently. This is so because there is no way of creating a deterministic experiment that would consistently result in a yes or no.

For the hypothesis of mind to be true in all respects, it would ideally comply with all three types of truth, and we would end up with a high degree of confidence that the hypothesis is true. For now, it's a statistical argument. As mentioned in Chapter 7, Dr. Dean Radin has shown that the mind's psychic ability is statistically true with a high degree of confidence, but he could be wrong. And so claim the skeptics. On the other hand, the skeptics are unable to adequately explain paranormal phenomena. More experiments and time will tell.

Skeptics may be laughing, sneering, or apoplectic at this point. They may rightly say that this book is filled with nonsense. But they might be wrong about that, too. Skeptics prefer the truth as practical value typically proven by traditional science. This type of truth is usually associated with the scientific method backed up by empirical evidence. It is the standard by which many skeptics declare a hypothesis to be conditionally true. The scientific method says that a theory proven by experiment must be verifiable by an independent and repeatable experiment that confirms the result. This result must continuously be subjected to experiments that could prove it false. Thus, most scientific theories are constantly being tested until they are generally accepted as true. Some theories, however, are not testable at all and must remain theories for a long time until we have the technology to create appropriate experiments. String theory is a case in point. This is the reason it is so controversial.

Anything to do with mind will remain in this unverifiable category for some time. Though we may claim that psychic phenomena are statistically true, we cannot be certain. There is a lot of evidence repeated, but it is not wholly reliable. For example, Newton's and Whitton's work on life-between-lives regressions is what I consider to be a series of independent "experiments" that provides some evidence that the soul exists. Their findings are consistent with what many religions say, especially Buddhism. Unless we are all experiencing a mass psychosis that has been repeated for thousands of years across all cultures and races, then skeptics should be skeptical about their own skepticism. Though I may be making a Type I error, skeptics may be making a Type II error!

Key Points and Summary

THE FOLLOWING are the key points in the book:

➢ Leadership contains an inconvenient truth. That truth is that we often require our leaders to satisfy our self-interest at the expense of others and the planet. This requirement is driven by our brain's design and our beliefs. Consequently, more often than not, leadership operates within a competitive framework. This competitive framework is about domination (i.e., winning and success), and many of our organizations reflect that type of self-interested behavior. This often results in hypocrisy and abuse of power. This is how social justice eludes us. For example, we want our nation's leader to represent our self-interests against those of all other nations. Negotiation is our preferred approach, but outright competition (i.e., war) is supported when necessary. As the world's population continues to increase and resources diminish, more conflict will erupt. Unless we change our traditional way of leading, it will not go well for humanity.

➢   Leadership is essentially based on inequality and the exploitation of differences enabled by inequality. At the same time, most of us want our leaders to work for social justice. Social justice is based, in part, on equality, freedom, and sovereignty of persons, and this includes people whom we consider as "them." Thus, leadership and social justice are effectively in conflict with each other. I believe that this is why social justice is so elusive within all of our organizations, and across humanity and the environment.

➢   Leadership, as practiced by most leaders today, is about propping up our existing systems and organizations. However, there are some leaders, much fewer in number, who are like voices in the wilderness. These are leaders who agitate for substantive changes to our existing systems and organizations and to how we lead. I am one of those voices in the wilderness.

➢   A system's rules drive behavior. A system can be very small (e.g., a person's central nervous system) to very large (e.g., the global economic system). A human being is a system with its own set of rules. A human's primary rule is physical survival. Survival trumps all other rules, which are secondary and only referred to once the primary rule has been satisfied. Thus, our brain is designed first and foremost to ensure survival of the body. The previous statement is a very key point. Since our organizations are created in our self-image, they have character, personality, and culture and behave as we do.

➢ To satisfy the primary rule of survival, the brain is designed to polarize all input in order to rapidly produce a decision. Polarized judgment is a binary decision-making process that happens in less than a second. It is framing all input to the brain as this *or* that. Only our logical (i.e., conscious) brain (approximately 10 percent of the brain's processing) can frame an issue as this *and* that, and only if we are self-aware. The key idea is that the brain naturally judges all things, and very quickly, and our subconscious makes that decision before the conscious or rational portion of our brain. We cannot deterministically predict what the outcome of this decision-making process will be because our brains are a nonlinear system, although the decision is biased by our beliefs and subconscious archetypes. This is essentially both humanity's greatest gift and its greatest misfortune. Polarized judgment has created our civilization as we know it; it is behind all progress and success, but is also the leading cause of our suffering. I believe that our traditional approach to leadership, which is largely based on unconscious processes, is no longer viable. Our intelligence and opposable thumbs have created technologies and organizations that enable us to satisfy our primary rule of survival. We are constantly competing with each other. As a species, we have been so successful that our own habitat is now seriously threatened. We have created our own trap because of how we are designed. We can't see it because it is hidden inside us. Escaping this trap requires a different approach to leadership than the one we have relied on in the past.

➤   Given the key ideas mentioned above, I am very critical of leadership that promotes the status quo way of doing things. Leaders have served us both very well and very badly. In a very crucial way, humanity is in denial. We are like alcoholics on a binge, and many of our leaders are not only giving us more alcohol, they are also joining us in the drinking. Some leaders are the worst "alcoholics." Any leader who dares to suggest removing the access to the "alcohol," or who is even courageous enough to do so, is removed because we hate them for pointing out our addiction and threatening our survival. We replace these "honest" leaders with others who will satisfy our cravings. For example, politicians have a habit of rolling out costly programs just before an election in an effort to buy votes. It usually works. You might consider how national debts are a reflection of our binging. As many people know, the first thing we must do to overcome an addiction, as with alcoholism, is recognize and admit to our problem. Consciousness is the method that allows us to do so.

➤   If we consider the traditional definitions of progress and success, we find that they are supportive of the primary rule of survival. That is quite appropriate and should be no surprise to anyone. However, sustainability has now been added to our vernacular as a modifier of progress and success. Sustainability has become a global concern because of population growth and resource consumption that are exceeding the planet's ability to reproduce certain renewable resources. Further, there is a social justice issue regarding the distribution of those resources that are available. So, to solve these issues, we have to do something about the global population and its consumption, as well as the leadership actions that cause distribution issues. As everyone knows, that would be too politically difficult, given the disparity between rich and poor around the world, and no one is going to tell anyone how many children they can or cannot have. Even China is looking to reverse its one-child policy. Traditional leadership approaches are failing us because traditional leadership beliefs about progress and success have created our global issues. I believe that traditional leadership often creates toxic organizations that leave broken people and damaged habitats in their wake.

➢   To do more of the same and expect a different result is, as the saying goes, a form of insanity. To take a fundamentally different approach to leadership requires an original idea and a redefinition of progress and success. All truly original ideas are usually met with skepticism, if not with outright hostility. I expect that transmutational leadership will be the subject of controversy because it suggests that the way out of our trap is a different view of mind and how it can be used to overcome our leadership issues.

➢   Over the years, would-be leaders have been told that they needed a high Intellectual Quotient (IQ), then they were told they also needed a high Emotional Quotient (EQ), then a high Systems Thinking Quotient (SYSQ), and now a high Spiritual Quotient (SQ). These are valid

points, in my opinion. Leadership competency
is becoming significantly more complex. The
transmutational leadership model incorporates
these four leadership competencies.

➤ I have termed the intentional and deliberate
oscillation of the brain and mind system the
Consciousness Quotient (CQ). A high CQ produces
more balanced decision making and more robust
organizations. A high CQ is similar to how
electronic circuits work. In electronic circuits the
higher the oscillation, the greater the bandwidth
or, if you wish, the more information available
for a given amount of time. Thus, a higher CQ
produces more possibilities because there is
more information available. Information can
be transformed into knowledge, and knowledge
is power. This means that an individual or
organization is able to learn more rapidly, be
more robust in the presence of a highly changing
and dynamic environment, and be more creative.
These attributes permit more possibilities to
emerge, and we become more aware of our
relationships and the impact of our activities on
the planet.

➤ Organizational survival is dependent on adapting
successfully to ongoing changes. Adaptation
is dependent upon learning. Our success has
been fueled by positive reinforcement. What we
have learned from this positive reinforcement
is now endangering our species and the planet.
Unfortunately, there are very deep barriers to
effective learning as a result of how our brains
operate. There is learning of the type that
reinforces "successful" behaviors that ultimately

lead to failure, and there is learning of the type that is a search for truth. The brain's number one rule of survival does not care for truth. Truth is often painful and requires courage and reconciliation. We tend to avoid this type of truth. It's quite natural to prefer pleasure over pain. The type of deep learning required to truly move all types of organizations forward is not easy to do. It is a significant challenge for both leaders and followers. CQ and transmutational leadership address this problem.

➢ Transmutational leadership is a model and a method for knowing our human and spiritual selves. It allows us to be authentic leaders. The transmutational leadership model helps explore what being authentic really means.

➢ CQ and the transmutational leadership model support, *in part only*, the Conscious Capitalism movement. This movement's underlying theme is that the historical leadership motivators of power and money are no longer viable. Needless to say, there are many critics of the Conscious Capitalism ideology and movement, and it is certainly not the dominant form of capitalism in the world today.

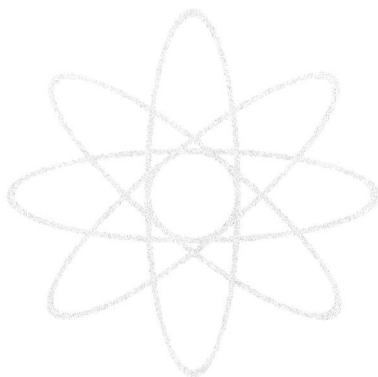

Endnotes

Chapter 1

1. Tzu, L. (2001). *Tao Te Ching: The Definitive Edition*. (J. Star, Trans.). New York: Jeremy P. Tarcher/Penguin. (Original work c. 300 BC). The Jonathan Star translation I reference here is wonderful, and I highly recommend it.

2. Wikipedia (2012). "Quantum Entanglement." Retrieved November 14, 2012 from http://en.wikipedia.org/wiki/Particle-wave_duality.

3. Chopra, D., MD, and Tanzi, R.E., PhD (2012). *Super Brain: Unleashing the Explosive Power of Your Mind to Maximize Health, Happiness, and Spiritual Well-Being*. New York: Random House Inc. Chopra and Tanzi report that people with hydrocephalus have varying degrees of cerebral fluid that fills their cranial cavity. This condition is usually fatal. However, there are some who survive whose cranial cavity is 95 percent fluid. Of these, half are severely retarded, whereas the other half have IQs over 100. In the case referenced, the individual has an IQ of 126. See page 27 in the work cited.

4. Ibid.

Chapter 2

1. Jung, C. G. (1964). *Man and his Symbols.* New York: Doubleday and Company.

2. Tolle, E. (2004). *The Power of Now: A Guide to Spiritual Enlightenment.* Vancouver, British Columbia: Namaste Publishing.

3. Tolle, E. (2006). *A New Earth: Awakening to Your Life's Purpose.* New York: Penguin Group.

4. Rychkun, E. (2012). *Planet Earth Inc: Empire Of The gods Deposed, Volume 2.* Rychkun's two-volume set is a tough read, and the version I read still required some editing, but it's worth it. Volume 2 is much better and more interesting than Volume 1 because it focuses more on solutions. To read it well, you need to set aside your innate brain-mind polarity thinking, which is a good exercise in and of itself. Also, Rychkun's economic philosophy is primarily libertarian, and the books should be read with that in mind.

5. Gleick, J. (1987). *Chaos: Making a New Science.* New York: Penguin Books.

6. Talbot, M. (2011). *The Holographic Universe: The Revolutionary Theory of Reality.* New York: HarperCollins.

7. Mackey, J. and Sisodia, R. (2013). *Conscious Capitalism: Liberating the Heroic Spirit of Business.* Boston: Harvard Business Review Press.

8. Hawken, P. (1994). *The Ecology of Commerce: A Declaration of Sustainability.* New York: HarperBusiness.

9. Kübler-Ross, E., and Kessler D. (2007). *On Grief and Grieving: Finding the Meaning of Grief Through the Five Stages of Loss.* New York: Scribner.

10. Note: I highly recommend the work of William Bridges, whose simple model of the human aspect of change is well worth

considering. For a process that leaders can use to effect change, I encourage you to read John Kotter's Harvard Business Review Classic *Leading Change: Why Transformation Efforts Fail.*

11. Note: I highly recommend the book *Beyond Change Management: How to Achieve Breakthrough Results Through Conscious Change Leadership* by Dean Anderson and Linda Ackerman Anderson (Pfeiffer, 2010).

Chapter 3

1. Arbiter, G.P. (ca 27 – 66 AD). *Gaius Petronius Arbiter Quotes.* Retrieved 31 January 2013 from http://www.famousquotes.com/author/arbiter.

2. Lipton, B. (2008). *The Biology of Belief: Unleashing the Power of Consciousness, Matter & Miracles.* Hay House Inc.

3. Wikipedia, (2013). Tragedy of the Commons. retrieved 28 January 2013 from http://en.wikipedia.org/wiki/Tragedy_of_the_Commons.

4. Durant, W. (1966). *The Story of Civilization, Volume II: The Life of Greece.* Simon and Schuster.

5. Francis, D. (2013). "Are 'extractive elites' sucking the life out of Canada's economy?" *Financial Post.* Retrieved 23 March 2013 from http://opinion.financialpost.com/2013/02/22/ are-extractive-elites-sucking-the-life-out-of-canadas-economy/.

6. Morgan, G. (1998). *Images of Organizations: The Executive Edition.* San Francisco: Berrett-Koehler.

7. Drucker, P. (2006). *Managing for Results.* New York: HarperBusiness.

8. Quinn, R. (2004). *Building the Bridge As You Walk On It: A Guide for Leading Change.* San Francisco: Jossey-Bass.

9. Oshry, B. (1996). *Seeing Systems: Unlocking the Mysteries of Organizational Life.* San Francisco: Berrett-Koehler.

10. Durant, W. and Durant A. (1968). *The Lessons of History*. New York: Simon and Schuster.

11. Bernard, C. (ca 1850). *Famous Quotes*. Retrieved 5 February 2013 from   http://www.famousquotes.com/author/bernard/4

12. Meadows, D. (2008). *Thinking in Systems: A Primer* (D. Wright, editor), White River Junction, Vermont: Chelsea Green Publishing Company.

13. Meadows, D., Randers, J., and Meadows, D., (2004). *Limits to Growth: The 30–Year Update*. White River Junction, Vermont: Chelsea Green Publishing Company.

14. Durant, W. and Durant, A. (1968). *The Lessons of History*. New York: Simon & Schuster.

15. Munro, M. (2013). "Plastic Waste Problem Persists—Despite efforts, less than half of garbage finds its proper place." *Vancouver Sun*. Tuesday, February 19, 2013. Section B, CanadaWorld.

16. MacLeod, I.C., (2013). Celebrate Freedom of the Press. *Maple Ridge News*. 6 March 2013.

17. Robinson, K., Sir. (2006). "Do Schools Kill Creativity?" Retrieved 6 February 2013 from http://www.youtube.com/watch?v=iG9CE55wbtY&list=PL70DEC2B0568B5469&index=1.

18. *Canadian Press* (2013). "Rebuilding trust in banking will take more than regulations, Carney says." Retrieved 25 February 2013 from http://globalnews.ca/news/397680/rebuilding-trust-in-banking-will-take-more-than-regulations-carney-says]

19. Ball, P. (2004). *Critical Mass: How One Thing Leads to Another*. New York: Farrar, Straus and Giroux.

20. Wikipedia (2013). "Prisoner's Dilemma." Retrieved 20 February 2013 from http://en.wikipedia.org/wiki/Prisoner%27s_Dilemma.

21. Tolle, E. (2004). *The Power of Now: A Guide to Spiritual Enlightenment*. Vancouver, British Columbia: Namaste Publishing.

22. Rychkun, E. (2012). *Planet Earth Inc.: Empire of The gods Deposed, Volume 2*. Ed Rychkun.

Chapter 4

1. Unknown Monk (ca 1100). *I Wanted to Change the World*. Retrieved 2 April 2013 from: http://www.scrapbook.com/poems/doc/12475/378.html.

2. Tzu, L. (2001). *Tao Te Ching: The Definitive Edition*. (J. Star, Trans.). New York: Jeremy P. Tarcher/Putnam. (Original work c. 300 BC).

3. Johnson, B. (1996). *Polarity Management: Identifying and Managing Unsolvable Problems*. Amherst, Massachusetts, HRD Press Inc.

4. Hawley, J. (2001). *The Bhagavad Gita: A Walkthrough for Westerners*.Novato, California: New World Library.

5. Anderson, D., and Ackerman Anderson, L. (2001). *Beyond Change Management: Advanced Strategies for Today's Transformational Leaders*. San Francisco: Jossey-Bass Pfeiffer.

6. Yukl, G. (2002). *Leadership in Organizations*. Custom Edition for LT516, Royal Roads University. Derived from Leadership in Organizations (5th Ed.), Upper Saddle River, New Jersey: Prentice-Hall Inc.

7. Manthorpe, J. (2013). "China's legislature a billionaire's club." *The Vancouver Sun*. Asia-Pacific Report, 11 March 2013.

8. Manthorpe, J. (2013). "Will Beijing impose cognac drought on North Korea?" *The Vancouver Sun*. Asia-Pacific Report, 11 March 2013.

9. Meadows, D., Randers, J., and Meadows, D., (2004). *Limits to Growth: The 30-Year-Update*. White River Junction, Vermont: Chelsea Green Publishing Company.

10. Rinpoche, S. (1992). *The Tibetan Book of Living and Dying*. New York: HarperCollins.

11. Newberg, A., MD, D'Aquili, E., MD, PhD, and Rause, V. (2001). *Why God Won't Go Away: Brain Science and the Biology of Belief.* New York: The Ballantine Publishing Group.

Chapter 5

1. Tolle, E. (2006). *A New Earth: Awakening to Your Life's Purpose.* New York: Penguin Group.

2. Rychkun, E. (2012). *Planet Earth Inc.: Empire of The gods Exposed ,Volume 1 and Planet Earth Inc.: Empire of The gods Deposed, Volume 2.* Ed Rychkun.

3. Cunningham, L. (2012). "Does it pay to know your type?" *Washington Post* – On Leadership. Retrieved 16 December 2012 from http://www.washingtonpost.com/national/on-leadership/myers-briggs-does-it-pay-to-know-your-type/2012/12/14/eae-d51ae-3fcc-11e2-bca3-aadc9b7e29c5_story_4.html.

4. Wikipedia (2012). "Myers-Briggs Type Indicator." Retrieved 21 December 2012 from http://en.wikipedia.org/wiki/MBTI.

5. Johnson, B. (1996). *Polarity Management: Identifying and Managing Unsolvable Problems.* Amherst, Massachusetts: HRD Press Inc.

6. Bridges, W. (2000). *Organizational Character Index.* Palo Alto, California: Consulting Psychologists Press Inc.

7. Wikipedia (2012). "Herrmann Brain Dominance Instrument." Retrieved 27 December 2012 from http://en.wikipedia.org/wiki/HBDI.

8. Bolman, L. G. and Deal, T. E. (2003). *Reframing Organizations: Artistry, Choice and Leadership,* 3rd Ed. San Francisco: Jossey-Bass.

9. Morgan, G. (1998). *Images of Organization: The Executive Edition.* San Francisco: Berrett-Koehler.

10. Mackey, J. and Sisodia, R. (2013). *Conscious Capitalism: Liberating the Heroic Spirit of Business.* Boston, Massachusetts: Harvard Business Review Press.

11. Robinson, K., Sir. (2006). "Do Schools Kill Creativity?" Retrieved 6 February 2013 from http://www.youtube.com/wat ch?v=iG9CE55wbtY&list=PL70DEC2B0568B5469&index=1.

Chapter 6

1. Chopra, D., MD, and Tanzi, R. E., PhD (2012). *Super Brain: Unleashing the Explosive Power of Your Mind to Maximize Health, Happiness, and Spiritual Well-Being.* New York: Random House.

2. Arntz. W., Chasse, B., and Vicente, M. (2005). *What The Bleep Do We Know: Discovering the Endless Possibilities for Altering Your Everyday Reality.* Deerfield Beach, Florida: Health Communications Inc.
Note: The brain's computational power is immense. Dr. Hameroff believes that microtubules are at interface between the physical and spiritual worlds and has developed a theory of consciousness with Penrose.

3. Schwartz, J., MD, and Begley, S., (2002). *The Mind and the Brain: Neuroplasticity and the Power of Mental Force.* New York: HarperCollins.

4. Durant, W. (1961). *The Story of Philosophy: The Lives and Opinions of the Greater Philosophers.* New York: Simon and Schuster.

5. Talbot, M. (2011). *The Holographic Universe: The Revolutionary Theory of Reality.* New York: HarperCollins.

6. Wikipedia, (2013). "Benoit Mandelbrot." Retrieved 5 March 2013 from: http://en.wikipedia.org/wiki/Benoit_Mandelbrot.

7. Wheatley, M. (1999). *Leadership and the New Science: Discovering Order in a Chaotic World.* San Francisco: Berrett-Koehler.

8. Arntz. W., Chasse, B., and Vicente, M. (2005). *What The Bleep Do We Know: Discovering the Endless Possibilities for Altering Your Everyday Reality*. Deerfield Beach, Florida: Health Communications Inc.

9. Talbot, M. (2011). *The Holographic Univers: The Revolutionary Theory of Reality*. New York: HarperCollins.

10. Ibid.

11. Wikipedia (2013). "Leonard Susskind." Retrieved 7 May 2013 from http://en.wikipedia.org/wiki/Leonard_Susskind.

12. Arntz. W., Chasse, B., and Vicente, M. (2005). *What The Bleep Do We Know: Discovering the Endless Possibilities for Altering Your Everyday Reality*. Deerfield Beach, Florida: Health Communications Inc.

13. Newton, M. (2012). *Journey of Souls: Case Studies of Life Between Lives*. 5th Ed., Woodbury Minnesota: Llewellyn Publications.

14. Newton, M. (2011). *Destiny of Souls: New Case Studies of Life Between Lives*. Woodbury, Minnesota: Llewellyn Publications.

15. Talbot, M. (2011). *The Holographic Universe: The Revolutionary Theory of Reality*. New York: HarperCollins.

16. Ibid.

Chapter 7

1. Taylor, J. B., PhD. (2006). *My Stroke of Insight: A Brain Scientist's Personal Journey*. New York: Penguin Group.

2. Newton, M. (2012). *Journey of Souls: Case Studies of Life Between Lives*. 5th Ed., Woodbury Minnesota: Llewellyn Publications.

3. Newton, M. (2011). *Destiny of Souls: New Case Studies of Life Between Lives*. Woodbury, Minnesota: Llewellyn Publications.

4. Wikipedia (2012). "Know Thyself." Retrieved November 15, 2012 from http://en.wikipedia.org/wiki/Know_thyself.

5. Durant, W. (1966). *The Story of Civilization Part II: The Life of Greece*. New York: Simon and Schuster.

6. Newton, M. (2012). *Journey of Souls: Case Studies of Life Between Lives*. 5th Ed., Woodbury Minnesota: Llewellyn Publications.

7. Newton, M. (2011). *Destiny of Souls: New Case Studies of Life Between Lives*. Woodbury, Minnesota: Llewellyn Publications.

8. Talbot, M. (2011). *The Holographic Universe: The Revolutionary Theory of Reality*. New York: HarperCollins.

9. Newton, M. (2012). *Journey of Souls: Case Studies of Life Between Lives*. 5th Ed., Woodbury Minnesota: Llewellyn Publications.

10. Newton, M. (2011). *Destiny of Souls: New Case Studies of Life Between Lives*. Woodbury, Minnesota: Llewellyn Publications.

11. Rinpoche, S. (1992). *The Tibetan Book of Living and Dying*. New York: HarperCollins.

12. Talbot, M. (2011). *The Holographic Universe: The Revolutionary Theory of Reality*. New York: HarperCollins.

13. Wilde, S. (2009). *Sixth Sense: Including the Secrets of the Etheric Subtle Body*. Hay House Inc.

14. Radin, D., Ph.D. (1997). *The Conscious Universe: The Scientific Truth of Psychic Phenomena*. New York: HarperCollins.

15. Radin. D. Ph.D. (2006). *Entangled Minds: Extrasensory Experiences in a Quantum Reality*. New York: Simon & Schuster.

16. Rychkun, E. (2012). *Planet Earth Inc.: Empire of The gods Deposed, Volume 2*. Ed Rychkun.

17. Wikipedia (2013). "Diffusion of Innovations." Retrieved 8 February 2013 from http://en.wikipedia.org/wiki/Diffusions_of_innovations.

18. Gladwell, M. (2002). *The Tipping Point: How Little Things Can Make a Big Difference*. New York: Little, Brown and Company.

19. Wilde, S. (2009). *Sixth Sense: Including the Secrets of the Etheric Subtle Body*. Hay House Inc.

20. Bridges, W. (2003). *Managing Transitions: Making the Most of Change*. 2nd ed. Cambridge, Massachusetts: Da Capo Press.

21. Bridges, W. (2001). *The Way of Transition: Embracing Life's Most Difficult Moments*. Cambridge, MA: Da Capo Press.

22. Kotter, J. (1995). "Leading Change: Why transformation efforts fail." *Harvard Business Review*. March-April 1995.

23. Anderson, D., and Ackerman Anderson, L. (2001). *Beyond Change Management: Advanced Strategies for Today's Transformational Leaders*. San Francisco: Jossey-Bass Pfeiffer.

24. Ball, P. (2006). *Critical Mass: How One Thing Leads to Another*. New York: Farrar, Straus and Giroux.

25. Radin, D., PhD (1997). *The Conscious Universe: The Scientific Truth of Psychic Phenomena*. New York: HarperCollins.

Chapter 8

1. Picard, M. (2008). *This Is Not a Book: Adventures in Popular Philosophy*. London, England: Quid Publishing.

2. Hunter, J. (2013). "Is mindfulness good for business?" *Mindful–Taking time for what matters* magazine. Washington, DC: Foundation for a Mindful Society Publishers.

3. Mackey, J. & Sisodia, R. (2013). *Conscious Capitalism: Liberating the Heroic Spirit of Business*. Boston, Massachusetts: Harvard Business Review Press.

Chapter 9

1. Augustine, N. R. (1997). *Augustine's Laws*. Reston, Virginia: American Institute of Aeronautics and Astronautics Inc.

Appendix B

1. Gleick, J. (1987). *Chaos: Making a New Science*. New York. Penguin Group.

2. Manthorpe, J. (2013). "Tudors' vilification of Richard III remains a model big lie for insecure leaders throughout the ages–Similar propaganda campaigns muddy the waters in the Middle East and East China Sea today." *Vancouver Sun*. 6 February 2013, p. B4.

3. Berreby, D. (2005). *Us and Them: Understanding Your Tribal Mind*. New York: Little Brown and Company.

4. Yukl, G. (2002). *Leadership in Organizations*. Custom Edition for LT516, Royal Roads University. Taken from *Leadership in Organizations* (5th Ed.), Upper Saddle River, New Jersey: Prentice-Hall Inc.

Appendix C

1. Picard, M. (2008). *This Is Not a Book: Adventures in Popular Philosophy*. London, England: Quid Publishing.

Bibliography

Anderson, D., and Ackerman Anderson, L. (2001). *Beyond Change Management: Advanced Strategies for Today's Transformational Leaders*. San Francisco: Jossey-Bass Pfeiffer.

Arntz. W., Chasse, B., and Vicente, M. (2005). *What The Bleep Do We Know: Discovering the Endless Possibilities for Altering Your Everyday Reality*. Deerfield Beach, Florida: Health Communications Inc.

Augustine, N. R. (1997). *Augustine's Laws*. Reston, Virginia: American Institute of Aeronautics and Astronautics Inc.

Ball, P. (2004). *Critical Mass: How One Thing Leads to Another*. New York: Farrar, Straus and Giroux.

Berreby, D. (2005). *Us and Them: Understanding Your Tribal Mind*. New York: Little Brown and Company.

Bolman, L. G. and Deal, T. E. (2003). *Reframing Organizations: Artistry, Choice and Leadership,* 3rd Ed. San Francisco. Jossey-Bass.

Bridges, W. (2000). *Organizational Character Index*. Palo Alto, California.: Consulting Psychologists Press Inc.

———— (2001). *The Way of Transition: Embracing Life's Most Difficult Moments.* Cambridge, Massachusetts: Da Capo Press.

———— (2003). *Managing Transitions: Making the Most of Change,* 2nd ed. Cambridge, Massachusetts: Da Capo Press.

———— and Mitchell, S. (2000). *Leading Transition: A New Model for Change.* Retrieved March 26, 2006 from http://www.hessel-beininstitute.org/knowledgecenter/journal.aspx?ArticleID=28.

Chopra, D. (2013). "The Conscious Lifestyle: A Leader Must Be Aware." Retrieved 7 February 2013 from http://www.linkedin.com/today/post/article/20130130233732-75054000-the-conscious-lifestyle-a-leader-must-be-aware?trk=eml-mktg-condig-0108-p1.

Chopra, D., MD, and Tanzi, R. E., PhD (2012). *Super Brain: Unleashing the Explosive Power of Your Mind to Maximize Health, Happiness, and Spiritual Well-Being.* New York: Random House.

Corporate Knights Magazine (Winter 2013). *Corporate Knights – The Magazine for Clean Capitalism.* Volume II, Issue 4, Toronto, Canada: Corporate Knights Inc.

Drucker, P. (2006). *Managing for Results.* New York: HarperBusiness.

Durant, W. (2002). *The Greatest Minds and Ideas of All Time.* Ed. John Little. New York: Simon and Schuster.

———— (1966). *The Story of Civilization Part II: The Life of Greece.* New York: Simon and Schuster.

———— (1961). *The Story of Philosophy: The Lives and Opinions of the Greatest Philosophers.* New York: Simon and Schuster.

———— and Durant A. (1968). *The Lessons of History.* New York: Simon and Schuster.

Eriksson, C. (2004). "The effects of change programs on employees' emotions." *Personnel Review, 33*(1), 110-126.

Fitzgerald, F. Scott (1936). *The Crack Up*. Retrieved from http://www.quotationspage.com/quote/90.html 15 Feb 2010.

Gallstedt, M. (2003). "Working conditions in projects: perceptions of stress and motivation among project team members and project managers." *International Journal of Project Management, 21*, 449-455.

Gladwell, M. (2002). *The Tipping Point: How Little Things Can Make a Big Difference*. New York: Little, Brown and Company.

Gleick, J. (1987). *Chaos: Making a New Science*. New York. Penguin Group.

Hardless, C., Nilsson, M., and Nulden, U. (2005). 'Copernicus' – Experiencing a failed project for reflection and learning. *Management Learning, 36*, 181-217.

Hawley, J. (2001). *The Bhagavad Gita: A Walkthrough for Westerners*. Novato, California: New World Library.

Hunter, J. (2013). Is mindfulness good for business? *Mindful – Taking time for what matters*. Washington, DC: Foundation for a Mindful Society Publishers.

Johnson, B. (1996). *Polarity Management: Identifying and Managing Unsolvable Problems.* Amherst, Massachusetts, HRD Press Inc.

Jung, C., von Franz, M. L., Henderson, J. L., Jacobi, J., Jaffe, A. (1964). *Man and his Symbols*. Garden City, New York: Doubleday and Company.

Kübler-Ross, E. and Kessler D. (2005). *On Grief and Grieving: Finding the Meaning of Grief Through the Five Stages of Loss*. New York: Scribner.

Lambright, L. (2001). "Group learning as viewed through the eyes of a software development project: An action research study." Retrieved December 15, 2006 from ProQuest Digital Dissertations database. (Publication No. AAT 3015955).

Lipton, B. (2008). *The Biology of Belief: Unleashing the Power of Consciousness, Matter & Miracles*. Hay House Inc.

Mackey, J. and Sisodia, R. (2013). *Conscious Capitalism: Liberating the Heroic Spirit of Business*, Boston, Massachusetts: Harvard Business Review Press.

MacLeod, I.C., (2013). "Celebrate Freedom of the Press." *Maple Ridge News*. 6 March 2013.

Meadows, D. (2008). *Thinking in Systems: A Primer.* (D. Wright, editor), White River Junction, Vermont: Chelsea Green Publishing Company.

———, Randers, J., and Meadows, D., (2004). *Limits to Growth: The 30-Year Update*. White River Junction, Vermont: Chelsea Green Publishing Company.

Morgan, G. (1998). *Images of Organizations: The Executive Edition*. San Francisco: Berrett-Koehler.

Newberg, A., MD, D'Aquili, E., MD, PhD and Rause, V. (2001). *Why God Won't Go Away: Brain Science and the Biology of Belief*. New York: Ballantine Books.

Newton, M. (2012). *Journey of Souls: Case Studies of Life Between Lives*. 5th Ed., Woodbury Minnesota: Llewellyn Publications.

——— (2011). *Destiny of Souls: New Case Studies of Life Between Lives*. Woodbury, Minnesota: Llewellyn Publications.

Oshry, B. (1996). *Seeing Systems: Unlocking the Mysteries of Organizational Life*. San Francisco: Berrett-Koehler.

Picard, M. (2008). *This Is Not a Book: Adventures in Popular Philosophy*. London, England: Quid Publishing.

Quinn, R. (2004). *Building the Bridge As You Walk On It: A Guide for Leading Change*. San Francisco: Jossey-Bass.

Radin, D., PhD (1997). *The Conscious Universe: The Scientific Truth of Psychic Phenomena*. New York: HarperCollins.

———— (2006). *Entangled Minds: Extrasensory Experiences in a Quantum Reality*. New York: Simon and Schuster.

Rinpoche, S. (1992). *The Tibetan Book of Living and Dying*. New York: HarperCollins.

Rychkun, E. (2012). *Planet Earth Inc: Empire of The gods Exposed Volume 1 and Planet Earth Inc: Empire of The gods Deposed Volume 2*. Ed Rychkun.

Smith, M. K. (2001). Chris Argyris: theories of action, double-loop learning and organizational learning. In *The Encyclopedia of Informal Education*. Retrieved December 15, 2006 from www.infed.org/.

Schwartz, J., MD, and Begley, S., (2002). *The Mind and the Brain: Neuroplasticity and the Power of Mental Force*. New York: HarperCollins.

Talbot, M. (2011). *The Holographic Universe: The Revolutionary Theory of Reality*. New York: HarperCollins.

Taylor, J. B., PhD. (2006). *My Stroke of Insight: A Brain Scientist's Personal Journey*. New York: Penguin Group.

Taylor, J. B., (2008). "Stroke of Insight: How it Feels to Have a Stroke." Available at http://www.youtube.com/watch?v=UyyjU 8fzEYU&list=PL70DEC2B0568B5469.

Tolle, E. (2004). *The Power of Now: A Guide to Spiritual Enlightenment*. Vancouver, British Columbia: Namaste Publishing.

———— (2006). *A New Earth: Awakening to Your Life's Purpose*. New York: Penguin Group.

Tzu, L. (2001). *Tao Te Ching: The Definitive Edition*. (J. Star, Trans.). New York: Jeremy P. Tarcher/Putnam. (Original work c. 300 B.C./2001).

Wheatley, M. (1999). *Leadership and the New Science: Discovering Order in a Chaotic World*. San Francisco: Berrett-Koehler.

Wikipedia. (2013). "Diffusion of Innovations." Retrieved 8 February 2013 from http://en.wikipedia.org/wiki/Diffusions_of_innovations.

Wikipedia. (2013). "Twelve Leverage Points." Retrieved 31 January 2013 from http://en.wikipedia.org/wiki/Twelve_leverage_points.

Wilde, S. (2009). *Sixth Sense: Including the Secrets of the Etheric Subtle Body*. Hay House Inc.

Yukl, G. (2002). *Leadership in Organizations*. Custom Edition for LT516, Royal Roads University. Taken from Leadership in Organizations (5th Ed.), Upper Saddle River, New Jersey: Prentice-Hall Inc.

Index

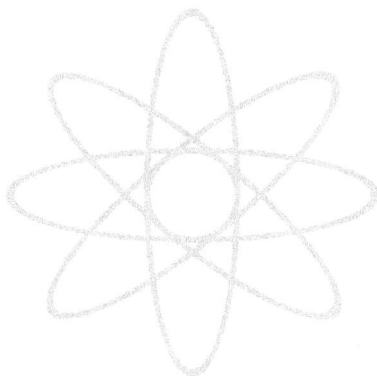

Acknowledgments

Writing this book has been a labor of love. Many of the ideas came from a deep part of me that emerged from reflection and meditation and by asking simple questions. I feel that much of the original work is not original per se—the knowledge preexisted and was given to me by the Infinite Mind in order to serve humanity and the planet, as were many of my poems that emerged from deep meditation. I'm simply the instrument for something that is greater than me.

Yet, I also recognize that much of what I know is a result of the work of many people who came before me. Where would we be without a written language? So, I'm grateful to all those who have had the courage to write down their knowledge and their truth through the ages. And I'm grateful to the oral history traditions in the world. Storytelling is just as valuable a history as the written word. A lot of what I know, I learned through hearing stories.

I'm also very grateful to those in my life who have contributed to who I am today: my grandparents, parents, teachers, friends, relatives, my ex-wife, my wife, my daughter, and my antagonists, too. Yes, I'm even grateful to those who taught me a mild lesson in what it's like to be an ethnic minority during a time of conflict. Know that all is forgiven, and I hope that I'm forgiven for the things I did that I'm not proud of today.

I also owe an intellectual debt to Royal Roads University's leadership faculty, particularly Dr. Marilyn Laiken, who was my faculty advisor during the Master of Arts Leadership and Training (MALT) program. I also thank Dr. Fred Jacques from the University of Calgary, my thesis advisor, who encouraged me to pursue a PhD. The knowledge I received at RRU and the lifelong learning it inspired have forever changed me. MALT is an outstanding program.

I'm particularly grateful to Susan and Danielle, who teach me the meaning of balance every day in so many ways. I'm also grateful to them for supporting my desire to pursue a doctorate late in life. I realize that supporting time away from family is support indeed. Thank you.

Finally, this book would not be what it is without those friends and acquaintances who have listened to my ideas and discussed them patiently with me. You know who you are. I single out and thank Steve Medd. Steve took a first crack at editing an early version of the manuscript and made valuable suggestions. I also thank Ken Leong and Ed Rychkun, who reviewed it and gave me excellent comments. I also thank Simone Gabbay, editor extraordinaire, whose keen eye and great skill made this book significantly better.

As many authors have said before me, I could not have done it without you. I'm eternally grateful.

www.ingramcontent.com/pod-product-compliance
Lightning Source LLC
Chambersburg PA
CBHW072049020426
42334CB00017B/1446